STOCKS FOR THE LONG RUN

A GUIDE TO SELECTING MARKETS FOR LONG-TERM GROWTH

Jeremy J. Siegel
Department of Finance
The Wharton School

Senior sponsoring editor: Amy Hollands Gaber
Project editor: Jane Lightell
Production manager: Jon Christopher
Interior designer: Larry J. Cope
Art coordinator: Mark Malloy
Compositor: TCSystems, Inc.
Typeface: 11/13 Century Schoolbook
Printer: Buxton-Skinner

Library of Congress Cataloging-in-Publication Data

Siegel, Jeremy J.
Stocks for the long run: a guide to selecting markets for long-term growth/by Jeremy J. Siegel.
p. cm.
Includes index.
ISBN 1-55623-804-5
1. Stocks. 2. Stocks—History. 3. Rate of return. I. Title.
HG4661.S53 1994
332.63′22—dc20 93-38979

Printed in the United States of America
6 7 8 9 BUX 1 0 9 8 7 6 5

PREFACE

The stock market has been called the world's greatest casino. Billions of dollars of gains or losses are realized every day in individual stocks. Newspapers tote up the exchanges' top winners and losers like they report daily lottery numbers. The ups and downs of the stock market seem like pure gambling, causing many investors to shun stocks.

But the stock market is far more than a game of chance. Stocks represent claims on the profits of the world's productive enterprises, enterprises which provide the goods we consume and drive growth and innovation. Despite the short-run instability of the market, great fortunes have been accumulated through stocks.

Three years ago I began to research the returns on financial assets to determine whether stocks did realize superior returns for the long-term investor. In the course of my research I came across a small volume, entitled *Common Stocks as Long Term Investments,* written in 1924 by Edgar Lawrence Smith, a New York investment banker. Smith set out to test the conventional wisdom in investment circles of his day. That wisdom said that although stocks may be better investments than bonds during inflation, bonds are superior when inflation is low and prices are stable or declining. Over the long run, investment in high-grade bonds is to be preferred over common stocks.

Surprisingly, Smith found the conventional wisdom to be completely wrong. Stocks were better investments whether or not commodity prices were rising or falling. In Smith's studies, which extended from the Civil War through the early 1920s, nearly all randomly selected portfolios of stocks outperformed bonds.

Smith's book provoked wide debate in both investment and academic circles, and was reviewed by the most prestigious economic journals and magazines. Irving Fisher and John Maynard Keynes, the greatest American and British economists of their time, praised Smith's work, calling his conclusions revolutionary. Others claimed that Smith's optimism fed the bull market of the 1920s, causing stocks to soar to heights that could not be justified on the basis of current or prospective earnings.

The crash of 1929 and subsequent depression extinguished all enthusiasm for equities. A whole generation shunned stocks, vividly remembering those who lost everything by investing with borrowed money. Smith's book was roundly attacked and his theories discarded.

The postwar bull market sparked renewed interest in stocks. Research showed that stocks may outperform bonds in the long run, but bonds are safer in the short run and should still be a substantial part of most investors' portfolio. Academic research tended to dismiss the recommendations commonly given by investment advisers that the young should hold a higher proportion of stocks in their portfolio than the old, claiming that it was based on the fallacious concept that the risks of stocks can be lowered over time.

But my examination into nearly two centuries of financial data reveals a different story. Although stocks are certainly riskier than bonds in the short run, over the long run the returns on stocks are so stable that stocks are actually *safer* than either government bonds or Treasury bills. The constancy of the long-term, after-inflation returns on stocks was truly astounding, while the returns on fixed-income assets posed higher risks for the long-term investor.

My excitement with these results prompted me to write this book. The chapters give practical advice on building wealth through buying stocks, but they also explain why, and not just how, the market reacts to economic forces. Understanding is the key to making the right investment choices.

To educate the readers about stock returns I have organized the book into five sections. The first section explains and interprets the historical returns on stocks and bonds over the past two centuries. It discusses the risk and return profile of stocks that makes stocks safer and more productive long-term investments.

The second section examines stock returns in greater detail. It explains how stock returns are calculated, the role of dividends and earnings in determining stock prices, the difference between large and small stocks and growth and value stocks, the significance of taxes, and the importance of including international equities to achieve superior investment returns.

Part 3 discusses the economic environment of investing and contains analysis which is rarely found in a book about the stock market. Emphasis is placed on the role of the monetary medium, the central bank, the inflation process, and the business cycle in determining stock prices. The importance of political cycles, war and peace, and the continuous flow of economic data which hit the markets are also explained.

Part 4 discusses stock fluctuations in the short run. Although investors should focus on the long run when choosing stocks, the drama of the market is clearly revealed by its short-term movements. I interpret the history of stock market volatility and why the stock crash of 1987 ended up so differently than that of 1929. I present simple technical trading rules and fascinating calendar patterns of stock returns which may enable investors to outperform the market.

Finally, the last section discusses how to build wealth through accumulating stocks. The chapter explains the reasons why money managers underperform the market and how difficult it is to distinguish luck from skill when examining investment results. The final chapter lists some simple rules for building a successful investment portfolio.

Although successful investing can be achieved by following the advice given in these chapters, this book is far more than just a guide to building wealth. The stock market is a reflection of psychology as well as earnings, dividends, and asset values. Economics is not an exact science, and human behavior can never be forecast with precision. Scientists can predict the paths of celestial objects flawlessly for the next thousand years, but no one has consistently been able to foretell what will happen to the market just one day, not to say one hour, in the future. But it is just this unpredictability which makes the market so fascinating and challenging. I hope this book makes a significant contribution toward understanding the mystery of the stock market.

ACKNOWLEDGMENTS

The idea for this book originated in 1989 when the New York Stock Exchange approached my Wharton colleague, Marshall Blume, and me to produce a work on the history of the Exchange, from both an economic and institutional perspective. A year later I began to gather data on the long-term returns on various securities, suspecting, and indeed confirming, that stocks outperformed all other financial assets over US history.

However, it soon became clear that my research was extensive enough to justify a separate book, one which would not just contain data on stock returns, but include a whole description of what influences stock prices. In conversations with friends and colleagues, I came to the conclusion that although there were dozens of publications about "How to Beat the Market" and several excellent books on how individual stock markets function, there wasn't any publication which explains the interaction of the stock market and other financial markets with political and economic events occurring both in the United States and around the world.

I was particularly encouraged by my long-time friend, Professor Robert Shiller of Yale University, to fill this gap by writing a book. His excitement and insistence that I publish my findings about stock returns in a volume geared to the informed public, and not only to academic specialists, motivated me to undertake this project.

But there are also others who encouraged my endeavors. Professor Paul Samuelson, my former teacher and graduate thesis adviser, now Nobel laureate and Professor Emeritus at M.I.T., corresponded with me extensively about the relation between the stock market and the business cycle, a subject which constitutes one of the chapters of the book. Professor Mark Grinblatt at UCLA made extensive remarks on an earlier draft and his forthright comments did much to improve both my organization and exposition. Professor Jay Ritter of the University of Illinois also provided me with valuable guidance, particularly on Chapter 5.

Academics were not the only ones imparting information and motivation. Peter Bernstein, the editor of the *Journal of Portfolio Management,* corresponded with me about historical asset returns, a topic which he has also researched. Conversations with John Bogle, chairman of the Vanguard Group of Investment Companies, whose recent book on mutual funds wonderfully complements the research presented here, were also extremely helpful. Others who have contributed their time freely were John Feeley of Lipper Analytical Services; Gregor Gielen, of Bayern-Invest of Munich, Germany; David Booth, of DFA Associates; Satya Pradhuman, of Merrill Lynch; and Larry Siegel, of Ibbotson Associates.

But this book would not be possible without research assistance, and I was blessed with the finest researchers that Wharton could supply. Peter Scherer, an MBA student, and Ashish Shah, an upperclassman at Wharton, helped collect and compute the historical returns which form the core of this book. Michael Rescorla, now an undergraduate at Harvard, helped me for two summers with both research and the final editing process. His comments were invaluable to the improvement in the exposition of the manuscript. Alex Gould, now a graduate student at Stanford University, also made important suggestions on how to tighten the arguments in the final draft.

My most important research association was unquestionably with Shaun R. Smith. Shaun, a finance major at the Wharton School, became my principal researcher for this book in early 1992, when he was only 19 years old. His computing, analytical, and expositional talents made the more than 70 charts and tables that are found in this book possible. I can say without hesitation that this volume would not have been written without his skills, motivation, and dedication to the project.

Of course, no book is written without an editor, and Amy Hollands Gaber from Irwin provided the encouragement and patience that was required to move my ideas from a loosely defined set of notes to a finished manuscript. Shirley Kessel fashioned a superb index, so important since this research covers many different topics. And every author knows the burdens that writing a book places on his family. Writing a book, especially one written without collaborators or co-authors, is a project more consuming than I ever dreamed possible. My wife, Ellen, and sons, Andrew and Jeffrey, both encouraged and endured. I hope in the future I can repay the time I took from them to write this book.

Jeremy J. Siegel

INDEX OF FIGURES AND TABLES

TABLE OF CONTENTS

PART 1
THE VERDICT OF HISTORY

PART 2
STOCK RETURNS

PART 1

THE VERDICT OF HISTORY

CHAPTER 1

STOCK AND BOND RETURNS SINCE 1802

I know of no way of judging the future but by the past.

Patrick Henry

"EVERYBODY OUGHT TO BE RICH"

In the summer of 1929, John J. Raskob, a senior financial executive at General Motors, was interviewed by Samuel Crowther about how the typical individual could build wealth by investing in stocks. In August of that year, Crowther published Raskob's ideas in a *Ladies' Home Journal* article with the audacious title "Everybody Ought to Be Rich."

In the interview, Raskob claimed that America was on the verge of a tremendous industrial expansion. He maintained that by putting just $15 per month into good common stocks, an investor could expect his wealth to grow steadily to $80,000 over the next 20 years. Such a return—24 percent per year—was unprecedented, but the prospect of effortlessly amassing a great fortune seemed plausible in the atmosphere of the 20s bull market. Investors were excited by stocks, and millions put their savings into the market seeking quick profit.

On September 3, 1929, a few days after Raskob's ideas appeared, the Dow-Jones Industrial average hit a historic high of 381.17. Seven weeks later, stocks crashed. The next 34 months saw the most devastating decline in share values in US history.

On July 8, 1932, when the carnage was finally over, the Dow Industrials stood at 41.22. The market value of the greatest corporations in America had declined an incredible 89 percent. Millions of investors were wiped out, and America was mired in the deepest economic depression in its history. Thousands who had bought stocks with borrowed money went bankrupt.

Raskob's advice was held up to ridicule for years to come. It was said to represent the insanity of those who believed that the market could go up forever and the foolishness of those who ignored the tremendous risks inherent in stocks. US Senator Arthur Robinson from Indiana publicly held Raskob responsible for the stock crash by urging common people to buy stock at the market peak.[1] In 1992, 63 years later, *Forbes* magazine warned investors of the overvaluation of stocks in its issue headlined "Popular Delusions and the Madness of Crowds." In a review of the history of market cycles, *Forbes* fingered Raskob as the "worst offender" of those who viewed the stock market as a guaranteed engine of wealth.[2]

The conventional wisdom is that Raskob's foolhardy advice epitomizes the mania that periodically overruns Wall Street. But is that verdict fair? The answer is decidedly no. If you calculate the value of the portfolio of an investor who followed Raskob's advice, patiently putting $15 a month into stocks, you find that his accumulation exceeded that of someone who placed the same money in Treasury bills after less than four years! After 20 years, his stock portfolio would have accumulated to almost $9,000, and after 30 years to over $60,000. Although not as high as Raskob had projected, $60,000 still represents a fantastic 13 percent return on invested capital, far exceeding the returns earned by conservative investors who switched their money to Treasury bonds or bills at the market peak. Those who never bought stock, citing the Great Crash as the vindication of their caution, eventually found themselves far behind investors who had patiently accumulated equity.[3]

---

[1] Irving Fisher, *The Stock Market Crash and After* (New York: Macmillan, 1930), p. xi.

[2] "The Crazy Things People Say to Rationalize Stock Prices," *Forbes*, April 27, 1992, p. 150.

[3] Raskob succumbed to investors in the 1920s who wanted to get rich quickly by devising a scheme by which investors borrowed $300, adding $200 of personal capital, to invest $500 in stocks. Although in 1929 this was certainly not as good as putting money gradually in the market, even this plan beat investment in Treasury bills after 20 years.

John Raskob's infamous prediction is indeed illustrative of an important theme in the history of Wall Street. But this theme is not the prevalence of foolish optimism at market peaks; rather, it is that over the last century, accumulations in stocks have always outperformed other financial assets for the patient investor. Even such calamitous events as the Great 1929 Stock Crash did not negate the superiority of stocks as long-term investments.

FINANCIAL MARKET RETURNS FROM 1802

This chapter reports and explains the returns on stocks and bonds over most of the history of the United States as well as other countries. Three shorter periods are also examined: the early period, from 1802 to 1870, when the US financial markets were in their infancy and stock markets, founded at the end of the 18th century, were just coming into their own;[4] the middle period, from 1871–1925, when the United States emerged as a great economic power and comprehensive stock indexes became available;[5] and finally the modern period, from 1926 to the present, when the economy went through boom and depression and for which exhaustive indexes of all types of financial instruments are readily available.[6]

Figure 1–1 tells the story. It depicts the total return indexes for stocks, long- and short-term bonds, gold, and commodities from 1802 through 1992. *Total returns* means that all returns, such as interest and dividends and capital gains, are automatically reinvested in the asset and allowed to accumulate over time.

It can be easily seen that the total return on equities dominates all other assets. Even the cataclysmic stock crash of 1929

[4] A brief description of the early stock market is found in the appendix. The stock data during this period are taken from Schwert (1990), though I have substituted my own dividend series. G. William Schwert, "Indexes of United States Stock Prices from 1802 to 1987," *Journal of Business* 63 (1990), pp. 399–426.

[5] The series used here are taken from Cowles indexes as reprinted in Shiller (1989). Robert Shiller, *Market Volatility* (Cambridge, Mass.: M.I.T. Press, 1989).

[6] The data from the third period are taken from the Center for the Research in Stock Prices (CRSP) value weighted indexes of all New York, American, and NASDAQ stocks.

FIGURE 1–1
Total Nominal Return Indexes (1802–1992)

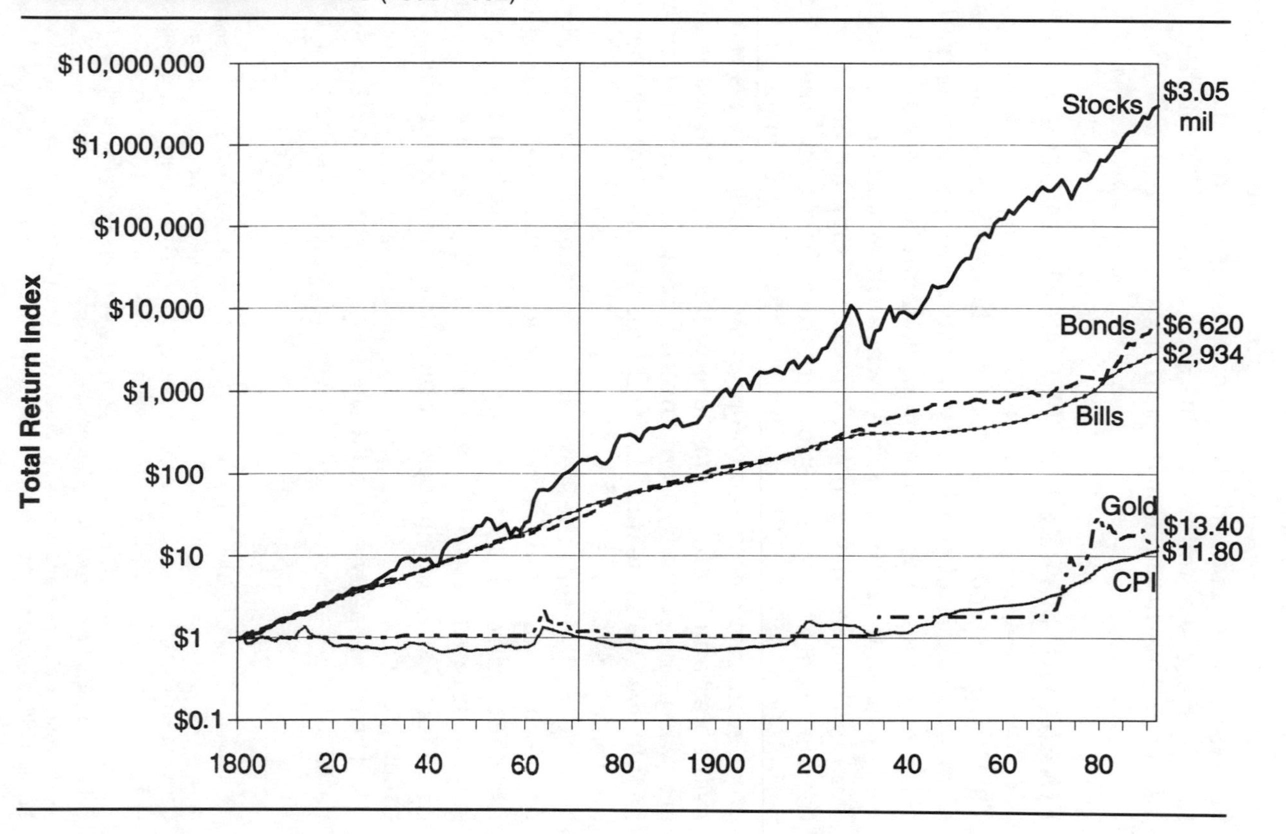

appears like a mere blip in the total returns index. Bear markets, which so frighten investors, pale in the context of the upward thrust of total stock returns. One dollar invested and reinvested in stocks since 1802 would have accumulated to $3,050,000 by the end of 1992.[7] Hypothetically, this means that $1 million, invested and reinvested during these 190 years, would have grown to the incredible sum of over $3 trillion in 1992. This nearly equals the entire capitalization of the US stock market!

One million dollars in 1802 is equivalent to about $12 million in today's purchasing power. This was certainly a large, though not overwhelming, sum of money to the industrialists and landholders of the early 19th century.[8] But total wealth in the stock market cannot accumulate as fast as the total return index. This is because investors consume most of their dividends and capital gains from the market.

It is rare for anyone to accumulate wealth for long periods of time without taking some income from their assets. The longest investors typically plan to hold assets without touching principal and income is when they are accumulating wealth in pension plans that will remain unbroken until retirement. Even those who bequeath fortunes untouched during their lifetimes to their heirs must realize that these accumulations are often dissipated in the next generation. The stock market has the power to turn a dollar into millions by the forbearance of generations—but few will have the patience or desire to let this happen.

HISTORICAL SERIES ON BONDS

Bonds are the most important financial assets competing with stocks. Bonds promise a fixed monetary payment over time. In contrast to equity, the cash flows from bonds have a maximum

---

[7] This figure is higher than I reported in my article, "The Equity Premium: Stock and Bond Returns Since 1802," *Financial Analysts Journal* 48, no. 1 (January/February, 1992), pp. 28–38. This is because of evidence that the dividend yield on stocks was higher than estimated earlier. See note 10 for a more complete explanation.

[8] Blodget, an early 19th-century economist, estimated the wealth of the United States at that time to be nearly $2.5 billion so that $12 million would only be about 0.5 percent of the total wealth. S. Blodget, Jr., *Economica,* "A Statistical Manual for the United States of America," 1806 ed., p. 68.

monetary value set by the terms of the contract and do not usually vary with the profitability of the firm.

The bond series we examine here are based on long- and short-term government bonds, when available. When government bonds were not available, interest rates on alternative highly rated securities were used. Default premiums were removed from all rates in order to obtain a comparable series over the entire period.[9]

Figure 1–2 displays the interest rates on long-term bonds and short-term bonds, called *bills,* over the entire period. Note that the most turbulent subperiod for interest rates is the last one, from 1926 through the present.

Refer back to Figure 1–1. By the end of the first subperiod, the total return in stocks beat bonds and bills, but not by much. It is in the second, and especially the third subperiods, when stocks clearly dominated fixed income assets. As a result, the final accumulations of bonds are dwarfed by those in equity.

GOLD AND COMMODITY PRICES

Financial assets are not the only investment for which good historical data are available. In the first two subperiods, the price of gold closely followed the price level. This was because the United States was on the gold standard, a system described in Chapter 9. Since the Great Depression, the United States has progressively abandoned the gold standard, and in 1970, the United States broke all links with gold. The price of gold soared in the 1970s and reached a high of $850 per ounce in January 1980. But the disinflation of the 1980s brought the price of gold back in line with other commodity prices by the end of the decade.

---

[9] See Siegel, "The Real Rate of Interest from 1800–1990: A study of the US and UK," *Journal of Monetary Economics* 29 (1992), pp. 227–52, for a detailed description of process by which a historical yield series was obtained.

FIGURE 1–2
US Interest Rates (1800–1992)

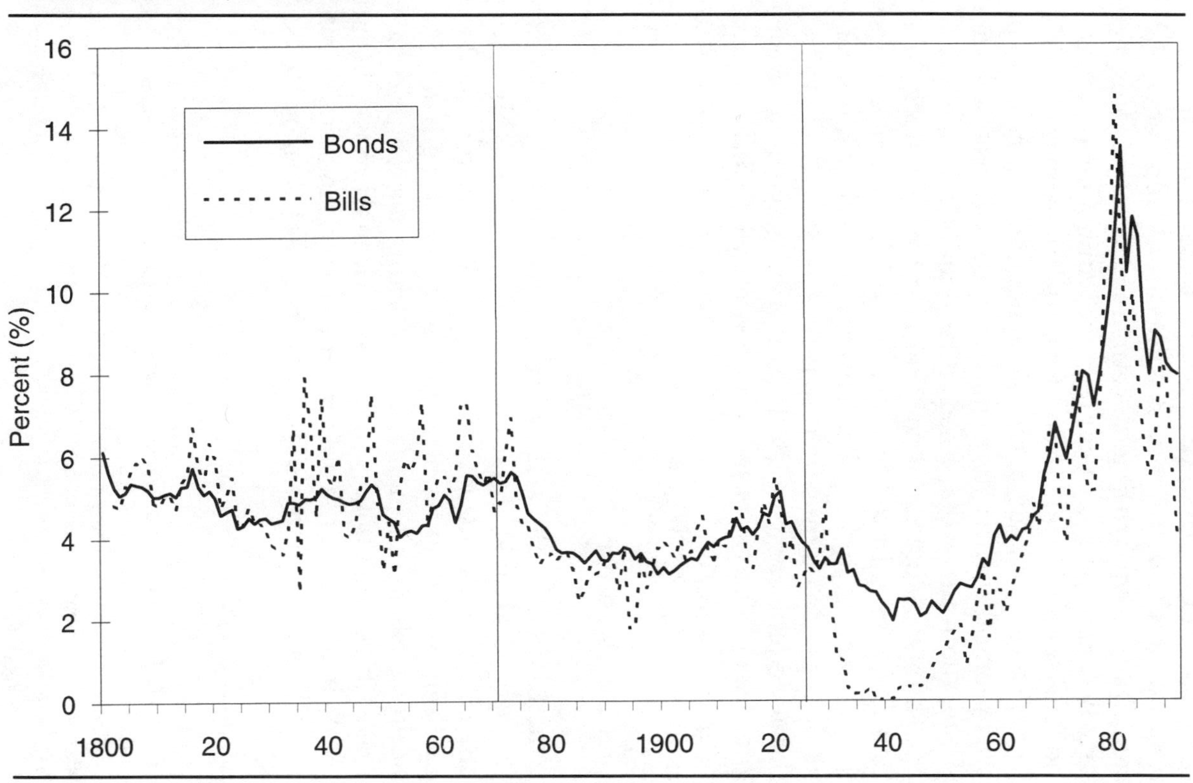

INTERPRETATION OF RETURNS

Nominal Stock Returns

Table 1–1 summarizes the returns to the stock market.[10] The nominal return is the return without any adjustment for inflation. The annual arithmetic return is the average expected return available over one year only and cannot be used to calculate the long-term accumulation of assets. As explained in Chapter 3, only the annual geometric, or compound, returns, can be realized by long-term investors who buy and hold assets and therefore will be the returns discussed in this chapter.

The average annual compound return on stocks has risen from 7.1 percent in the first period, to 7.2 percent in the second, and 9.9 percent in the third. This rising trend in stock returns is not due, as one might think, to increased growth of productivity, increased efficiency, or the improved management of corporate enterprises. The overwhelming reason why stock returns have risen faster in the last seven decades is the increased rate of inflation.

Real Stock Returns

In the 1950s and 1960s, it was common to regard stocks as excellent hedges against inflation. But in the 1970s this perception collapsed, right along with the market. The conventional wisdom had been turned on its head. Inflation appeared bad for stocks, and investors found themselves yearning for the price stability of the 1950s and 1960s, when the stock market was booming.

As it turns out, the old conventional wisdom is still compatible with the experience of the 1970s. Stocks turn out to be great

---

[10] The dividend yield for the first subperiod has been estimated by statistically fitting the relation of long-term interest rates to dividend yields in the second subperiod, yielding results which are closer to other information we have about dividends during the period. See Walter Werner and Steven Smith, *Wall Street* (New York: Columbia Univ. Press, 1991), for a description of some early dividend yields. See also a recent working paper by William Goetzman and Roger Ibbotson, "A Broad Based Index of NYSE Stocks from 1815 to 1871" unpublished manuscript, 1993.

TABLE 1–1
Annual Stock Market Returns

		Total Nominal Return (%)			Nominal Capital Appreciation (%)			Dividend	Total Real Return (%)			Real Capital Appreciation (%)			Real Gold Return	Consumer Price Inflation
		Geo	Arith	*Risk*	Geo	Arith	*Risk*	Yield	Geo	Arith	*Risk*	Geo	Arith	*Risk*		
Periods	1802-1992	**8.1**	9.5	*17.6*	**2.6**	4.1	*17.4*	**5.5**	**6.7**	8.3	*18.2*	**1.3**	2.9	*17.9*	**0.1**	**1.3**
	1871-1992	**8.7**	10.3	*18.6*	**3.7**	5.4	*18.4*	**5.0**	**6.6**	8.3	*19.0*	**1.7**	3.4	*18.7*	**0.0**	**2.0**
Major Sub-periods	I 1802-1870	**7.1**	8.1	*15.5*	**0.7**	1.8	*15.5*	**6.4**	**7.0**	8.3	*16.9*	**0.6**	1.9	*16.6*	**0.2**	**0.1**
	II 1871-1925	**7.2**	8.4	*15.7*	**1.9**	3.1	*16.1*	**5.2**	**6.6**	7.9	*16.8*	**1.3**	2.7	*17.1*	**-0.8**	**0.6**
	III 1926-1992	**9.9**	12.0	*20.7*	**5.2**	7.2	*20.0*	**4.8**	**6.6**	8.6	*20.7*	**2.0**	4.0	*20.0*	**0.7**	**3.1**
Post-War Periods	1946-1992	**11.4**	12.7	*16.8*	**6.9**	8.1	*16.1*	**4.5**	**6.6**	8.1	*17.5*	**2.4**	3.8	*16.8*	**-0.1**	**4.5**
	1966-1981	**6.6**	8.3	*19.5*	**2.6**	4.3	*18.7*	**4.1**	**-0.4**	1.4	*18.7*	**-4.1**	-2.4	*18.0*	**8.8**	**7.0**
	1966-1992	**10.1**	11.5	*17.3*	**6.0**	7.3	*16.6*	**4.2**	**4.2**	5.6	*17.1*	**0.3**	1.7	*16.5*	**1.9**	**5.7**
	1982-1992	**15.4**	16.1	*13.0*	**11.1**	11.8	*12.5*	**4.3**	**11.1**	11.8	*12.9*	**7.0**	7.7	*12.5*	**-7.4**	**3.8**

Geo = geometric compound annual return
Arith = arithmetic average of annual returns
Risk = standard deviation of arithmetic returns

long-term hedges against inflation even though they are often poor *short-term* hedges.

Figure 1–3 displays the total real return index—the nominal return shown in Figure 1–1 corrected for inflation. Over the past two centuries, the average *real,* or after-inflation, compound return on stocks has been 6.7 percent per year. This means that the purchasing power of investments in stocks doubles every 10 years and 6 months. After 21 years the stock market will produce a fourfold increase in one's real wealth. After 42 years, a bit less than two generations, wealth accumulated in the stock market will have undergone a 16-fold increase in purchasing power.

What is most remarkable about all this is the persistence and stability of the real return on stocks over time. Table 1–1 shows that over the major subperiods, the real returns on stocks have been 7.0 percent, 6.6 percent, and 6.6 percent respectively. During this time we have evolved from an agricultural to an industrial and now to a postindustrial service and technology-oriented economy. Information which once took weeks to cross the country is now instantaneously and simultaneously broadcast around the world. Yet despite the mammoth changes that have occurred in our economy since 1800, the basic factors generating wealth for shareholders have shown an astounding persistence.

Gold and Commodity Prices

Figure 1–3 shows that since 1802 the dollar dropped to nine cents in purchasing power, while the price of gold has risen slightly, relative to commodity prices. Ironically, well-preserved paper money from the early 19th century is worth many times its face value on the collectors' market, far surpassing gold bullion as a long-term investment. An old mattress containing 19th-century paper money is a better find for the antique hunter than the equivalent amount hoarded in gold bars!

Capital Appreciation and Dividends

Total returns on any asset can be divided into capital appreciation and income. Capital appreciation is the return due to the change in the price of the asset, while income is the annual cash

FIGURE 1–3
Total Real Return Indexes (1802–1992)

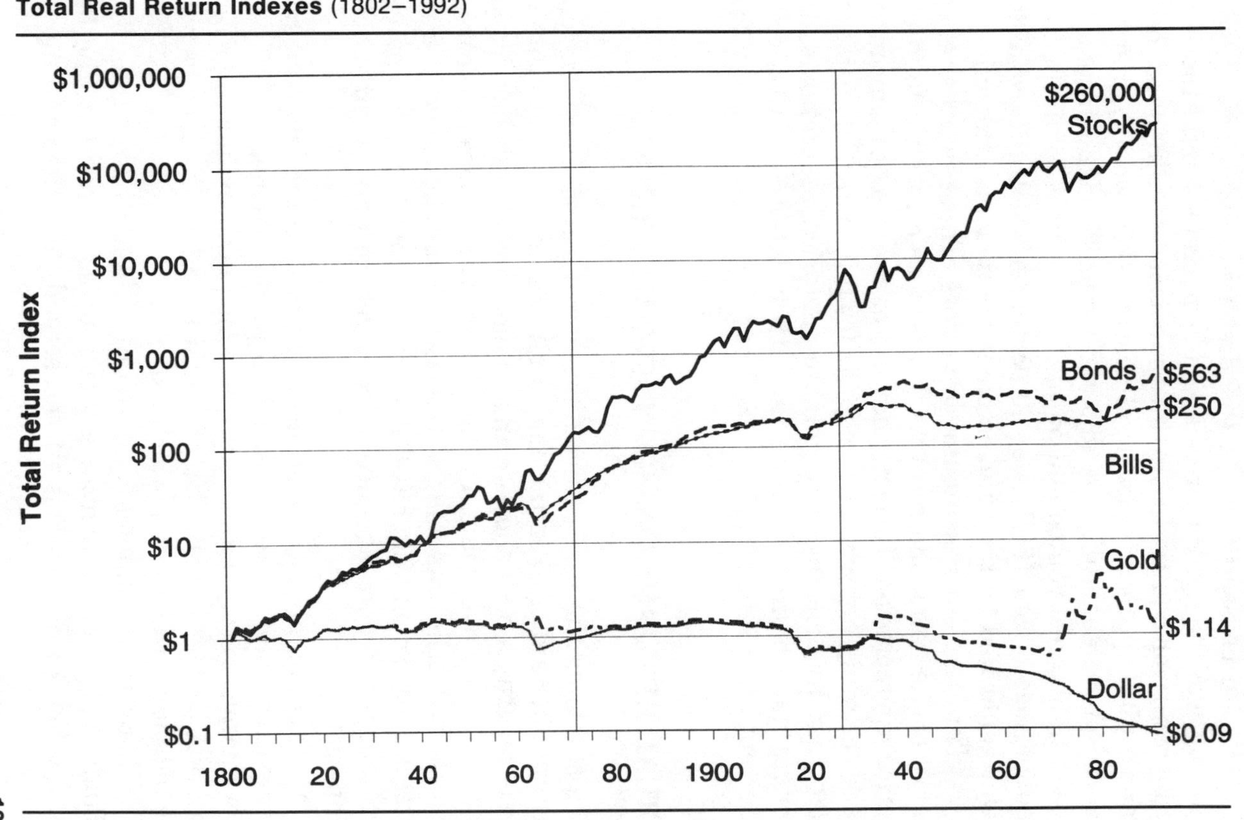

return—dividends for stocks and interest for bonds. Table 1–1 notes that over the entire period, the average dividend yield on stocks has been 5.5 percent, declining somewhat in recent years, a phenomenon analyzed in Chapter 4.

It can be seen that in the first two subperiods, dividend income was the lion's share—about 80 percent—of the total nominal return on equity. In the third subperiod, the dividend income and capital appreciation were almost equal. However, when measured on a real, inflation-adjusted basis, dividend income has been the largest component of total real returns in all the major subperiods. From 1802, over 80 percent of the total *real* return was generated by the reinvestment of dividend income.

This fact surprises many investors. There is a belief that most of the gains one receives from stocks comes through their price appreciation. In fact, that is not the case by any means, and certainly not when one adjusts for inflation. Yet despite the fact that dividend income dominates historical real returns, stock *prices* have more than kept up with inflation—increasing 1.3 percent after inflation since 1802 and 2.1 percent since 1925.

REAL RETURNS ON FIXED-INCOME ASSETS

As stable as the real returns have been for equities, the same cannot be said of fixed-income assets. Table 1–2 shows that the real return on both short-term and long-term bonds has dropped precipitously over time. In the 19th century, the real return on bonds and bills was substantial. Over time, however, the real annual return on bills has fallen from 5.1 percent to 3.2 percent to a bare 0.5 percent since 1926, a return only slightly above inflation.

If the historical rate of return on bills in the last subperiod were extrapolated into the future, it would take nearly 140 years for an investor to double his purchasing power by holding money market assets. In contrast, it would take less than 11 years to double his purchasing power in stocks.

Long-term bonds have fared only slightly better than bills. Their real return fell from a generous 4.8 percent in the first subperiod, to 3.7 percent in the second, and then to only 1.7

TABLE 1–2
Fixed-Income Returns

		Long Term Governments							Short Term Governments				Consumer Price Inflation
		Coupon Rate (%)	Nominal Return (%)			Real Return (%)			Nominal Rate (%)	Real Return (%)			
			Geo	Arith	*Risk*	Geo	Arith	*Risk*		Geo	Arith	*Risk*	
Periods	1802-1992	**4.7**	**4.7**	4.9	*5.6*	**3.4**	3.7	*8.6*	**4.3**	**2.9**	3.1	*6.2*	**1.3**
	1871-1992	**4.6**	**4.6**	4.8	*6.7*	**2.6**	2.9	*8.6*	**3.8**	**1.7**	1.8	*4.7*	**2.0**
Major Sub-Periods	I 1802-1870	**4.9**	**4.9**	4.9	*2.8*	**4.8**	5.1	*8.3*	**5.2**	**5.1**	5.4	*7.7*	**0.1**
	II 1871-1925	**4.0**	**4.3**	4.4	*3.0*	**3.7**	3.9	*6.4*	**3.8**	**3.2**	3.3	*4.8*	**0.6**
	III 1926-1992	**5.1**	**4.8**	5.2	*8.6*	**1.7**	2.1	*10.1*	**3.8**	**0.5**	0.6	*4.3*	**3.1**
Post-War Periods	1946-1992	**6.0**	**4.9**	5.3	*9.8*	**0.4**	0.9	*10.7*	**4.9**	**0.4**	0.4	*3.5*	**4.5**
	1966-1981	**7.2**	**2.5**	2.8	*7.1*	**-4.2**	-3.9	*8.1*	**6.9**	**-0.2**	-0.1	*2.1*	**7.0**
	1966-1992	**8.1**	**7.4**	8.0	*11.6*	**1.6**	2.3	*12.7*	**7.0**	**1.3**	1.3	*2.6*	**5.7**
	1982-1992	**9.6**	**14.9**	15.5	*13.0*	**10.6**	11.3	*13.0*	**7.3**	**3.3**	3.3	*2.0*	**3.8**

Geo = geometric compound annual return
Arith = arithmetic average of annual returns
Risk = standard deviation of arithmetic returns

percent in the third. If the return in the third subperiod is projected into the future, it would take nearly 45 years in order to double one's wealth in bonds, four times the time it takes in stocks.

A better picture of the trends in returns can be found by taking averages of yearly returns. Figure 1–4 shows the 30-year average real geometric returns on stocks and bonds from 1802 to the present. The decline in the average real return on fixed-income securities is striking. In any 30-year period beginning with 1888, the average real rate of return on short-term government securities has exceeded 2 percent only three times. Since the late 19th century, the real return on bonds and bills over *any* 30-year horizon has seldom matched the average return of 4.5 to 5 percent reached during the first 70 years of our sample. From 1879, the real return on long-term bonds has never reached 4 percent over any 30-year period, and exceeded 3 percent during only 12 years.

One has to go back 1½ centuries, to the period from 1831 through 1861, to find any 30-year period where the return on either long- *or* short-term bonds exceeded that on equities! The dominance of stocks over fixed-income securities is overwhelming for investors with long horizons.

EXPLANATIONS FOR THE FALL IN FIXED-INCOME RETURNS

We have seen that although the returns on equities have more than compensated stock investors for the increased inflation since World War II, the returns on fixed-income securities have not. One possible explanation for this is that the postwar inflation was not anticipated by bondholders when they committed their funds. Bond buyers in the 1960s and early 1970s could have scarcely imagined the double-digit inflation which ravaged the real value of their bonds.

Although this explanation for the fall in returns seems reasonable for long-term bonds, unanticipated inflation should be a less important factor for money market instruments in which lenders can adjust much more quickly to the increased inflation-

FIGURE 1–4
Real Returns—Stocks and Bonds (30-Year Centered Geometric Moving Average 1816–1992)

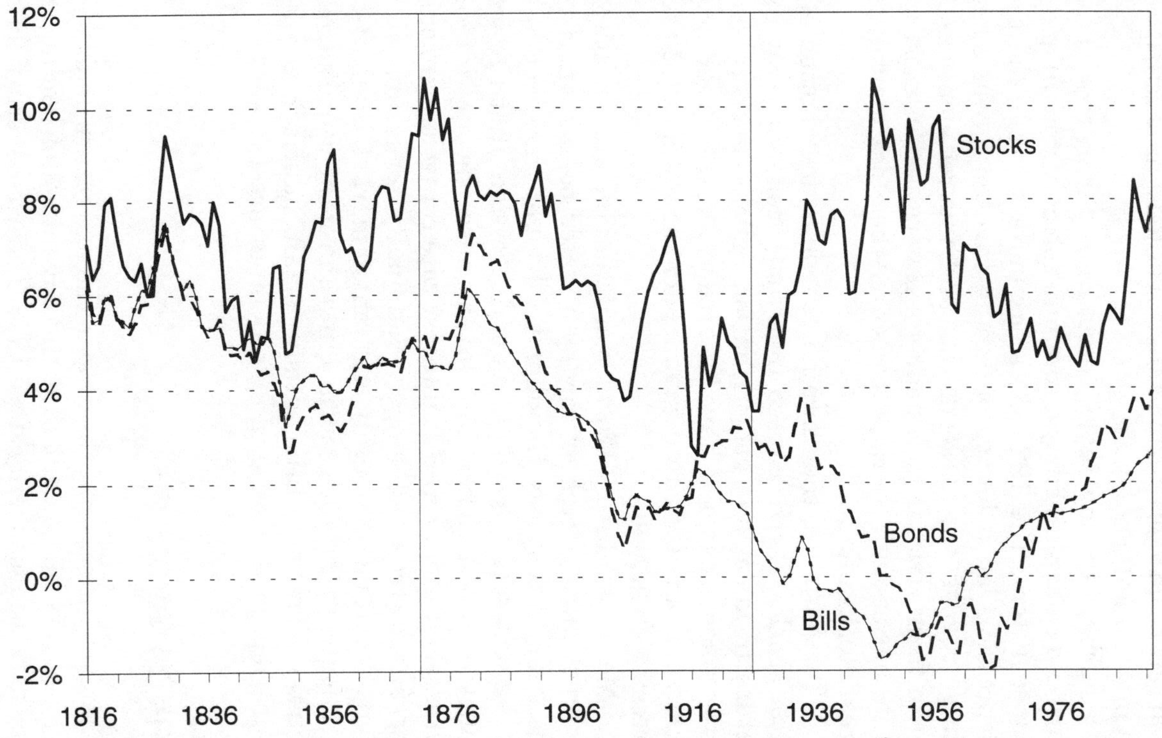

ary pressures. Shifts in the inflation outlook give short-term lenders an opportunity to demand a premium in the rate of interest when they negotiate their loans. Accordingly, short-term bonds should better protect investors against unanticipated inflation than longer-term bonds. Yet in the third subperiod, the real return on short-term bonds fell at least as much, if not more, than on long-term bonds.

Perhaps the low real interest rates during much of this century can be explained by a combination of historical and institutional factors. The 1929–32 stock market crash and the Great Depression left a legacy of fear in investors, causing many to cling to government securities and insured deposits, driving down their yield. It took nearly a generation for most investors to gather enough courage to reenter the stock market after the great stock collapse.

Furthermore, the more homogenous distribution of wealth after World War II, caused by strong economic growth, a high return to labor, and redistribution policies undertaken by the government, may also have lowered real rates. Savers with more modest means tend to demand safer money market assets, depressing their yield.

Moreover, during World War II and the early postwar years, interest rates were kept low by a stated bond support policy of the Federal Reserve. Bondholders bought these bonds because of the widespread predictions of depression after the war. This policy was abandoned in 1951 because the low interest rate threatened inflation. But interest rate controls, particularly on deposits, lasted much longer. And finally, one cannot ignore the transformation of a highly segmented market for short-term instruments in the 19th century into one of the world's most liquid markets. Treasury bills satisfy certain fiduciary and legal requirements not possessed by any other asset.

EQUITY PREMIUM

Whatever the reasons, the drop in the real return on fixed-income investments has meant that the advantage of holding equities has increased markedly since 1926. The excess return for holding

FIGURE 1–5
Equity Risk Premium (30-Year Centered Geometric Moving Average 1816–1992)

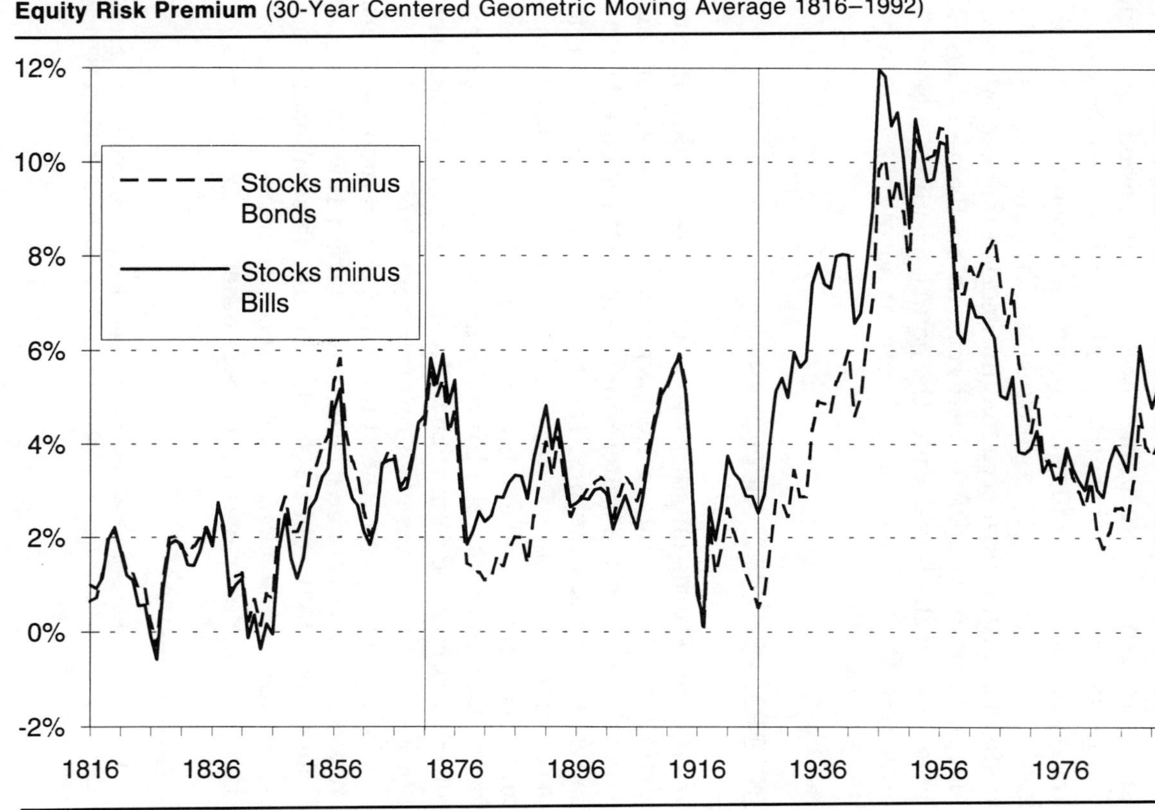

equities over short-term bonds is referred to as the *equity risk premium,* or simply the *equity premium,* and is plotted in Figure 1–5. The equity premium averaged 1.9 percent in the first subperiod, 2.8 percent in the second subperiod, and 6.1 percent in the final period.

The low real rates on bonds may have contributed to higher equity returns in the immediate postwar period. Since firms finance a large part of their capital investment with bonds, the low real cost of obtaining such funds increased returns to shareholders. It may not be a coincidence that the highest 30-year average equity return occurred in a period marked by very low real returns on bonds. As real returns on fixed-income assets have risen in the last decade, the equity premium appears to be returning to the 2 percent to 3 percent norm that existed before the postwar surge.

INTERNATIONAL RETURNS

Why have returns on stocks so outpaced bonds during most of history? Certainly in the 19th century not all investors anticipated that the United States would become the greatest economic power in the next century. But the superior long-term returns to equity hold not only for the United States, but also for foreign countries. Figure 1–6 displays the cumulative stock return index for the United States, the United Kingdom, and Germany.[11] The returns are charted from 1926 to the present, our third subperiod, while the inset traces total returns from 1871.

It is striking that the cumulative real returns on German and UK stocks over the 67-year period from 1926 through 1992 come so close to that of the United States. The compound annual real returns on stocks in each of these countries are all within about one percentage point of each other.

---

[11] The German returns are obtained from Gregor Gielen, "120 Jahre Deutscher Aktiemarkt," unpublished manuscript, 1993. British returns are from Shiller (1989) and updated from various sources.

FIGURE 1–6
Total Real Stock Returns (US, UK, and Germany 1926–92)

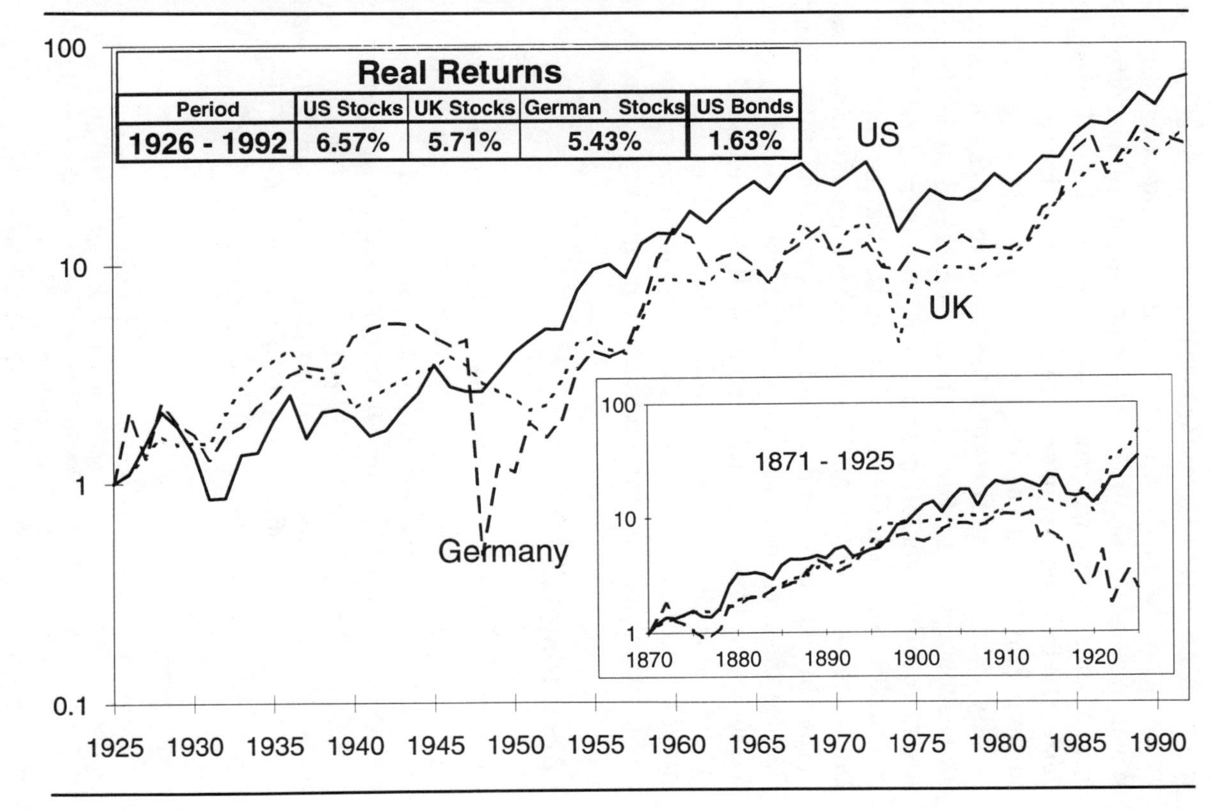

Real Returns				
Period	US Stocks	UK Stocks	German Stocks	US Bonds
1926 - 1992	6.57%	5.71%	5.43%	1.63%

Germany

There is no question that the First World War and the interwar period devastated German stocks. By the end of 1922, stocks were selling in real terms for less than 20 percent of their prewar value. And the real value of German stocks after the Second World War fell to about 1/10 their prewar level. Despite the ravages of these wars, investors were not wiped out. Investors who patiently held equity were rewarded with the tremendous returns in the postwar period.[12]

By 1958, the total return for German stocks had surpassed its prewar level. In the 12 years from 1948 to 1960, German stocks rose by over 30 percent per year in real terms. Indeed, from 1939, when the Germans began the war in Poland, through 1960, the real return on German stocks nearly matched those in the United States and exceeded those in the United Kingdom. Despite the total devastation that the war visited on Germany, the long-run investor made out as well in defeated Germany as in victorious Britain or the United States. The data powerfully attest to the resilience of stocks in the face of seemingly destructive political, social, and economic changes.

United Kingdom

Over the long run, the returns in British equities are just as impressive as in the American market. In contrast to the US experience, the greatest stock crash in Britain occurred in 1973 and 1974 not in 1929. The collapse, caused by rampant inflation as well as political and labor turmoil, brought the capitalization of the British market down to a mere $50 billion. This was less than the yearly profits of the OPEC oil-producing nations that year.[13] In other words, the OPEC nations could have purchased

---

[12] Of course, not everyone in Germany was able to realize the German postwar miracle. The stock holdings of many who resided in the eastern sector, controlled by the Soviet Union, were totally confiscated. Despite the reunification with the West, it is uncertain whether any of those claims will be recovered.

[13] "The défi Opec" (no author), *The Economist,* December 7, 1974, p. 85.

a controlling interest in every publicly traded British corporation at the time with less than one year's cash flow!

It's lucky for the British that they didn't. The British market increased dramatically since the 1974 crash and outstripped the dollar gains in all other major world markets, including Japan. Again, those rewards went to those who held on to British stocks through this crisis.

Japan

The postwar rise in the Japanese market is now legendary. The Nikkei Dow Jones stock average, patterned after the US Dow Jones averages and containing 225 stocks, was first published on May 16, 1949. The day marked the reopening of the Tokyo Stock Exchange, which had been officially closed since August of 1945. On the opening day, the value of the Nikkei was 176.21—virtually identical to the US Dow-Jones Industrials at that time. By August of 1993, the Nikkei average was over 20,000, after reaching nearly twice that value at the end of 1989.

But the gain in the Japanese market measured in dollars far exceeds that measured in yen. The yen was set at 360 to the dollar three weeks before the opening of the Tokyo Stock Exchange—a rate that was to hold for more than 20 years. By August, the dollar fell to nearly 100 yen. So in dollar terms, the Nikkei average climbed to over 70,000 in 1993. Since 1948 the Nikkei has increased nearly 20 times its American counterpart!

Shareholders in Japan, like those in Germany, did not see their assets wiped out by World War II. By the end of 1945, stock prices stood at about 35 percent of their level just prior to the Japanese surrender. But from that point they rapidly increased. The postwar Japanese inflation sent wholesale prices up nearly 60-fold, and shares were actively bought for protection against inflation.[14] Like Germany, investors in equities managed to retain their wealth while fixed-income holders suffered badly.

---

[14] T. F. M. Adams and Iwao Hoshii, *A Financial History of the New Japan* (Tokyo: Kodansha International Ltd., 1972), p. 39.

FIGURE 1–7
International Total Real Return Indexes

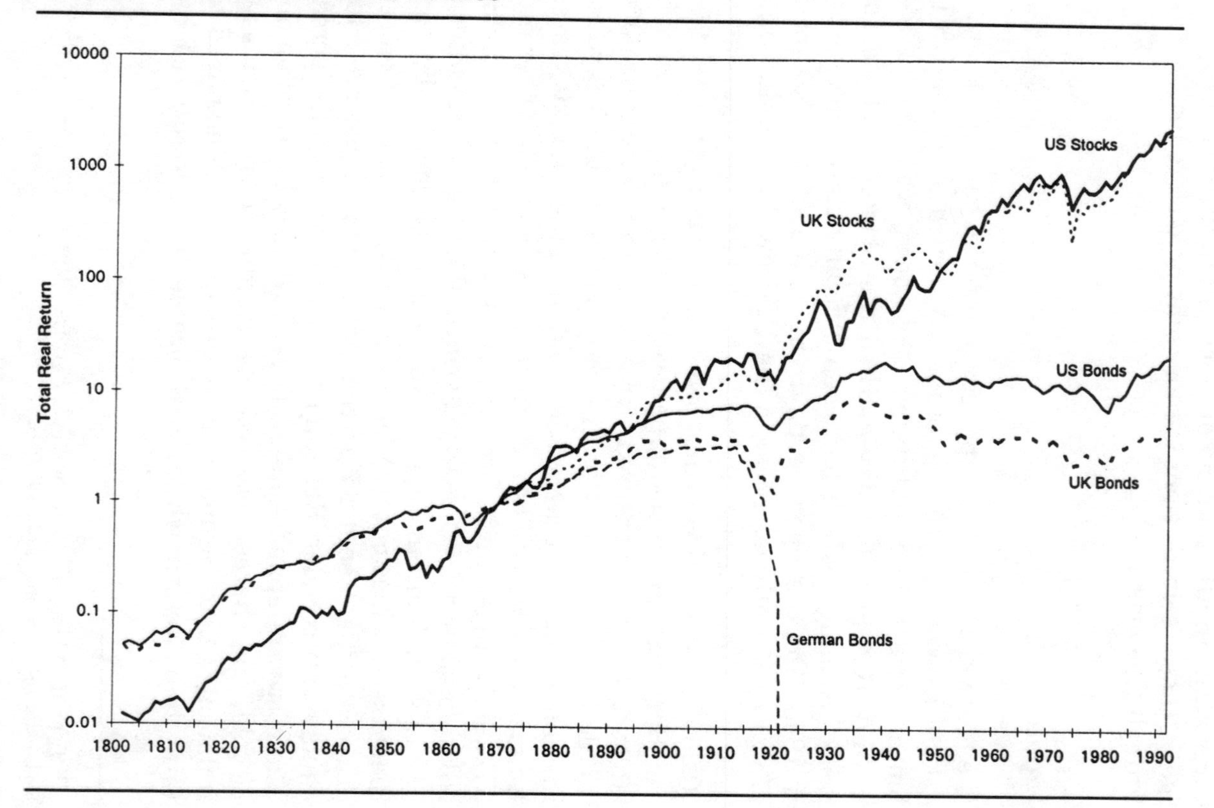

What appeared to be the safe asset in the short run turned out to be far riskier in the long run.

Foreign Bonds

Figure 1–7 summarizes the return on foreign bonds as well as stocks. German bondholders were wiped out by the 1922–23 hyperinflation, an event weathered far better by German stockholders. Hyperinflation will devastate bonds, leaving stocks relatively untouched, while political revolution can make both bonds and stocks worthless.

The superior returns to equity over the past two centuries might be explained by the growing dominance of nations committed to free-market economics. Who might have expected the triumph of market-oriented economies 100 or even 50 years ago? The superior returns to equity over the past 200 years may reflect the emergence of the golden age of capitalism—a system whose fortunes may decline in the next century. But even if capitalism declines, it is unclear which assets, if any, will retain value.

CONCLUSIONS

The superiority of stocks to fixed-income investments over the long run is indisputable. The compound annual real return on stocks has exceeded 6 percent over the past 190 years, remaining remarkably constant over time. In contrast, the real rate of return on fixed-income assets has declined markedly, averaging over 5 percent from 1802–70, but only 0.5 percent since 1926.

Given the special circumstances that occurred subsequent to the stock boom of the 1920s—the Great Crash and Depression, war, government controls—it is reasonable to assume that the low real returns on fixed-income assets over the past 70 years will not be characteristic of the future. As investors recognized the inflationary consequences of a government-managed monetary system, they came to demand an interest premium to boost their return. In the future, as long as inflation does not accelerate significantly, the equity premium will shrink from the levels reached over the past several generations.

Yet the surprising constancy of the historical real return on equity cannot be denied. It may reflect economic forces far beyond our usual concepts of capital and investment. The superior long-term returns to German and Japanese equities appear to indicate that the traditional view of the basis of stock returns—investment in plant and equipment and traditional capital goods—is far too narrow.

The ability to create value springs from skillful management, a stable political system which respects property rights, and a desire to increase wealth by providing value to consumers. Although stocks are legally just the residual claim on the firm after all creditors are satisfied, stocks turn out to be much more than that. The returns to equity are the returns to entrepreneurship which motivate production and growth. Perhaps that is why stock returns transcend the radical political, economic, and social changes that have impacted the world over the past two centuries.

APPENDIX

STOCKS FROM 1802 TO 1871

The first actively traded US stocks, floated in 1791, were two banks: The Bank of New York and the Bank of the United States.* Both offerings were enormously successful and were quickly bid to a premium. But they collapsed the following year when Alexander Hamilton's assistant at the Treasury, William Duer, attempted to manipulate the market and precipitated a crash. It was from this crisis that the antecedents of the New York Stock Exchange were born on May 17, 1792.

---

* The oldest continuously operating firm is Dexter Corp., founded in 1767, a Connecticut maker of special materials; the second is Bowne & Co. (1775) which specializes in printing; the third is CoreStates Financial Corp., founded in 1782 as the First National Bank of Pennsylvania; and the fourth is the Bank of New York Corp., founded in 1782, which was involved in the successful 1791 stock offering with the Bank of the United States that was eventually involved in the crash of 1792.

Joseph David, a historian of the 18th-century corporation, claimed that equity capital was readily forthcoming not only for every undertaking likely to be profitable, but, in his words, "for innumerable undertakings in which the risk was very great and the chances of success were remote.** Although over 300 business corporations were chartered by the states before 1801, fewer than 10 had securities that traded on a regular basis. Two thirds of those chartered before 1801 were connected with transportation: wharves, canals, turnpikes, and bridges.

But the important stocks of the early 19th century were financial institutions—banks and, later, insurance companies. Bank and insurance companies held loans and equity in many of the manufacturing firms which, at that time, did not have the financial standing to issue equity. The fluctuations in the stock prices of financial firms in the 19th century reflected the health of the general economy and the profitability of the firms to whom they lent.

The first large nonfinancial venture was the Delaware and Hudson Canal, issued in 1825, which also became an original member of the Dow-Jones Industrial average 60 years later. In 1830, the first railroad, the Mohawk and Hudson, was listed and for the next 50 years railroads dominated trading on the major exchanges.

** Werner and Smith, *Wall Street,* p. 82.

CHAPTER 2

STOCKS, BONDS, AND LONG-TERM RISK

It seems that the market overrates the safety of "safe" securities . . . and it mistakes the steadiness of money income from a bond for the steadiness in real income which it does not possess.

Irving Fisher, 1925

RISK AND LONG-TERM RETURNS

Many investors avoid stocks because they cannot bear to buy an asset which stands a good chance of falling in price. For these investors the assets of choice are bank CDs, Treasury bills, and money market mutual funds. But one pays dearly for assets which are "safe"—assets with which it is impossible, at least in money terms, to end up with less than one puts in. The first chapter showed that over the long run the returns on these assets have lagged substantially behind those of equities, and in the long run money markets are not nearly as safe as they appear.

Despite the long-run superiority of stocks, those who invest in equities can expect some rocky years along the way. Market declines strongly influence the public's attitude toward stocks. The crash of 1929 affected the public's investing habits for at least a generation. The 89 percent drop in the Dow-Jones Industrial average from September 1929 through July 1932 did not tell the whole story. The Dow utilities, once considered conservative by so many investors, also fell 89 percent, while the Rail average plummeted 93 percent! And the Dow consisted of the "blue chip" stocks—the slaughter of the smaller stocks was even greater, as many fell 95 percent or became completely worthless.

Clearly, almost anyone who had invested in 1929 with borrowed money, using stocks as collateral, would have found himself under water for many years. But what of those who held stocks through the crash—those who didn't panic and weren't forced to liquidate their investments? It may have taken more than 25 years—until November 23, 1954—for the Dow Industrial average to surpass its 1929 highs. But because of the generous dividend yield on stocks during the 1930s, the waiting period for stockholders to recover their original investment was about 15 years. And it took 21 years for stocks to beat all other financial assets, just one year longer than Raskob's recommended 20-year waiting period to enjoy the fruits of stock investing.

Figure 2–1 shows the total return on $100,000 invested in stocks, bonds, or bills after 30 years, adjusted for the rate of inflation. The dominance of stocks over all the subperiods is quite evident. But it may surprise many that money put in stocks at the August 1929 market peak accumulated to a greater sum over 30 years than money put into bonds over the same period. Even the *worst* 30-year post-1926 returns for stocks, which occurred from 1960 to 1990, is almost three times the *best* 30-year returns for bonds and bills. You can mix and match any 30-year period in stocks to any in bonds and bills and find it impossible not to find stocks coming out on top.

Table 2–1 provides a simple comparison of the frequency that the historical returns on stocks beat bonds or bills. Over the entire period, stocks outperform bonds and bills only about 60 percent of the time on a year-to-year basis, but this rises to over 99 percent for bills and 97 percent for bonds over a 30-year horizon. Since 1871 stocks have *never* underperformed bonds or bills over a 30-year horizon! Even with holding periods as short as five years, stocks outperform long- and short-term bonds by a four-to-one margin since 1926 and more than a two-to-one margin since 1872.

COMPARISON OF STOCK AND BOND RETURNS

It is widely known that stock returns, on average, exceed bonds in the long run. But it is little known that in the long run, the risks in stocks are *less than* those found in bonds or even bills!

FIGURE 2–1
30-Year Holding Period Real Returns ($100,000 Initial Investment)

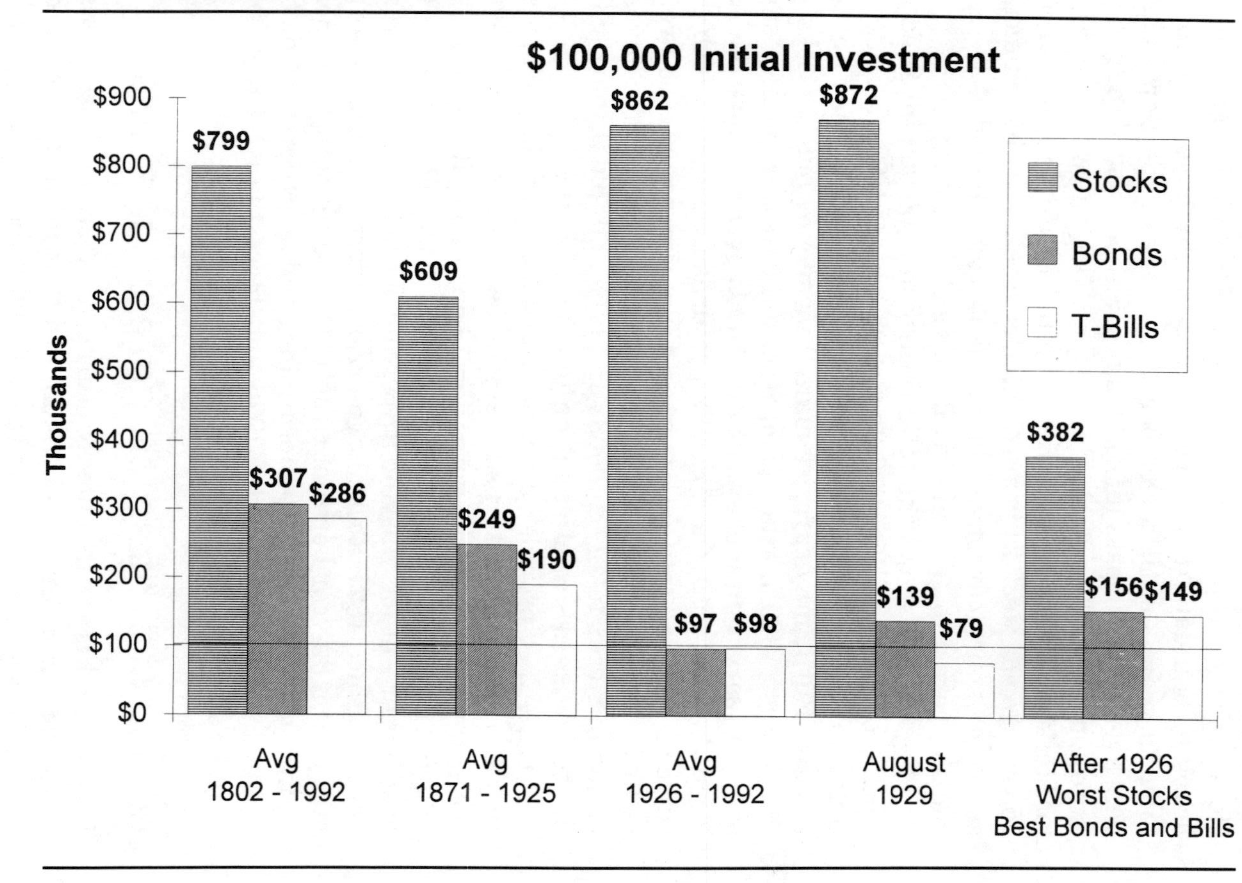

TABLE 2–1
Holding Period Comparisons (Percentage of Periods When Returns on One Asset Exceed Another Asset)

Holding Period	Time Period	Stocks Outperform Bonds	Stocks Outperform T-Bills	Bonds Outperform T-Bills
1 Year	1802-1992	60.21	61.26	49.74
	1871-1992	59.02	63.93	52.46
2 Years	1802-1992	64.74	64.74	53.16
	1871-1992	64.46	68.60	58.68
5 Years	1802-1992	69.52	72.73	51.87
	1871-1992	71.19	74.58	60.17
10 Years	1802-1992	79.67	79.12	52.75
	1871-1992	82.30	84.07	59.29
20 Years	1802-1992	91.28	94.19	51.74
	1871-1992	94.17	99.03	59.22
30 Years	1802-1992	99.38	96.91	46.91
	1871-1992	100.00	100.00	58.06

Figure 2–2 summarizes the ranges of stock and bond returns for the period from 1802–1992. Real stock returns are substantially more volatile than the returns of bonds and bills over short-term periods. But as the horizon increases, the range of stock returns narrows far more quickly than for fixed-income assets. In fact, the 8.0 percent range between the highest and lowest 30-year average real holding period returns for stocks is smaller than *either* bonds or bills!

FIGURE 2–2
Maximum and Minimum Real Holding Period Returns (1802–1992)

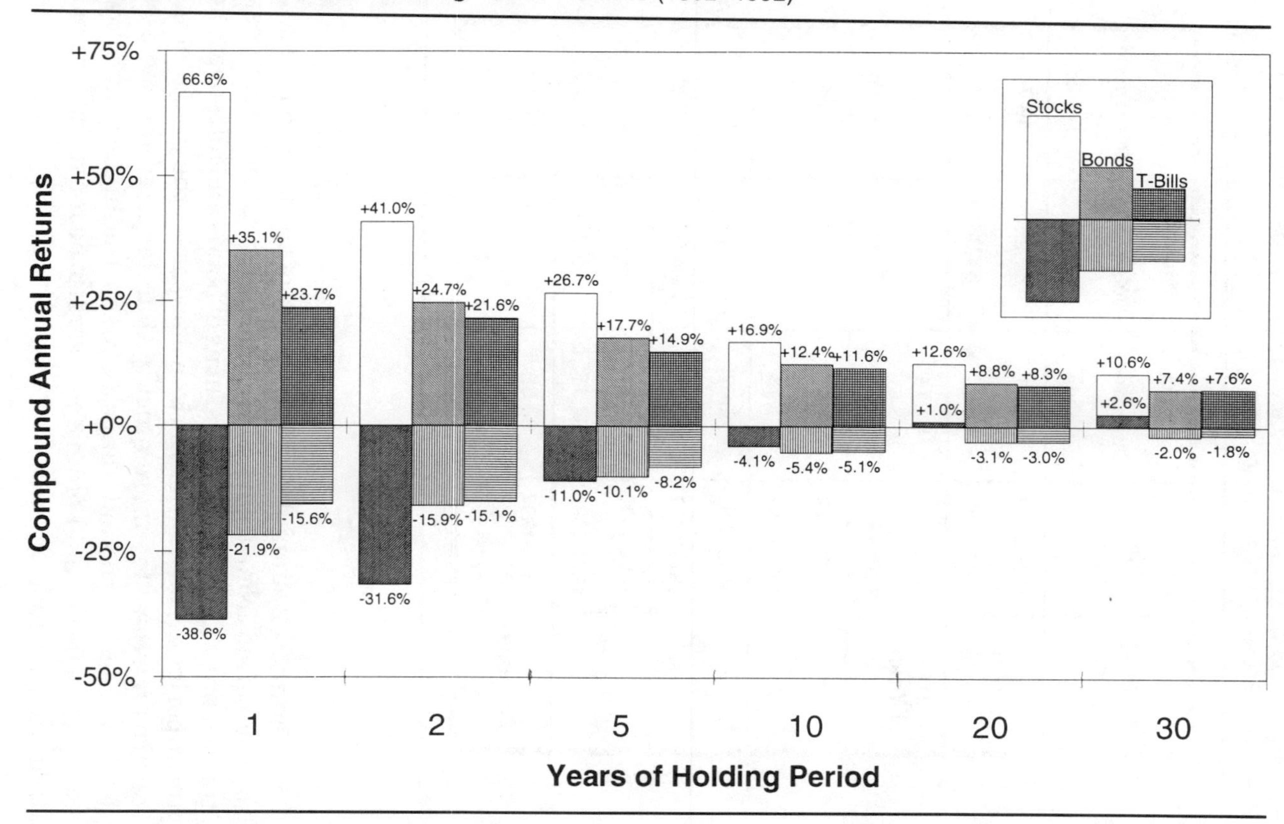

The fact that stocks, in contrast to bonds or bills, have never offered investors a negative real holding period return yield over 20 years or more is also extremely significant. Although it might appear to be riskier to hold stocks than bonds, precisely the opposite is true: the safest long-term investment has clearly been stocks, not bonds.

Figure 2–3 explicitly calculates the dispersions (measured by the standard deviation, and described in the appendix) of the average real holding period annual returns on stocks, bonds, and bills. For one-year holding periods, the dispersion of stock returns is more than twice that of bonds and about three times that of bills. As the holding period increases, the dispersion of the average annual return on both stocks and bonds falls, but it falls far faster for stocks than bonds. In fact, for a 20-year holding period, the dispersion of stock returns is less than for bonds and bills, and becomes even smaller as the holding period increases.

Figure 2–3 also displays (with dashed lines) the risk to a long-term investor based solely on the variability of one-year returns. The results illustrate why portfolios based on the one-year variability of returns are inappropriate for longer-term investors. The risk of holding stocks for 30-year holding periods is significantly less than would have been predicted on the basis of yearly returns, while the risks to bonds and bills are significantly higher. Stocks have what economists call *mean-reverting* returns, meaning that over long periods of time, high returns seem to be followed by periods of low returns and vice versa. On the other hand, over time, real returns on fixed-income assets become relatively less certain. For horizons of 20 years or more, bonds are riskier than stocks.

THE HISTORICAL STUDIES OF STOCK RETURNS

The superiority of stocks over bonds as long-term investments is not a new finding. Edgar L. Smith, a financial analyst and investment manager of the 1920s, was the first to demonstrate

FIGURE 2–3
Holding Period Risk for Annual Real Returns (Historical Data and Theoretical (Dashed Line) 1802–1992)

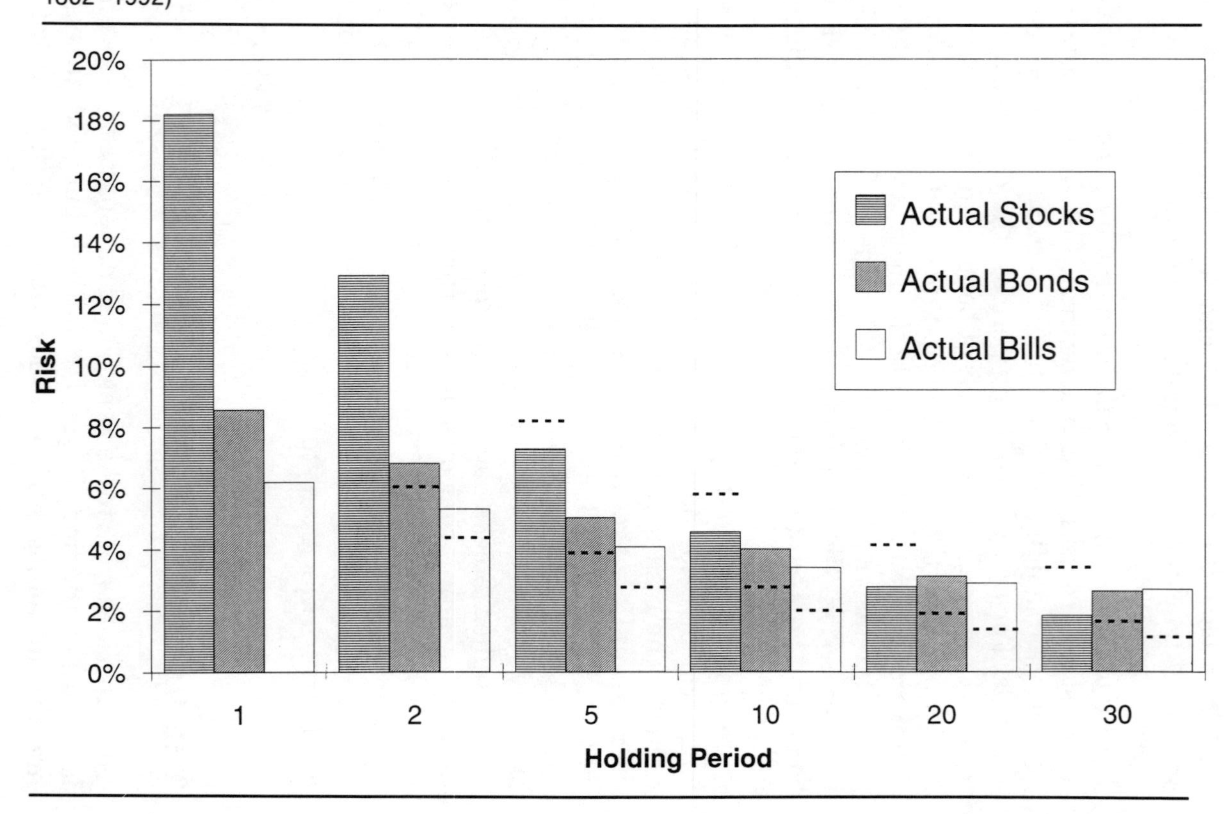

how accumulations of a diversified portfolio of stocks beat bonds. Smith showed that stocks outperformed bonds not only in times of rising commodity prices but also when prices were falling. These results surprised investors since stocks were thought to outperform bonds only in inflationary times.

Smith published his studies in 1924 in a book entitled *Common Stocks as Long-Term Investments*. In it he stated:

> Even if we have bought [stocks] at the very peak, there is definitely to be expected a period in which we may recover as many dollars as we have invested. Our hazard even in such extreme cases appears to be that of time alone.[1]

Smith stated that on the basis of his historical analysis, there was only a 6 percent chance that one would have to wait as long as 6 to 15 years before having an opportunity to liquidate one's stocks on even terms. Smith's conclusion was right, not only historically, but even prospectively. It took just over 15 years to recover the money invested at the 1929 peak, following a crash far worse than Smith had ever examined. And since World War II the recovery period for stocks has been better than Smith's wildest dreams. The *longest* it has even taken since 1945 to recover one's original investment in the stock market was the 3½-year period from December 1972 to June 1976.

Smith wrote his book at the onset of one of the greatest bull markets in our history. Its conclusions caused a sensation in both academic and practical investing circles. *The Economist,* in a review of the book, stated, "Every intelligent investor and stockbroker should study Mr. Smith's most interesting little book, and examine the tests individually and their very surprising results.[2]

Irving Fisher, a professor of economics at Yale and widely considered America's leading economist, praised Smith's research. Fisher summarized:

---

[1] Edgar L. Smith, *Common Stocks as Long-Term Investments* (New York: Macmillan, 1925), p. 81.

[2] "Ordinary Shares as Investments," *The Economist,* June 6, 1925, p. 1141.

> It seems, then, that the market overrates the safety of "safe" securities and pays too much for them, that it underrates the risk of risky securities and pays too little for them, that it pays too much for immediate and too little for remote returns, and finally, that it mistakes the steadiness of money income from a bond for a steadiness of real income which it does not possess. In steadiness of real income, or purchasing power, a list of diversified common stocks surpasses bonds.[3]

Smith's ideas quickly crossed the Atlantic and were the subject of much discussion in Britain. John Maynard Keynes, the great British economist and originator of the business cycle theory which became the accepted paradigm for generations, reviewed Smith's book with much excitement. Keynes stated,

> The results are striking. Mr. Smith finds in almost every case, not only when prices were rising, but also when they were falling, that common stocks have turned out best in the long-run, indeed, markedly so. . . . This actual experience in the United States over the past fifty years affords prima facie evidence that the prejudice of investors and investing institutions in favour of bonds as being "safe" and against common stocks as having, even the best of them, a "speculative" flavor, has led to a relative over-valuation of bonds and under-valuation of common stocks.[4]

Money managers were quick to realize the impact of Smith's work. Hartley Withers wrote in *The London Investors Chronicle and Money Market Review:*

> Old-fashioned investors and their old-fashioned advisers have so long been in the habit of looking on all holdings of ordinary shares or common stocks as something rather naughty and speculative, that one feels a certain amount of hesitation in even ventilating the view that is now rapidly gaining acceptance that ordinary shares, under certain conditions, are really safer than [bonds], even

---

[3] From foreword by Irving Fisher in Kenneth S. Van Strum, *Investing in Purchasing Power* (New York: Barrons, 1925), p. vii. Van Strum, a writer for *Barron's* weekly, followed up and confirmed Smith's research.

[4] J. M. Keynes, "An American Study of Shares versus Bonds as Permanent Investments," *The Nation & The Athenaeum,* May 2, 1925, p. 157.

though the latter may be of the variety which is commonly called "gilt-edged."[5]

A RADICAL SHIFT IN SENTIMENT

But the glorious days for common stocks did not last. The crash pushed the image of stocks as good investments into the doghouse and with it the credibility of Smith's contention that stocks were the best long-term investments. Lawrence Chamberlain, an author and well-known investment banker, stated *"Common stocks, as such, are not superior to bonds as long-term investments, because primarily they are not investments at all. They are speculations."*[6]

The common-stock theory of investment, which is what Smith's theory of stocks had come to be known, was attacked from all angles. In 1934 Benjamin Graham, an investment fund manager and David Dodd, a finance professor at Columbia University, wrote what was to become the bible of the value-oriented approach to analyzing stocks and bonds, entitled *Security Analysis: Principles and Techniques*. Through its many editions, the book has had lasting impact on students and market professionals alike.

Graham and Dodd clearly blamed Smith's book for feeding the bull market mania of the 1920s by proposing plausible-sounding but fallacious theories to justify the purchase of stocks. They wrote:

> The self-deception of the mass speculator must, however, have its element of justification. . . . In the new-era bull market, the "rational" basis was the record of long-term improvement shown by diversified common-stock holdings.
>
> [There is] a small and rather sketchy volume from which the new-era theory may be said to have sprung. The book is entitled

---

[5] Quoted by Edgar Lawrence Smith in *Common Stocks and Business Cycles* (New York: The William-Frederick Press, 1959), p. 20.

[6] Lawrence Chamberlain and William W. Hay, *Investment and Speculations* (New York: Henry Holt & Co., 1931), p. 55.

Common Stocks as Long-Term Investments, by Edgar Lawrence Smith, published in 1924.[7]

POST-CRASH VIEW OF STOCK RETURNS

The crash left the impression that stocks could not be worthy long-term investments. So much had been written about so many who had been wiped out by the market that the notion that stocks could still beat other financial assets was regarded as ludicrous.

In the late 1930s, Alfred Cowles 3rd, founder of the Cowles Commission for economic research, constructed stock indexes back to 1871 of all stocks traded on the New York Stock Exchange. Cowles found that stocks offered superior returns and concluded:

> During that period [1871–1926] there is considerable evidence to support the conclusion that stocks in general sold at about three-quarters of their true value as measured by the return to the investor.[8]

Yet Cowles squarely placed the blame for the crash of 1929 on the shoulder of the government, claiming that increased taxation and government controls rationally drove prices downward.

As stocks slowly recovered from the depression, their returns seemed to warrant a new look. In 1964, two professors from the University of Chicago, Lawrence Fisher and James H. Lorie, examined stock returns through the stock crash of 1929 and the Great Depression.[9]

Fisher and Lorie concluded that stocks offered significantly higher returns (which they reported at 9.0 percent per year) than

---

[7] Benjamin Graham and David Dodd, *Security Analysis,* 2nd ed. (New York: McGraw-Hill, 1940), p. 357.

[8] Alfred Cowles 3rd and associates, *Common Stock Indexes 1871–1937* (Bloomington, Indiana: Pricipia Press, 1938), p. 50.

[9] "Rates of Return on Investment in Common Stocks," *Journal of Business* 37 (January 1964), pp. 1–21.

any other investment media during the entire 35-year period 1926 through 1960. They even factored taxes and transaction costs into their return calculations and concluded:

> It will perhaps be surprising to many that the rates have consistently been so high. . . . The fact that many persons choose investment with a substantially lower average rate of return than that available on common stocks suggests the essentially conservative nature of those investors and the extent of their concern about the risk of loss inherent in common stocks.[10]

Ten years later, Roger Ibbotson and Rex Sinquefield published an even more extensive review of returns in an article entitled, "Stocks, Bonds, Bills, and Inflation: Year-by-Year Historical Returns (1926–74)."[11] They acknowledged their indebtedness to the Lorie and Fisher study and confirmed the superiority of stocks as long-term investments. Their summary statistics are frequently quoted and have often served as the return benchmarks for the securities industry.

CONCLUSION

The news of crashes and panics grabs so many of the headlines and causes many investors to be preoccupied with the short-run volatility of the market, ignoring its long-run potential. And in that long run, the risk of stocks is not only reduced, but actually becomes lower than holding fixed-income assets.

The doctrine that common stocks provide the best way to accumulate wealth, first expounded 70 years ago by Edgar Smith, still remains valid today. In fact, the more data we analyze, the more confident we are that stocks are superior long-term investments. In the long run, the true risk resides with fixed-income investments, not with common stocks.

---

[10] *Ibid.*, p. 20.

[11] *Journal of Business* 49 (January 1976), pp. 11–43.

APPENDIX

MEASURES OF RISK

A common measure of risk is the *standard deviation* of yearly returns. The standard deviation is defined as $\sigma = \{[(r_1 - r_A)^2 + (r_2 - r_A)^2 + \ldots (r_n - r_A)^2]/n\}^{1/2}$, where $r_1, r_2 \ldots r_n$ are the individual yearly returns and r_A is the average, or *mean* of the yearly returns (σ^2 is called the *variance*). If yearly returns follow a normal distribution, popularly known as the *bell-shaped curve,* then about two thirds of the time the asset will have a return equal to the mean plus or minus one standard deviation. That is, the return on the asset will be within one standard deviation of its average, or mean, about two thirds of the time. About 95 percent of the time, the return on the asset will be within two standard deviations of its mean.

PART 2

STOCK RETURNS

CHAPTER 3

STOCKS, STOCK AVERAGES, AND STOCK RETURNS

It has been said that figures rule the world.

Johann Wolfgang Goethe, 1830

MARKET AVERAGES

The Dow-Jones

"How's the market doing?" one stock investor asks another.

"It's having a good day—it's up 25 points."

Exchanges like this are made thousands of times a day throughout the United States. No one asks, "What's up 25 points?" Everyone knows the answer: the Dow-Jones Industrial average, the most quoted stock average in the world. This index, popularly called the "Dow," is so renowned that the news media often call the Dow "the stock market." No matter how imperfectly the index describes the movement of share prices—and virtually no money manager pegs his or her performance to it—it is the way that most investors think of the stock market.

The Dow-Jones averages were created in the late 19th century by Charles Dow, one of the founders of Dow Jones & Co., which also publishes *The Wall Street Journal.* On February 16, 1885, he began publishing a daily average of 12 stocks (10 rails and 2 industrials) which represented active and highly capitalized stocks. Four years later, Dow published a daily average based on 20 stocks—18 rails and 2 industrials.

As industrial and manufacturing firms succeeded railroads in importance, the Dow Industrial average was created on May 26, 1896 from the 12 stocks shown on Table 3–1. The old index

TABLE 3–1
The Dow-Jones Industrial Average

1896	1916	1928	1993 Dow Companies	1993 Price Weight	1993 Market Value Wgt
American Cotton Oil	American Beet Sugar	Allied Chemical	Allied-Signal	4.22%	1.26%
American Sugar	American Can	American Can	Aluminum Co. of America	4.27%	0.79%
American Tobacco	Am. Car & Foundry	American Smelting	American Express	1.87%	1.90%
Chicago Gas	American Locomotive	American Sugar	American Tel & Tel	3.88%	10.98%
Dist. & Cattle Feeding	American Smelting	American Tobacco	Bethlehem Steel	1.15%	0.22%
General Electric	American Sugar	Atlantic Refining	Boeing	2.43%	1.74%
Laclede Gas	American Tel & Tel	Bethlehem Steel	Caterpillar	4.78%	1.02%
National Lead	Anaconda Copper	Chrysler	Chevron	5.57%	3.82%
North American	Baldwin Locomotive	General Electric	Coca-Cola	2.60%	7.15%
Tenn. Coal & Iron	Central Leather	General Motors	Walt Disney	2.69%	3.03%
U.S. Leather pfd.	General Electric	General Railway Signal	Du Pont	3.15%	4.48%
U.S. Rubber	Goodrich	Goodrich	Eastman Kodak	3.37%	2.33%
	Republic Iron & Steel	International Harvester	Exxon	4.13%	10.81%
	Studebaker	International Nickel	General Electric	6.01%	10.81%
	Texas Co.	Mack Trucks	General Motors	2.70%	4.04%
	U.S. Rubber	Nash Motors	Goodyear	2.44%	0.75%
	U.S. Steel	North American	IBM	3.11%	3.74%
	Utah Copper	Paramount Publix	International Paper	4.13%	1.07%
	Westinghouse	Postum, Inc.	McDonald's	3.11%	2.35%
	Western Union	Radio Corp.	Merck	2.33%	5.61%
		Sears, Roebuck	Minn. Mining	6.84%	3.15%
		Standard Oil (N.J.)	J.P. Morgan	4.23%	1.72%
		Texas Corp.	Philip Morris	3.02%	5.57%
		Texas Gulf Sulphur	Procter & Gamble	3.11%	4.47%
		Union Carbide	Sears Roebuck	3.42%	2.51%
		U.S. Steel	Texaco	4.05%	2.21%
		Victor Talking Machine	Union Carbide	1.21%	0.39%
		Westinghouse Electric	United Technologies	3.45%	0.90%
		Woolworth	Westinghouse Electric	0.93%	0.68%
		Wright Aeronautical	Woolworth	1.81%	0.50%

created in 1889 was reconstituted and renamed the *Rail average* on October 26, 1896. In 1916, the Industrial average was increased to 20 stocks and in 1928 the number was expanded to 30. The Rail average, whose name was changed in 1970 to the *Transportation average,* is comprised of 20 stocks, as it has been for almost a century.

The early Dow stocks were centered around commodities: cotton, sugar, tobacco, lead, leather, rubber, etc. Six of the 12 companies have survived in much the same form, but only one—General Electric—has both retained its membership in the Dow Industrials *and* not changed its name. Chicago Gas Co., an original member of the 12 Dow stocks, became Peoples Energy, which is a current member of the Dow Utilities.

Almost all of the original Dow stocks thrived as large and successful firms, even if they did not remain in the index (see Appendix A for details). The only exception was US Leather Corp., which was liquidated in the 1950s. Shareholders received $1.50 plus one share of Keta Oil & Gas, a firm acquired earlier. But in 1955, Keta's assets were looted by the president, Lowell Birrell, who later fled to Brazil to escape US authorities. Shares in US Leather, which in 1909 was the seventh-largest corporation in the United States, became worthless.

Figures 3–1 and 3–2 plot the monthly high and low of the Dow-Jones Industrial average from its inception in 1885. Each vertical line represents the high and low for the month. Figure 3–1 displays the actual levels of the Dow, while Figure 3–2 shows the real Dow-Jones average, which is the actual levels corrected for inflation.

It surprises many to note that the real Dow is currently far below the peak reached in 1966 and not much above the peak reached in 1929. The decline in the real value of the Dow Industrials from the mid 1960s to the early 1980s was almost 75 percent, second only to the Great Crash of 1929 to 1932.

The real Dow-Jones average appears to move in a channel with an average growth rate of 1.65 percent per year. This is the rate at which the Dow stocks appreciated after inflation. The Dow-Jones average, like most other popular averages, excludes dividends, so that this growth rate of the Dow Industrial index greatly understates the total return on the Dow stocks.

The channel drawn in Figure 3–2—plus or minus 67 percent of the midpoint—contains the real Dow Industrials three quarters of the time. When prices move out of the channel to the upside, as they did in 1929 and again in the mid-1960s, stocks subsequently suffered poor returns. On the other hand, when stocks penetrated the band on the downside, they subsequently experienced superior returns.

The current upper limit of the channel is near 5000 on the

FIGURE 3–1
The Dow-Jones Industrial Average (Feb. 1885–May 1993)

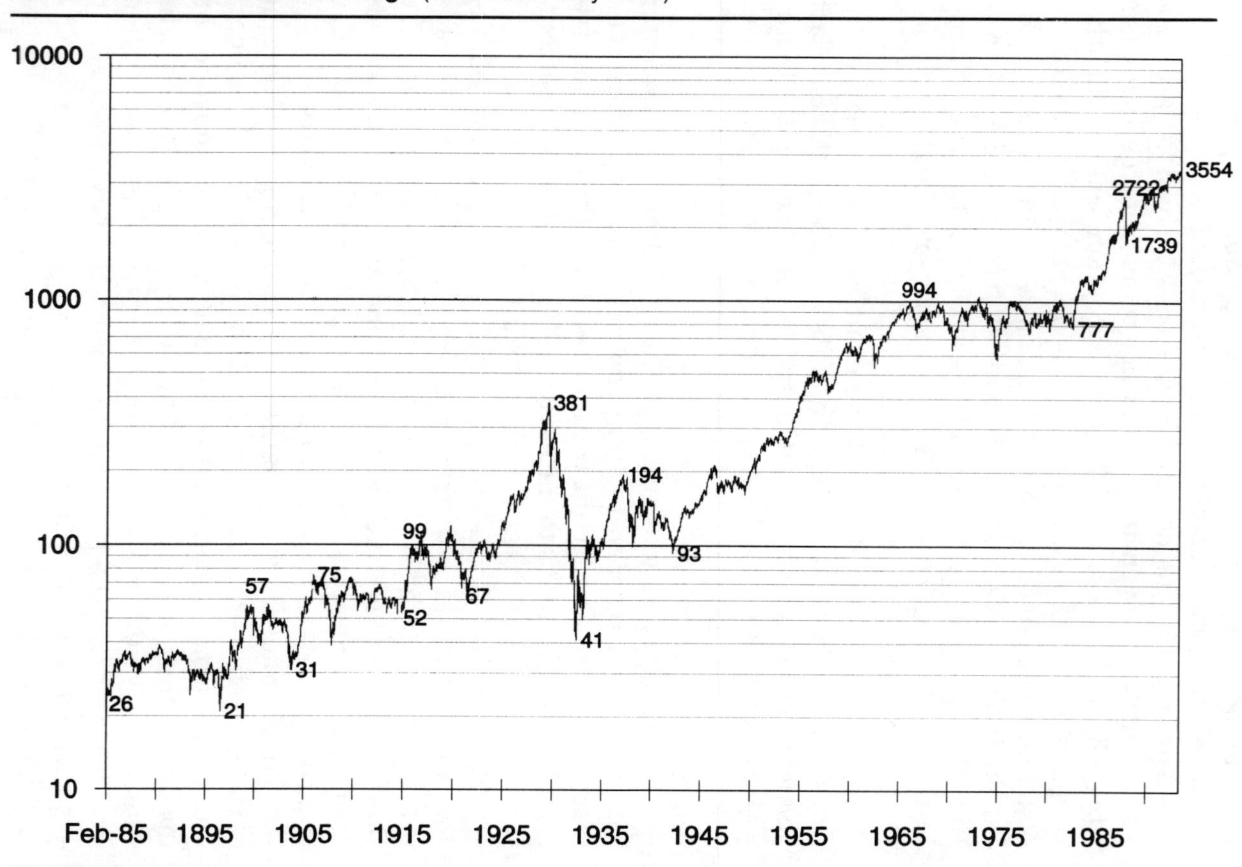

FIGURE 3–2

The Real Dow-Jones Industrial Average (Feb. 1885–May 1993—In 1993 Dollars)

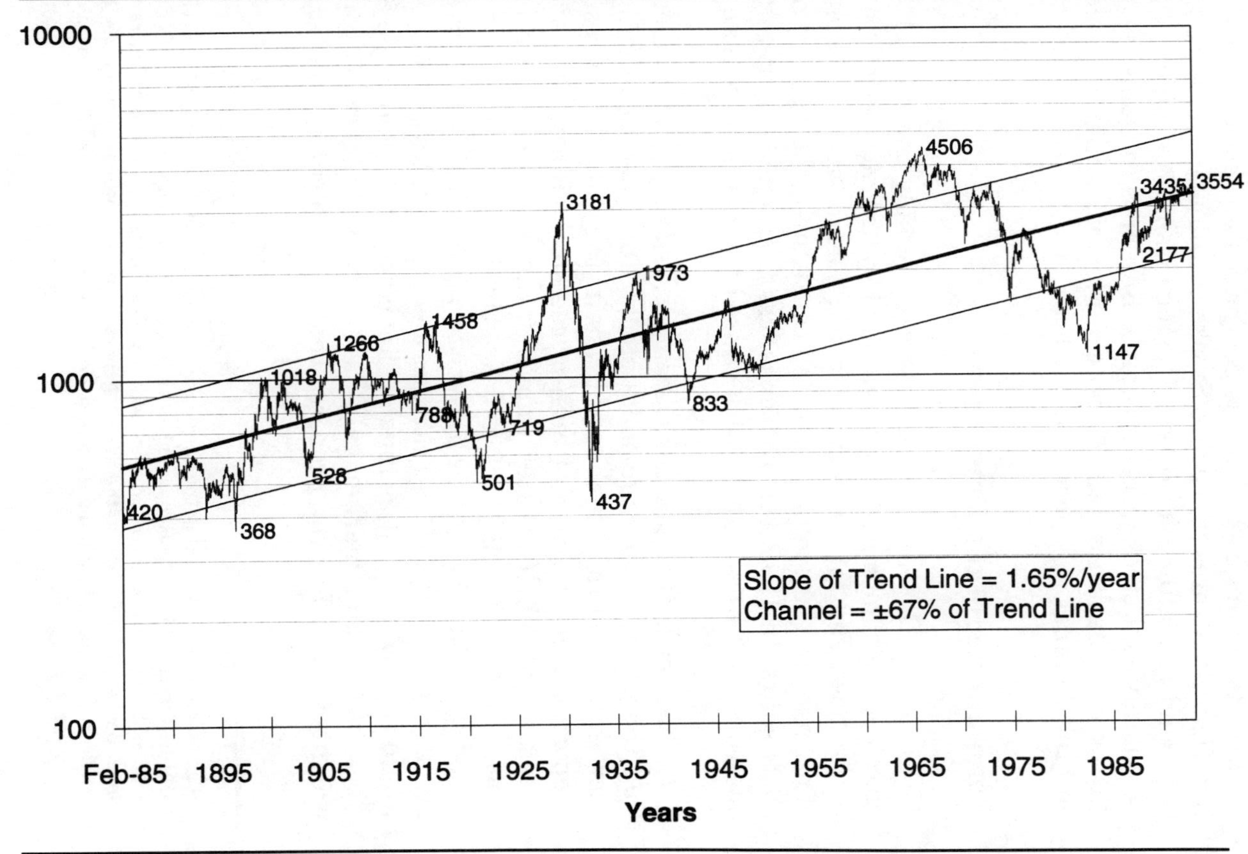

Dow Industrials. But using channels and trend lines to predict future returns, however tempting, can be misleading. Long-standing trends have been broken in the past. Applying such a channel to Figure 3–1, where stock prices are not corrected by inflation, illustrates this point. Stocks permanently broke above the trend line after World War II, since rising consumer prices ultimately sent stock prices upwards. But since consumer prices did not come back down to their prewar levels, neither did stocks and the channel was permanently broken.

Computation of the Dow Index

The original Dow-Jones averages were simply the sum of the prices of the component shares divided by the number of stocks in the index. But this divisor had to be adjusted over time because of changes in the companies which constituted the average and stock splits. In 1993, the divisor is less than one half, so that a one-point rise in any Dow stock caused the average to increase over two points.[1]

The Dow Industrials is a *price-weighted* index, which means that the prices of the component stocks are added together and then divided by the number of firms in the index. As a result, proportional movements of high-priced stocks in the Dow averages have a much greater impact than those of lower-priced stocks. A stock which is 100 and rises by 1 percent, or one point, would cause the Dow to rise by over two points (using the current divisor), while if a $50 stock rises by 1 percent, then the Dow would rise by one-half as much. This is the case even if the $50 stock has greater market value than the $100 stock. A price-weighted index has the property that when a component stock

[1] The procedure for computing the Dow-Jones averages when a new (or split) stock is substituted is as follows: the component stock prices are added up before and after the change and a new divisor is determined which yields the same average as before the change. Because of stock splits, the divisor generally moves downward over time, but the divisor could increase if a higher-priced stock is substituted for a lower-priced one in the average.

splits, the split stock has a reduced impact on the average, and all the other stocks a slightly increased impact.[2]

Because of the nature of price-weighted averages, equal percentage changes in the prices of the Dow stocks can have very different impacts on the Dow averages. Table 3–1 displays the June 1993 weighting of each Dow stock. Westinghouse Electric has the lowest weight, under 1 percent, while Minnesota Mining and Manufacturing has the highest weight—nearly 7 percent, about eight times greater. This is only because the price of 3M shares is about eight times that of Westinghouse. If 3M were to split eight-for-one, both stocks would have the same weight in the index.

But the price of each stock has little to do with the *market* value of the company. As of June 1993, AT&T, the largest component firm, comprised 10.98 percent of the market capitalization of the 30 Dow stocks, while Bethlehem Steel comprised only 0.22 percent, or one 50th that of AT&T. But AT&T's price impact is only about three times that of Bethlehem Steel's. A 1 percent move of 3M has nearly twice the impact on the Dow as does the same change for AT&T, although AT&T has almost four times the market value. The Dow Industrial average, in effect, gives more weight to some of the smaller blue chips than would a capitalization-weighted index.

VALUE-WEIGHTED INDEXES

The Cowles Index

Although the Dow averages were published in 1885, they were certainly not comprehensive. Many important companies were not included in the indexes and historical prices of the component

---

[2] Before 1914, the divisor was left unchanged when a stock split and the stock price was multiplied by the new number of shares when computing the index. This led to rising stocks having greater weight in the average, something akin to value-weighted stock indexes today.

stocks were not computed. In 1939, Alfred Cowles, founder of the Cowles Foundation for Economic Research, constructed a stock index back to 1871 which consisted of all stocks listed on the New York Stock Exchange. This index was the first to weight each stock's performance by its capitalization, or market value, a technique now recognized as giving the best indication of the direction of the overall market.

Standard & Poor's Index

The Cowles index became the basis of what is currently the most important benchmark among portfolio analysts, the S&P 500 Index. This, like the Cowles index, is a capitalization-weighted index of 500 of the largest US corporations.

The Standard & Poor's stock price index was inaugurated on March 4, 1957. At that time, the S&P 500 Index contained 500 heavily capitalized stocks, whose value comprised about 90 percent of all NYSE-listed stocks. The 500 stocks contained 425 industrials, 25 railroad, and 50 utility corporations. In 1988, the Standard & Poor's Corporation dropped any fixed weighting between different industries.

The S&P 500 Index was calculated back to 1926, although for many years before 1957 the index did not contain 500 stocks. A base value of 10 was chosen for the average index value from 1941 to 1943 so that when the index was first published in 1957, the average price of a share of stock (which stood between $45 and $50) was approximately equal to the value of the index. An investor at that time could easily identify with the changes in the S&P 500 Index, since a 1-point change approximated the price change for an average stock, while in 1954 the Dow Industrials was already many times the average stock price.

The S&P 500 Index does not contain the 500 largest stocks nor are all the stocks in the index United States-based corporations. For example, Microsoft, one of the largest stocks in the United States, is not in the S&P 500 Index, while Royal Dutch Petroleum, a Dutch-based oil firm which ranks among the top 10 US corporations in market capitalization, is included. On the other hand, the S&P 500 Index has a number of firms that are quite small, representing companies that have fallen in value and have yet to be replaced. In June 1993, three stocks in the S&P 500 Index had a market value less than $100 million, which ranks them below the top 2,000 firms traded in the United States. Currently the S&P 500 constitutes less than three quarters of the value of all stocks traded in the United States.

Market Capitalization

The history of large corporations reflects the history of industrial America. In 1909, US Steel was by far the largest American corporation, with assets approaching $2 billion. It was followed by Standard Oil Co. (only one fifth the size of US Steel), American Tobacco, International Mercantile Marine (later US Lines), and International Harvester (now Navistar).

Table 3–2 lists the largest corporations in terms of market value of equity since 1956, when General Motors took the honor. From 1961 through 1989 the top position alternated between IBM and AT&T. Since then, the number one spot has gone to Philip Morris and Exxon, heir of the Standard Oil dynasty that was in second place in the early part of this century.

As of June 1993, AT&T regained its position as the largest US corporation ranked by market value—$82.6 billion—with Exxon and General Electric very close behind. The only firm worldwide that beats it is its sister in Japan, Nippon Telephone and Telegraph, which in 1993 had a market value of $140 billion.

But consider how large AT&T would be without the 1984 divestiture of the regional Bell companies. In June 1993 the total market value of the Baby Bells, as the regional companies are known, is $152.9 billion, almost twice that of Ma Bell. Adding the babies to the parent would form the world's largest corporation, three times the size of any other in the United States and larger than its Japanese counterpart.

A noteworthy trend is the tendency of the largest companies to represent a smaller fraction of the market value of all listed stocks. The top five firms constituted over 22 percent of the market value of all stocks in 1956, but that declined to less than 9 percent in 1993. No longer do a few solitary giants dominate the American corporate landscape. There is always room for

TABLE 3–2

Largest Capitalized Stocks (Selected years, 1956–1993, dollars in billions)

Rank	1993			1992			1991		
1	**AT&T**	**$82.6**	**2.1%**	**Exxon**	**$80.3**	**2.1%**	**Philip Morris**	**$70.9**	**2.0%**
2	Exxon	81.3	2.0	AT&T	78.4	2.1	Exxon	68.0	2.0
3	GE	81.3	2.0	Walmart	75.2	2.0	GE	67.6	1.9
4	Walmart	57.8	1.4	GE	75.8	2.0	Wal-Mart	61.2	1.8
5	Coca-Cola	53.8	1.3	Philip Morris	57.3	1.5	Merck	56.9	1.6
		$356.8	8.9%		$366.9	9.7%		$324.6	9.4%

Rank	1990			1985			1980		
1	**Exxon**	**$72.1**	**2.7%**	**IBM**	**$95.7**	**5.0%**	**IBM**	**$39.6**	**3.1%**
2	Philip Morris	64.4	2.4	Exxon	40.3	2.1	AT&T	36.1	2.9
3	IBM	63.8	2.4	GE	33.2	1.7	Exxon	34.8	2.8
4	GE	57.8	2.2	AT&T	26.7	1.4	Std. Oil Ind.	23.4	1.9
5	Wal-Mart	42.4	1.6	GM	22.3	1.2	Schlumberger	22.3	1.8
		$300.5	11.3%		$218.1	11.4%		$156.3	12.4%

Rank	1975			1965			1956		
1	**IBM**	**$33.6**	**5.0%**	**AT&T**	**$34.8**	**6.3%**	**GM**	**$12.3**	**5.7%**
2	AT&T	29.4	4.4	GM	28.3	5.1	Std. Oil (NJ)	11.5	5.4
3	Exxon	19.9	2.9	Std. Oil (NJ)	16.8	3.0	AT&T	9.8	4.6
4	Kodak	17.1	2.5	IBM	16.1	2.9	DuPont	8.8	4.1
5	GM	16.5	2.4	DuPont	10.7	1.9	GE	5.2	2.4
		$116.5	17.3%		$106.7	19.3%		$47.6	22.3%

newcomers: Witness Wal-Mart's climb from obscurity a generation ago to the fourth-largest US corporation in 1992, while erstwhile giants, such as IBM, fell.

Composition of Stock Indexes

Of the eight largest US stocks, all but Wal-Mart are represented in the Dow Industrials. But not all the Dow stocks are large. There are 9 stocks in the 30 Dow Industrials which rank *below* the top 100 stocks in market capitalization. (The smallest Dow stock by market capitalization is Bethlehem Steel, which ranked about 370th in 1993.)

The top 100 stocks in the S&P 500 Index comprise about two thirds of the market value of the Index, while the top 200 comprise about five sixths of the value. To show how small stocks become when one goes down the list, the smallest 100 stocks of the S&P 500 Index make up less than 2 percent of the index's value.

Yet the S&P 500 Index does not make up the whole market—not by a wide margin. Figure 3–3 shows the size and total market value in June of 1993 of the largest 3,000 domestic corporations. The top 500 stocks comprise 80 percent of the $4.0 trillion market value of the largest 3,000 domestic corporations. The value of the S&P comprises about 78 percent and the Dow stocks less than 20 percent of market value of the top 3,000 stocks.

The largest comprehensive index is the Wilshire 5000, which, although created with 5,000 stocks in 1974, now includes over 6,000 firms with readily available price data.[3] The S&P 500 Index comprises only about 70 percent of the value of the Wilshire 5,000. So if one wants to hold the entire US market, an investor must invest 30 percent of his portfolio in small stocks and 70 percent in the S&P 500 Index.

---

[3] There are over 7,000 listed stocks on US exchanges, excluding some 20,000 "penny stocks" which are infrequently traded.

FIGURE 3–3
Market Capitalization of the 3,000 Largest Stocks

Rank	Percent of Market	Dollar Value (in billions)
1 - 500	80.0%	$77.13 - 1.46
501 - 1,000	11.3	1.46 - 0.53
1,001 - 1,500	4.6	0.53 - 0.25
1,501 - 2,000	2.3	0.25 - 0.13
2,001 - 2,500	1.2	0.13 - 0.08
2,501 - 3,000	0.7	0.08 - 0.04

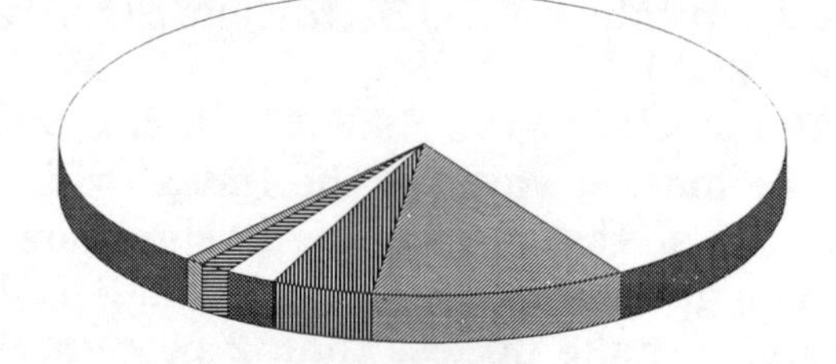

TOTAL RETURNS INDEXES

Although stock indexes are useful for short-run measurement of returns, they are quite inadequate over the longer run. This is because stock price indexes do not include the dividend paid by the stocks. To take account of dividends, one must construct a *total return index*. This index can be calculated for any asset by adding the cash returns (such as dividends or interest) to the change in the price of the asset. A total return index measures the accumulation of wealth if all returns are continually reinvested in the asset.[4]

Asset Price Indexes

In contrast to a total return index, an *asset price index* measures the appreciation or depreciation of the price of an asset or, more frequently, a collection of assets over time *without* any reinvest-

[4]The measurement of the total returns index for an asset which pays no dividends or interest is simply the difference between the initial and terminal prices.

ment of cash flows. Asset price indexes for a group of stocks are called *stock price indexes*. This is the type of index represented by any of the popular indexes, such as the Dow-Jones averages or the S&P 500 Index.[5] All of these indexes compute the average price of a group of individual stocks (some weighted by value, others not) without reinvesting the cash dividends paid to the investor.

Stock returns *cannot* be calculated from the stock index alone, but must include dividends. This means that when choosing money managers or mutual funds, an investor must compare their reported returns to stock indexes which include the reinvestment of dividends, not to simple indexes such as the S&P 500 or the Dow Industrials.

ARITHMETIC AND GEOMETRIC RETURNS

Many mutual fund or money managers report average annual rates of return on the assets under their management. It might appear that the higher the average return, the better off an investor would be. But this is not necessarily so. Arithmetic returns can give an extremely misleading view of investment performance over time.

A simple example will suffice. Imagine a money manager whose portfolio goes from 100 to 50 in one year, and back to 100 the next. In the first year the return is minus 50 percent, while in the second year the return is plus 100 percent, as the portfolio doubled in value. The average annual return on the portfolio is therefore plus 25 percent, even though the value of the portfolio is the same as it was two years ago. In contrast, imagine another manager whose portfolio goes from 100 to 110 at the end of the first year and then to 121 in the second year: an average annual 10 percent gain in value. Clearly you would be better off with the second manager, although his average annual return is lower than the first.

---

[5] The only important exception is the American Stock Exchange's Market Value Index, which adds dividends to its value.

To understand how this can be, it is important to distinguish two methods of calculating returns. The first and simplest is the *average annual arithmetic return.* The average annual arithmetic return is the simple average of individual total yearly returns. The yearly return is the sum of (1) the percentage gain (or loss) in the value of your portfolio due to changes in asset prices and (2) any dividends or other cash distributions, expressed as the percent of invested assets.

The second method of calculating returns is the *average annual geometric* or *compound return.* The average geometric return is far more important than the average arithmetic return if one is analyzing the long-run return on assets. The average annual geometric return is the rate at which the sum you invested at the beginning of the period will accumulate to a given sum at the end of the period by the process of *compounding,* or continuously reinvesting your dividends and capital gains. A characteristic of the compound return is that it depends *only* on the initial and final values of the portfolio—not at all on the path by which that value was realized.

For a one-year holding period, the arithmetic and geometric returns are identical, since both calculate the total return over one year. But over longer holding periods, the geometric average return is *always* less than the arithmetic return except when all the individual yearly returns are exactly the same, in which case the geometric return equals the arithmetic return.

Given the initial and final value of a portfolio, an investment manager can always increase the average annual return by *increasing* risk. As noted above, a manager who takes your portfolio from 100 to 50 and back to 100 again achieves an average arithmetic return of plus 25 percent, beating the zero return from a manager who keeps your portfolio at 100 each year. Yet every investor should prefer the second manager to the first. Geometric returns are the only way to compare long-term accumulations. Unless one is a superior market timer, reducing your stock portfolio before the market goes down and increasing it before it goes up, it is impossible to accumulate wealth at average arithmetic returns. A buy-and-hold strategy always leads to an accumulation of wealth at the geometric or compound rate of return. Appendix A discusses the statistical relation between arithmetic and geometric returns.

DIVERSIFICATION: INCREASE RETURN AND REDUCE RISK

There are two major factors to be considered in any investment: expected return and risk. Investors seek the highest level of return for a given level of risk or, alternatively, the lowest risk for a given level of return. The choice between risk and return is called the risk-reward trade-off. The simplest and most effective means of improving the risk-reward trade-off is by diversifying your portfolio.

The benefits of diversification have been long recognized in the academic literature. James Tobin, upon winning the Nobel Prize in 1981, was asked to summarize the essence of his work. He responded, "Don't put all your eggs in one basket." But as often as this is said, it is not often followed. Despite the indisputable evidence that diversification lowers risk, many investors own very few stocks and indeed put most of their eggs in one big basket.

Those who doubt the value of diversification concede that it may prevent serious overall losses, but it also reduces the chances for the large gains many investors seek. Most market players are more likely to follow the advice of Andrew Carnegie, who back in the 19th century said that the best way to accumulate wealth was "to put all your eggs in one basket and watch that basket very closely." Yet unless you are very certain which of those eggs will hatch, this strategy is almost never right.

The advantages of diversification are straightforward. Since stock prices are not perfectly synchronized, combining several stocks, some moving up while others move down, lowers the overall variability of one's portfolio. An example of a diversified portfolio would be combining both airline stocks, which are hurt when oil prices rise, with stocks of firms with large oil reserves, whose value will increase with higher oil prices. By combining stocks of both of these industries into one portfolio, an investor has hedged the effects of oil shocks and reduced the variability of returns.

The more assets one buys, the lower is the risk of the average return on the portfolio. The reduction in risk depends on two factors: the number of stocks in the portfolio and the correlation of the returns among these stocks.

Diversification works because asset prices are not exactly synchronized—when one asset goes up another may go down. The lower the correlation of returns between assets, the more likely it is that gains and losses will offset each other. When correlations are high, meaning that the prices of different assets move in tandem with one another, the gains from diversification are significantly reduced.

Although the risk-reducing benefit of diversification is well documented, diversification also increases the expected *compound return* of a portfolio. Recall the money manager that achieved a fantastic 25 percent average annual arithmetic return by alternatively doubling and halving the value of your portfolio. But the final wealth, and average geometric return, are zero for this risky strategy. By diversifying, the manager should have been able to achieve positive expected portfolio growth—and a positive expected compound return—even though he may have a lower average arithmetic return.

SUMMARY

Popular stock averages represent the return on equities *before* dividends are considered. They are convenient yardsticks for judging short-term fluctuations in the market. But total return indexes which include reinvested dividends, are the way to judge the performance of stocks over long periods of time.

The best way to judge long-term returns is by using the geometric or compound rate of return. The average arithmetic return, which is calculated as a simple average of a series of yearly returns on the market, cannot be replicated over time by an investor without superior market timing. The geometric return, in contrast, can be achieved by a simple buy-and-hold strategy.

Diversification not only reduces risk but also increases the expected geometric return of a portfolio. The long-term returns on assets that have been discussed in the first two chapters can only be achieved through a widely diversified portfolio of common stocks. To realize long-term wealth accumulation, this is by far the best strategy.

APPENDIX A

WHAT HAPPENED TO THE ORIGINAL 12 DOW INDUSTRIALS?

Two stocks (General Electric and Laclede) retained their original name (and industry), five (American Cotton, American Tobacco, Chicago Gas, National Lead, and North American) became large public companies in their original industries, one (Tennessee Coal and Iron) was merged into the giant US Steel, two (American Sugar, US Rubber) went private—both in the 1980s. Surprisingly, only one (Distilling and Cattle Feeding) changed its product line (from alcoholic beverages to petrochemicals, although it still manufactures ethanol), and only one (US Leather) liquidated.

1. *American Cotton Oil*—became Best Food in 1923, Corn Products Refining in 1958, and finally *CPC International* in 1969—a major food company with operations in 51 countries. Current market value: $6.2 billion.
2. *American Sugar*—became *Amstar* in 1970, went private in 1984, and now manufactures, markets, and distributes portable electric power tools.
3. *American Tobacco*—changed its name to American Brands in1969, a global consumer products holding company; core business in tobacco, liquor, office products, and home improvements. Current market value: $6.7 billion.
4. *Chicago Gas*—became Peoples Gas Light and Coke Co. in 1897, and then *Peoples Energy Corp.,* a utility holding company in 1980. Peoples Energy Corp. has a market value of $1.1 billion and is a member of the Dow-Jones Utility average.
5. *Distilling and Cattle Feeding*—became American Spirits Manufacturing and then Distiller's Securities Corp. Two months

after the passage of Prohibition, the company changed its charter and became US Food Products Corp. and then National Distiller's and Chemical. Became *Quantum Chemical Corp.* in 1989, a leading producer of petrochemicals and propane. In July 1993 received a $3.2 billion buyout bid from Hanson, an Anglo-American conglomerate. Market value of equity: $660 million.

6. *General Electric*—founded in 1892, the only stock still in the Dow Industrials. A huge manufacturing and broadcasting conglomerate (owns NBC). Market value: $82 billion, one of the top three in the United States
7. *Laclede Gas*—retained its original name and is a retail distributor of natural gas in the St. Louis area. Market value: $360 million.
8. *National Lead*—changed its name to *NL Industries* in 1971, manufactures titanium dioxide and specialty chemicals. Market value: $200 million.
9. *North American*—became *Union Electric Co.* in 1956, provides electricity in Missouri and Illinois. Market value: $4.2 billion.
10. *Tennessee Coal and Iron*—bought out by US Steel in 1907, now *USX–US Steel Group,* has a market value of $2.4 billion.
11. *US Leather*—one of the largest makers of shoes in the early part of this century liquidated in January 1952, paying its shareholders $1.50 plus stock in an oil and gas company that was to become worthless.
12. *US Rubber*—became *Uniroyal* in 1961 and was taken private in August of 1985.

APPENDIX B

THE RELATION BETWEEN ARITHMETIC AND GEOMETRIC RETURNS

The average arithmetic return, r_A, is the average of each yearly return. If r_1 to r_n are the *n* yearly returns, $r_A = (r_1 + r_2 \ldots + r_n)/n$. The average geometric return, r_G, is the nth root of the product of one year total returns. Mathematically this is expressed as $r_G = [(1+r_1)(1+r_2)$

$\ldots (1 + r_n)]^{1/n} - 1$. An asset that achieves a geometric return of r_G will have accumulated to $(1 + r_G)^n$ times the initial investment over n years.

The average geometric return is always less than the average arithmetic return except when all yearly returns are exactly equal. This difference is related to the risk of yearly returns, defined in the appendix of Chapter 2. The geometric return is approximately equal to the arithmetic return minus one-half the standard deviation squared, or $r_G = r_A - \frac{1}{2} \sigma^2$.

CHAPTER 4

STOCK PRICES, DIVIDENDS, AND EARNINGS

> Even when the underlying motive of purchase [of common stocks] is mere speculative greed, human nature desires to conceal this unlovely impulse behind a screen of apparent logic and good sense.
>
> *Benjamin Graham and David Dodd*[1]

AN EVIL OMEN RETURNS

In the summer of 1958, an event of great significance took place for those who followed long-standing indicators of stock market value. For the first time in history, the interest rate on long-term government bonds exceeded the dividend yield on common stocks.

Business Week noted this event in an August 1958 article entitled "An Evil Omen Returns," warning investors that when yields on stocks approached those on bonds, a major market decline was in the offing.[2] The stock crash of 1929 occurred in a year when stock dividend yields came within 0.5 percent of bond yields. The stock crashes of 1907 and 1891 also followed episodes when the yield on bonds came within 1 percent of that on stocks.

Prior to 1958, the dividend yield on stocks had *always* been higher than long-term interest rates, and most analysts thought that this was the way it was supposed to be. Stocks were riskier

---

[1] "The Theory of Common-Stock Investment," in *Security Analysis,* 2nd ed., 1940, p. 343.

[2] *Business Week,* August 9, 1958, p. 81.

than bonds and therefore should command a higher yield in the market. Under this reasoning, whenever stock prices went too high and brought stock yields down close to that of bonds, it was time to sell.

But things did not work this way in 1958. Stocks returned over 30 percent in the 12 months after dividend yields fell below bond yields and continued to soar into the early 1960s. There were good economic reasons why this famous benchmark fell by the wayside. Inflation increased the yield on bonds to compensate lenders for rising prices, while investors regarded stocks as the best investment to protect against the eroding value of money. As early as September 1958, *Business Week* noted that "the relationship between stock and bond yields was clearly posting a warning signal, but investors still believe inflation is inevitable and stocks are the only hedge against it.[3]

Yet many on Wall Street were still puzzled by the "great yield reversal." Nicholas Molodovsky, vice president of White, Weld & Co. and editor of the *Financial Analysts Journal* observed:

> Some financial analysts called [the reversal of bond and stock yields] a financial revolution brought about by many complex causes. Others, on the contrary, made no attempt to explain the unexplainable. They showed readiness to accept it as a manifestation of providence in the financial universe.[4]

Imagine the value-oriented investor who pulled all his money out of the stock market in August of 1958 and put it into bonds, vowing never to buy stocks again unless dividend yields rose above those on high-quality bonds. Such an investor would still be waiting to get back into stocks. After 1958, stock dividend yields never again exceeded those of bonds. (See Figure 4–1.) Yet, from August 1958 onward, overall stock returns overwhelmed the returns on fixed-income securities for *any* holding period.

---

[3] "In the Markets," *Business Week*, Sept. 13, 1958, p. 91.

[4] "The Many Aspects of Yields," *Financial Analysts Journal* 18, no. 2 (March-April 1962), pp. 49–62.

FIGURE 4–1
Earnings Yields, Dividend Yields, and Nominal Bond Yields (1871–1992)

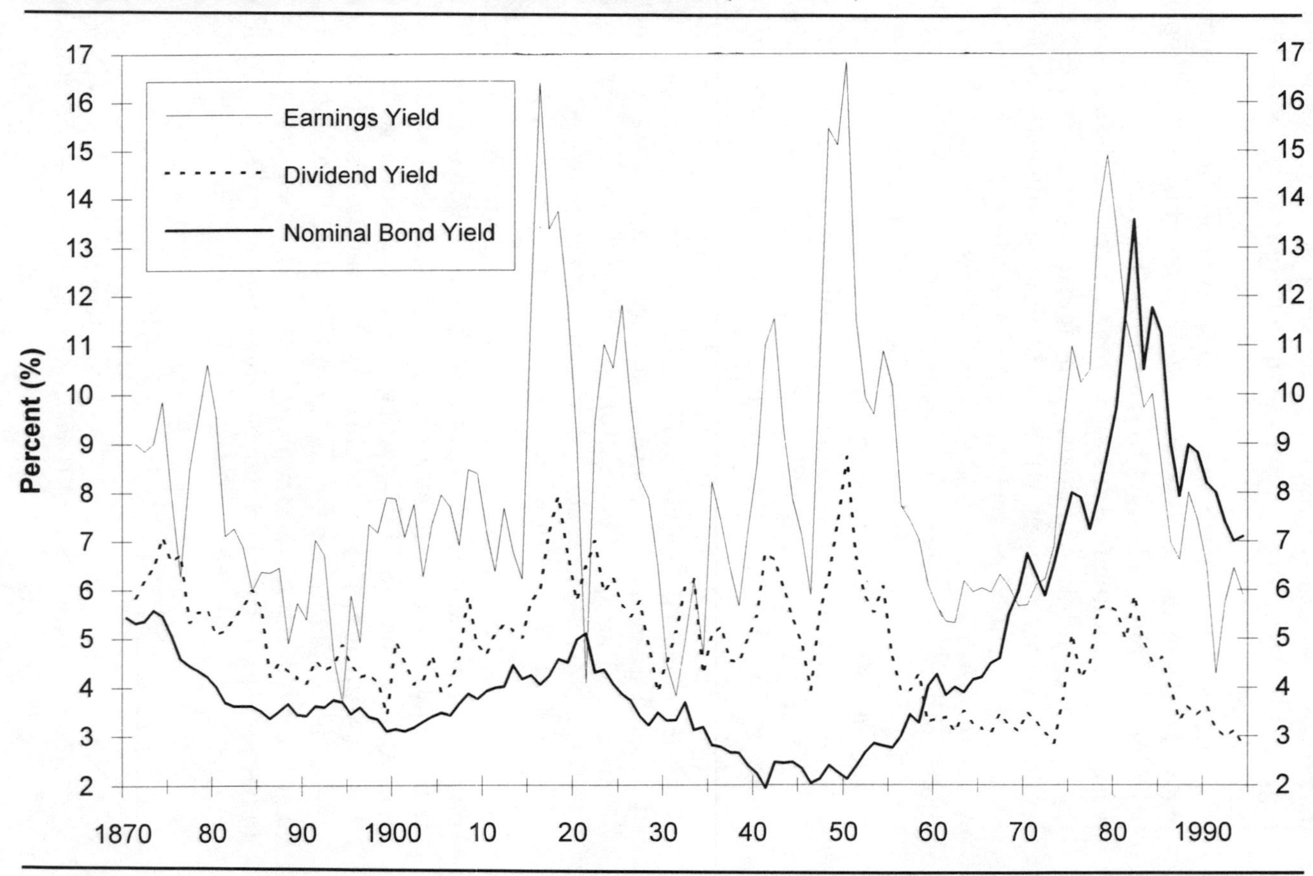

Benchmarks for valuation are valid only as long as the institutions of the economy do not change. The chronic postwar inflation, resulting from a switch to a paper money standard, changed forever the way investors judged the yields on stocks and bonds.

VALUATION—FUNDAMENTALS OR SENTIMENT?

Often one hears an investment adviser comment that the market is "too high" or not a good "buy." But what exactly does this mean? Jim Rodgers, a well-known and successful international investor, stated during the 1992 Latin America stock market boom: "I didn't invest in Mexico because every day on the front pages of Mexican newspapers, there were stories about a journalist, an elevator operator, or whoever, making a fortune in the stock market."[5] During the US stock boom in 1929, some busboys and waiters were said to have made fortunes by speculating on hot tips overheard while serving tables. For many speculators, it is the ebb and flow of investor sentiment such as fear and greed, not stock earnings and dividends, which determine movements in the market.

For example, some investors become concerned whenever the market passes a historical landmark. On November 23, 1954, when the Dow-Jones Industrial average finally scaled its September 3, 1929, peak which had held for over 25 years, *The Wall Street Journal* devoted its "Abreast of the Market" column to soothing investor fears of an impending crash. The *Journal* reported how much both the market and the companies which constitute the Dow averages had changed in the past 25 years. The message was clear: "'Things are different now' and the current level of the market is not a cause of alarm."

Valuation of Cash Flows from Stocks

Despite the use of investor sentiment as a guide to investing, most financial advisers rely on the fundamental building blocks of stock value—the dividends and earnings of firms—to direct

---

[5] Kathryn M. Welling, "Track of the Bear?" *Barron's*, June 22, 1992, p. 12.

their market decisions. In contrast to a work of art—which can be bought for its own enjoyment as well as an investment—stocks have value only because of the potential cash flows, called *dividends,* which a stockholder expects to receive from her share of the ownership of the firm.[6] It is by forecasting and valuing potential future dividends and earnings that one can judge the investment value of shares.

The value of any asset is determined by the *discounted value of all future expected cash flows. Discounted* means that future cash flows are not valued as highly as current flows. For stocks, cash flows come primarily in the form of dividends, but occasionally from other distributions resulting from the sale of assets or other transactions. For most assets—and especially for all stocks—the future cash flows are uncertain and depend on the financial circumstances of the firm. Even the cash flows from corporate bonds are uncertain—either because of the potential default of the issuing firm or the premature payoff (called the *call*) of the bonds' principal value. The only assets with certain cash flows are noncallable federal government bonds.

The future cash flows from assets are discounted because cash received in the future is not worth as much as cash received in the present. There are many reasons for this: the innate *preferences* of most individuals to enjoy their consumption now rather than wait for tomorrow; *productivity,* which allows funds invested today to yield a higher return tomorrow; *inflation,* which reduces the future purchasing power of cash received in the future; and the *uncertainty* associated with any event which takes place in the future. The rate at which future cash flows from stocks are discounted is called the *discount rate for stocks.*

The nature of the cash flows from an investment is one of the hallmarks that distinguishes assets. For bonds, the cash flows are very simple. The bondholder receives a fixed payment (called the *coupon*) each year until maturity, at which time a

[6] There may be some psychic value to holding a controlling interest, above and beyond the returns accrued. In that case, the owner values the stock more than minority shareholders.

principal payment (usually $1000 per bond) is paid, extinguishing the firm's obligation to the bondholder. In contrast, the stockholder receives dividends from the earnings and profits of the firm for as long as the firm is in operation, which may be indefinitely. Since dividends generally increase over time, the value of most stocks depends on what may happen many decades hence.

Estimates of *all* future cash flows are important for the valuation of equity—not only the ones received during the time the investor holds the asset. However, for a short-term investor, the return on an investment will depend not only on *his* assessment of the cash flows but also on the *market's* assessment of the cash flows at the time of the sale. This is because a large part of the return for a short-term stockholder comes from the proceeds of the sale of the asset and not from the dividends received. Unless one intends to hold the asset forever, one must take into account how much other investors in the market will value the asset at the time of sale in order to estimate one's return.

As a consequence, for most investors, the return on an asset is composed of two parts: the cash flows received while holding the asset and the change in the valuation of the asset by the market from the time of purchase to the time of sale. An investor might be enthusiastic about the dividend prospects of a certain stock, but if he expects to sell the stock next year, he is at the mercy of what *other* investors will think of the firm's prospects at that time.

Most investors attempt to profit in the market by buying a stock with what they consider attractive future returns, hoping that other investors will come to agree with their judgment. If this comes to pass, the price of the stock will rise. In fact, the fastest way to make money in the market is to successfully forecast how *other* investors might change the basis on which *they* make judgments about stocks' value in the near future. For example, if you think that other investors will turn optimistic about technology stocks, then you may make money buying such stocks whether or not you believe they are a good value.

Accordingly, success for short-term investors comes primarily from discerning how the public will view stocks in the future, and quite secondarily from the cash flows realized by the investment itself. The tension between investing in the long run and the short run was best described by John Maynard Keynes over 50 years ago when he wrote:

> Most of these [professional investors and speculators] are, in fact, largely concerned, not with making superior long-term forecasts of the probable yield of an investment over its whole life, but with foreseeing changes in the conventional basis of valuation a short time ahead of the public. They are concerned, not with what an investment is really worth to a man who buys it "for keeps," but with what the market will value it at, under the influence of mass psychology, three months or a year hence.[7]

The game of forecasting future investor sentiment is difficult and deters many from investing in stocks. But, as the last chapter indicated, you need not forecast market sentiment in order to profit in stocks. Although investment advice geared to the short run hinges on predicting the judgment of other investors, in the long run one can ride out the waves of investor sentiment and profit from your own predictions. It is far easier to buy and hold and thereby reap the gains that stocks realize over time. Winning with stocks requires only patience, not special foresight.

EARNINGS AND DIVIDEND YIELDS

The cash flows which are received by shareholders come primarily from dividends, and these dividends in turn come from earnings. Obviously, then, two of the most important financial statistics about stocks are earnings and dividends. The earnings per share divided by the current stock price is referred to as the *earnings yield* on the stock. Many investors prefer to think in terms of the inverse of the earnings yield—called the *price/earnings*, or *P/E ratio*. The P/E ratio, also called the *earnings multiple,* measures how many times current (or prospective) earnings the market is paying for a stock. The P/E ratio is the most popular fundamental variable for valuing both stocks and the market.

---

[7] John Maynard Keynes, *General Theory (of Employment, Interest, and Money)*, (Org. Pub. 1936) (New York: Harcourt, Brace & World, 1965 ed.), p. 155.

But the dividend and cash flows from the stock are rarely identical to the earnings. Some earnings are usually retained by management to generate funds for future operations or expansion, or sometimes used to repurchase shares. The current cash return to the stockholder is called the *dividend yield* and is represented by the dividend per share divided by the current share price.

Earnings that are not paid out as dividends are called retained earnings. Management has two uses to which such retained earnings can be put. One is the purchase of either real or financial assets. As long as these assets are productive, their acquisition will increase future earnings and hence the future price of the shares. The second use of retained earnings is the purchase of the firm's own shares in the open market. Reducing the number of shares will also increase future per-share earnings and dividends and hence the future price of the shares. Therefore if the firm buys productive assets or buys its own shares, per-share earnings and dividends will increase from retained earnings.

Figure 4–2 displays the real, inflation-corrected dividend and earnings per share on the S&P 500 Index, along with the ratio of dividends paid to earnings—called the *dividend payout ratio*. One can see that there is greater variability in earnings than dividends, especially in the post–World War II period. The smoothing of dividends is a conscious act of management designed to cater to the preference of shareholders for receiving a constant or rising dividend stream. By keeping the payout ratio below 100 percent in good times, firms will be able to maintain dividend payments when earnings fall temporarily, such as during recessions.

It can be seen from Figure 4–2 and Table 4–1 that the dividend payout ratio has declined since World War II. Before 1948, the dividend payout ratio averaged 71.5 percent while after 1948 the ratio averaged 51.8 percent. One of the reasons for the decrease in the ratio is the income tax which, as we shall see in Chapter 7, makes it more desirable for the shareholder to receive income in the form of lightly taxed capital gains than in the form of fully taxable dividends. Another reason may be the increased desire of management to stabilize dividends, necessitating a larger cushion between earnings and dividends.

FIGURE 4–2
Real Dividends, Earnings, and S&P 500 (1871–1994)*

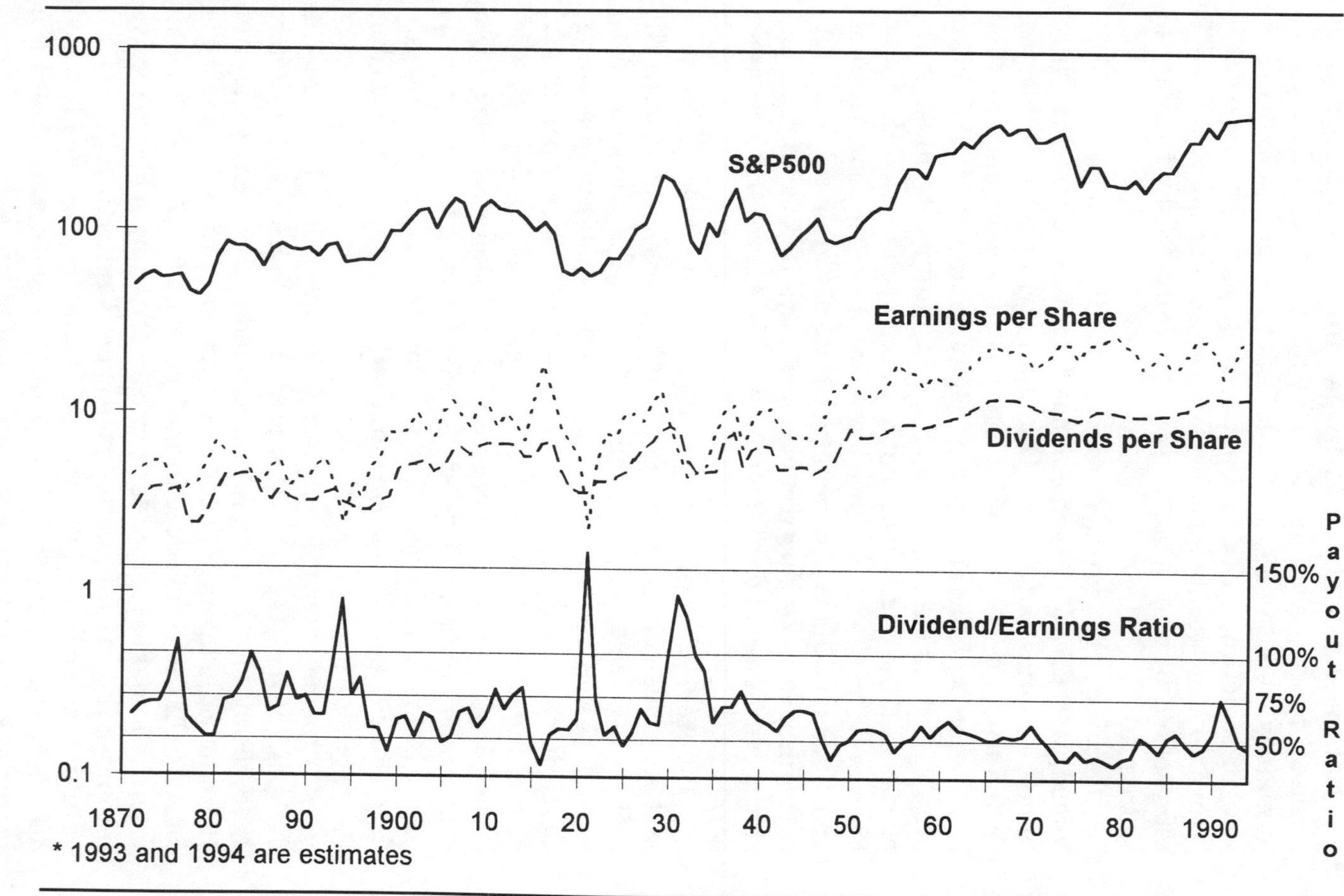

* 1993 and 1994 are estimates

TABLE 4–1
Historical Averages of Dividends and Earnings

Period	*Dividend Yield (%)*	*Price/ Earnings*	*Earnings Yield (%)*	Period	*Dividend/ Earnings (%)*	*Growth of Real Dividends (%)*	*Growth of Real Earnings (%)*	*Growth of Real S&P (%)*
1871 - 1994*	4.9%	13.6	8.1%	**1871 - 1994***	64.0%	1.2%	1.5%	1.8%
1871 - 1958	5.3	13.4	8.2	**1871 - 1947**	71.5	0.7	1.0	0.8
1959 - 1994*	3.8	14.1	7.8	**1948 - 1994***	51.8	2.0	2.1	3.4

Note: Averages in last three columns are annual compound geometric means.

* 1993 and 1994 are estimated.

DO STOCK PRICES DEPEND ON EARNINGS OR DIVIDENDS?

We have said that the price of a stock depends primarily on the present discounted value of all expected future dividends. But the level of dividends depends on the payout ratio determined by the management, so it appears that the payout ratio is critical in determining the value of stocks.

In theory, this should not be the case. If management invests retained earnings in a way that is *as profitable as* the return shareholders currently receive on the stock, then it makes absolutely no difference what payout ratio the management chooses. The present value of dividends, and hence the price of the stock, will be invariant with respect to the dividend policy. The reason for this is that dividends not paid today are reinvested by the firm and paid as even larger dividends in the future.

Of course the dividend payout policy does influence the timing of the dividend payments. The lower the dividend payout ratio, the smaller will be the dividends received in the near future, but over time dividends will rise and eventually exceed the dividend path associated with a higher payout ratio. But the present value of these dividend streams will be identical no matter what payout ratio is chosen. The appendix shows why the value of the firm is unaffected by the dividend ratio.

A key assumption needed to obtain this result is that the firm earns the same return on its retained earnings as the earnings yield demanded by investors on the stock. If the firm earns a higher or lower return on its retained earnings, then the stock price will depend on the dividend payout ratio. If the firm earns a lower return, then the price of the stock will fall when the payout ratio falls. The reason for this is that with a lower payout ratio, the firm will retain more earnings, and if the profit rate on these earnings is lower than the return demanded by shareholders, future dividends will not rise as fast as needed to compensate investors for the lower current level of dividends.

Note that whether or not the firm earns the same return on retained earnings as the earnings yield on the stock, the price of the stock is always equal to the present value of all future *dividends* and not the present value of future earnings. Earnings not paid to investors can only have value if they are paid as dividends at a later date. To value stock as the present discounted value of future *earnings* is manifestly wrong and greatly overstates the value of a firm, unless all the earnings are always paid out as dividends.

John Burr Williams, one of the greatest investment analysts of the early part of this century and author of the classic *The Theory of Investment Value,* argued this point persuasively in 1938. He wrote:

> Most people will object at once to the foregoing formula for valuing stocks by saying that it should use the present worth of future *earnings,* not future *dividends.* But should not earnings and dividends both give the same answer under the implicit assumptions of our critics? If earnings not paid out in dividends are all successfully reinvested at compound interest for the benefit of the stockholder, as the critics imply, then these earnings should produce dividends later; if not, then they are money lost. Earnings are only a means to an end, and the means should not be mistaken for the end.[8]

HISTORICAL DATA ON DIVIDENDS AND EARNINGS

When predicting future returns on the market, the price-to-earnings ratio and the dividend yield, compared to historical standards, are the most frequently cited criteria for judging the valuation of the market.

Table 4–1 displays the dividend and earnings yields on stocks represented by the S&P 500 Index. We can see that the average historical earnings yield since 1871 is 8.11 percent or an average P/E ratio of 13.61.[9] This means that investors still price stocks on average at about 12 to 15 times their annual earnings, a figure that has shown only a slight upward movement over time. Despite the stability of the average, the P/E ratio has

---

[8] John Burr Williams, *The Theory of Investment Value,* (Cambridge, Mass.: Harvard University Press, 1938), p. 30.

[9] Because of the statistical properties of the average of the inverse of numbers, the average P/E ratio must be greater than 1 over the average earnings yield.

shown considerable annual variation, ranging from a high of 27 in 1894 to a low of 6 in 1950.

Another yardstick used to judge the future of the market is the dividend yield. The dividend yield has averaged 4.89 percent from 1871, with a high of 8.71 percent in 1959 and a low of 2.85 percent in 1973. As noted above, the dividend yield shows far less variability than the earnings yield, as managers pursue policies to stabilize the cash payouts to stockholders.

In contrast to the long-term stability of the earning yield, the dividend yield has fallen significantly in recent years. Since 1959, the average dividend yield is 3.83 percent, while from 1871 to 1958 it averaged 5.32 percent. The primary cause of the reduction in the dividend yield is not the higher valuation of shares, but the reduction in the dividend payout ratio—the fraction of earnings firms pay as dividends. As noted earlier, the increase in personal and corporate taxes has made it advantageous for firms to retain earnings, rather than pay them to stockholders in the form of taxable dividends.

Can Dividend Yields Be Used to Predict Future Returns?

Can one use dividend yields to predict subsequent returns on the stock market? Table 4–2 shows the historical evidence. The real holding period returns on stocks are calculated subsequent to various levels of dividends reached at the *beginning* of the holding period. Dividend yields are sorted in percentile groupings: for example, the lowest 10 percent of all annual dividend yields range from 2.85 percent (the lowest) to 3.33 percent, while the highest 10 percent of dividend yields range from 6.47 percent to 8.71 percent. Returns are calculated for 1-, 5-, and 30-year holding periods.

Table 4–2 does demonstrate that low dividend yields appear to be followed by periods of low return, while higher dividend yields appear to be followed by periods of higher returns. For example, for 30-year returns, stocks have a 4.78 percent compound annual return if stocks start with a dividend yield in the lowest decile, while they have a 7.52 percent return if the holding periods starts with a dividend yield in the highest decile. The

TABLE 4–2
Subsequent Real Holding Period Returns Sorted by Dividend Yield in the Initial Year (1871–1992)

		1 Year Return			5 Year Return			30 Year Return		
Percentile	Dividend Range	Stocks	Bonds	Bills	Stocks	Bonds	Bills	Stocks	Bonds	Bills
0% - 10%	2.85% - 3.36%	4.31%	0.54%	0.60%	1.04%	-1.45%	0.09%	4.78%	1.24%	1.33%
10 - 20	3.38 - 3.94	2.49	2.28	1.90	5.03	-0.75	0.86	6.50	1.25	0.76
20 - 40	3.94 - 4.53	12.96	4.36	2.61	8.42	3.23	2.36	5.96	1.20	1.13
40 - 60	4.53 - 5.17	0.45	1.31	1.23	3.97	1.39	0.55	6.03	1.59	0.79
60 - 80	5.23 - 5.86	13.41	4.10	2.21	5.75	3.92	2.25	6.81	1.75	1.18
80 - 90	5.96 - 6.47	13.68	2.57	0.04	10.77	4.18	1.92	7.45	1.68	0.67
90 - 100	6.61 - 8.71	9.76	3.34	2.42	15.69	3.89	2.05	7.52	1.69	1.12

effects of dividend yields on subsequent returns are even more marked for 5-year holding periods—stocks have a measly 1 percent return over the next five years when dividend yields are near their low, while they experience nearly 15 percent annual returns when dividend yields are very high.

This evidence looks persuasive: lighten up on stocks when dividend yields are low and plunge into equities when such yields are high. This and similar studies have had powerful influence on the investing community and are often used to determine what proportion of a portfolio should be allocated to stocks. But studies such as these have an inherent bias which overstates their importance.

A simple experiment can illustrate the problem. Examine a chart of the price of a stock over the past year. Then do a study by recording all past prices, ranking them from highest to lowest, and determine the subsequent return on the stock from each price range.

It is easy to see that the subsequent returns will be poor when the return was calculated from high stock prices and the return will be high when calculated from low prices. But this is because we have, *after the fact,* identified the high and low prices for the stock. Once the high price has been identified, all subsequent prices must be lower, assuring poor returns. Similarly, the subsequent returns from low prices will be high. This is because of how the test is constructed. It makes no difference what process, random, or deterministic, determines stock prices.

The same problem arises from examining future stock returns by sorting by dividend yields. In 1993, for example, the yields on stock averages approached historic lows. But there is no reason to believe that what are low yields today will not become the norm in the future. Certainly in the next decade or two we will know whether this is the case. If today's low yields indeed are seen as low in the future, then it will either be because stock prices have declined, dividends have risen, or some combination of the two. But if yields go even lower, then the year 1993 will no longer stand out as a year of extremely low yields. Sorting on historical value factors is biased towards finding criteria which appear to predict future returns.

The biases inherent in these procedures can explain the two percentage point difference in subsequent returns for 30-year holding periods between high and low dividend yields. Yet it cannot explain the sharp differences for intermediate holding periods such as 5 years. The returns for five-year holding periods sorted by the dividend yields show differences that are greater than the bias these tests display.

Even if current dividend yields predict returns five years out, it still does not mean an investor should pull his money from stocks when the dividend yield is low. Table 4–2 indicates that the returns on fixed-income assets are also low when the dividend yields on stocks are low. While it is true that stocks do not outperform bonds or bills by as much in these circumstances, stocks have still outperformed fixed-income assets, no matter what the dividend yield.

CONCLUSIONS

Any yardstick for stock valuation, even one with a sound theoretical basis or one that has worked for more than a century, can stop working. It was reasonable to monitor the relation between bond and stock yields during a period when inflation was not a permanent factor in our economy. But when chronic inflation becomes the order of the day, the age-old relation between nominal bond yields and dividend yields was thrown out.

Will any of the current yardsticks, such as earning or dividend yields, also fail to be good future indicators of returns? Perhaps. In recent decades the dividend yield has turned lower due to lower firm payout ratios, motivated by higher income taxes on dividends compared to capital gains. Stock earnings yields may also go lower, and stock prices higher, as investors better understand the superior long-run returns on stocks. For these reasons, investors are best advised to hold stocks for the long run rather than try to use historical yardsticks to beat the market.

APPENDIX

THE INVARIANCE OF PRICE TO THE PAYOUT RATIO

Assume that investors demand a 10 percent annual return on equity, so that they will pay $100 for a stock which is earning $10 per year. If the firm pays out its entire earnings as dividends, the firm can pay out $10 per year indefinitely. The present value of $10 per year, discounted at 10 percent, is $100, which equals the value of the stock.

If the firm decides to reduce its payout to only one half of its earnings, then in the first year the dividend will be $5, and $5 will be retained earnings. The next year the firm will earn $10 on its original assets plus 50 cents (10 percent of $5 on its reinvested earnings), for a total of $10.50. If the firm continues to pay one half of its earnings as dividends, the dividend will rise to $5.25.

The next year the firm has $5.25 per share of retained earnings to invest. With a 10 percent earnings yield, the additional retained earnings from the past year will generate an additional 52.5 cents of earnings next year, so that earnings will rise to $11.025, dividends will rise to $5.5125, and the price of the share will rise to $110.25.

If dividends are set at one half of earnings, the dividend rates, of course, will start out at one half the level it would have been if the firm paid out all its earnings as dividends. But dividends, earnings, and the price of the stock will rise at 5 percent per year thereafter. The total return on the stock will be 10 percent—5 percent from capital accumulation and 5 percent from the dividend yield—the same 10 percent return an investor would receive if all the earnings were paid out as dividends. Therefore, the choice of payout ratio does not change the current price of the stock.

CHAPTER 5

LARGE STOCKS, SMALL STOCKS, VALUE STOCKS, GROWTH STOCKS

Security analysis cannot presume to lay down general rules as to the "proper value" of any given common stock. . . . The prices of common stocks are not carefully thought out computations, but the resultants of a welter of human reactions.

Benjamin Graham and David Dodd[1]

OUTPERFORMING THE MARKET

What factors can investors use to choose individual stocks with superior returns? Earnings, dividends, cash flows, book values, capitalization, and price, among others, have all been investigated to find stocks that will beat the market. But if the stock market is *efficient,* which means that all known factors influencing the stock are already included in the price of the shares, then all these factors should not be useful in explaining future stock returns.

There is one factor, however, which should influence stock returns—the *risk,* or expected volatility of future returns. Riskier stocks should reward shareholders with higher returns since investors need to be compensated for investing in a stock with a more uncertain future. The trade-off between risk and return has become the fundamental tool of financial analysis.

---

[1] "Price Earnings Ratios for Common Stocks" in *Security Analysis,* 2nd ed. (New York: McGraw-Hill, 1940), p. 530.

It has been shown that the proper theoretical measure of risk for an individual stock is the variability of the stock's returns *relative* to the overall market. This risk measure became known as *beta,* and it can be estimated statistically by correlating a stock's historical returns with the market.[2] Beta represents the risk to an asset's return that cannot be eliminated in a well-diversified portfolio. Hence it is the risk which the market must reward. Risk which can be diversified, and hence eliminated, does not warrant extra return.

Unfortunately, beta has not been very successful at explaining many of the differences between the historical returns of individual stocks. Although there is some evidence that high beta stocks have higher returns, the explanatory power of beta proved weak. Some economists interpreted the weak association between risk and return as indicative of the inherently unpredictable nature of stock returns, and gave up further search.

SMALL-STOCK PREMIUM

But the search for factors explaining returns did not end with beta. In 1981 Rolf Banz, a young finance professor who received his degree from the University of Chicago, began analyzing the returns on stocks based on the size, or market capitalization, of the company. He found that small stocks systematically outperformed large stocks, even after adjusting for risk.

Using the data base provided by the Center for the Research in Security Prices (CRSP) at the University of Chicago, Banz showed that small stocks—defined as the lowest 20 percent in market capitalization on the New York Stock Exchange—sported an arithmetic return that exceeded large

---

[2] Greek letters have long been used in mathematics to designate the coefficients of regression equations. Beta, the second coefficient, is calculated from the correlation of an individual stock's return with the market. The first coefficient estimated is the average historical return on the stock and is termed *alpha.*

stocks, such as defined by the S&P 500 Index, by over 6 percent per year. Even the geometric return on small stocks was over 2 percent higher than that of large stocks.

These differences are shown in Figure 5–1, which sorts the stocks traded on the New York Stock Exchange by market capitalization and reports their returns from 1926 through 1992. The results are striking. The average arithmetic return on smallest stocks (smallest 10 percent market value) is more than double the return on large stocks, while the geometric return is almost five percentage points more than that of the largest stocks. The excess of the return of small stocks over large stocks is called the *small-stock premium.*

Research has been done on the small-stock premium in foreign markets as well. It is positive in every country where it has been tested and quite significant in most of them. It is particularly strong in Japan, the world's second-largest capital market.

What can explain such superior performance of small stocks? Certainly, they are riskier than large stocks. The standard deviation of the annual returns on the smallest stocks is more than twice that of large stocks. But most of the risks to holding small stocks are diversifiable, which means that a large part of the variability of small-stock returns is independent of returns in large stocks. We noted that diversifiable risk should not be rewarded, and so the return on small stocks is far greater than can be explained on the basis of standard risk and return theory.

Risks from Investing in Small Stocks

But these superior returns are not the only factor one should take into account when investing in small stocks. There are also some negative factors. The transaction costs of acquiring small stocks are far greater than those for large stocks. It has been estimated that the average buy-sell or bid-ask spread for stocks in the S&P 500 Index is only 0.45 percent, while the spread on stocks in the Russell 2000 (the 2,000 smallest stocks among the

FIGURE 5–1
Market Capitalization Returns (1926–92)

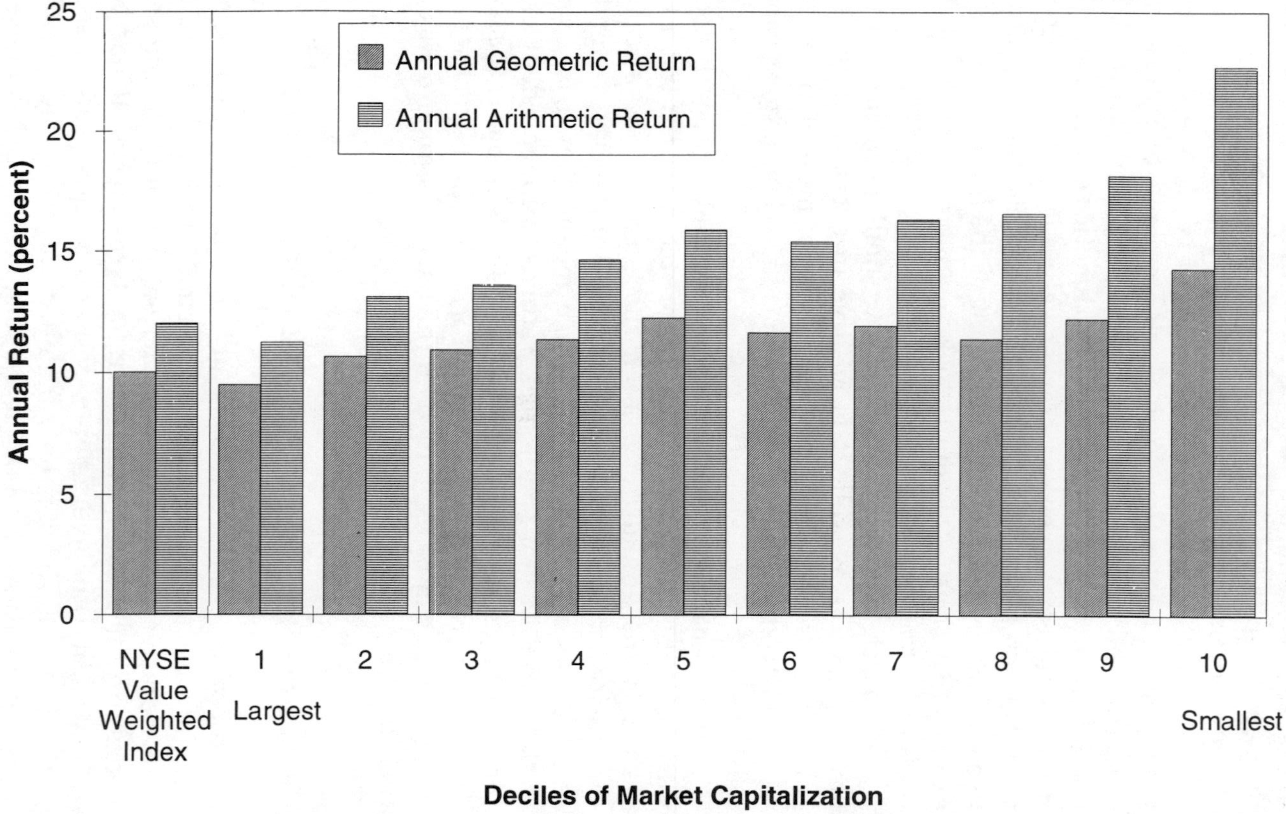

Annual Geometric Return
Annual Arithmetic Return

Annual Return (percent)

25
20
15
10
5
0

NYSE Value Weighted Index
1 Largest
2
3
4
5
6
7
8
9
10 Smallest

Deciles of Market Capitalization

top 3,000 traded) is 2.75 percent, more than six times as large.[3] So it is not possible to receive the total returns found for small stock indexes which ignore transactions costs.

To get around this problem, some of the recent small stock indexes use the actual return on the Dimensional Fund Advisors 9/10 Fund, which invests in the bottom quintile (9th and 10th deciles) of stocks ranked by market value. Costs of running this fund average 0.65 percent per year.[4] So taking trading costs into consideration reduces, but far from eliminates, the small-stock premium.

But there may be far more serious problems for investors in small stocks. The magnitude of the small-stock premium waxes and wanes over time. Small stocks experience periods of several years when they are in favor with investors, but then fall out of favor.

Figure 5–2 displays the ups and downs of small-stock returns since 1926. Small stocks recovered smartly from their beating in the Great Depression, but still underperformed large stocks from the period from the end of World War II until almost 1960. In fact from 1926, the cumulative total return on small stocks (measured by the bottom quintile of market capitalization) did not overtake large stocks until 1959. Even by the end of 1974, the average annual compound return on small stocks exceeded large stocks by only about 0.5 percent per year, not nearly enough to compensate most investors for their extra risk.

But from 1975 to the end of 1983, small stocks exploded. During these years, small stocks averaged a 35.3 percent compound annual return, more than double the 15.7 percent return on large stocks. Total returns during these nine years exceeded 1,400 percent in small stocks. Then they hit a dry period. Small stocks faltered and, excepting 1988, did not outperform large

---

[3] Richard Bernstein and Staya Pradhuman, *Merrill Lynch Quantitative Viewpoint,* March 2, 1993.

[4] This information was provided to me by David Booth of DFA Inc. DFA has largely avoided paying the bid-ask spread on small stocks by skillfully buying and selling blocks of stocks, a strategy not usually available to small investors.

FIGURE 5–2

Total Returns to Small Stocks and Large Stocks 1926–92 (Including and Excluding years 1975–83)

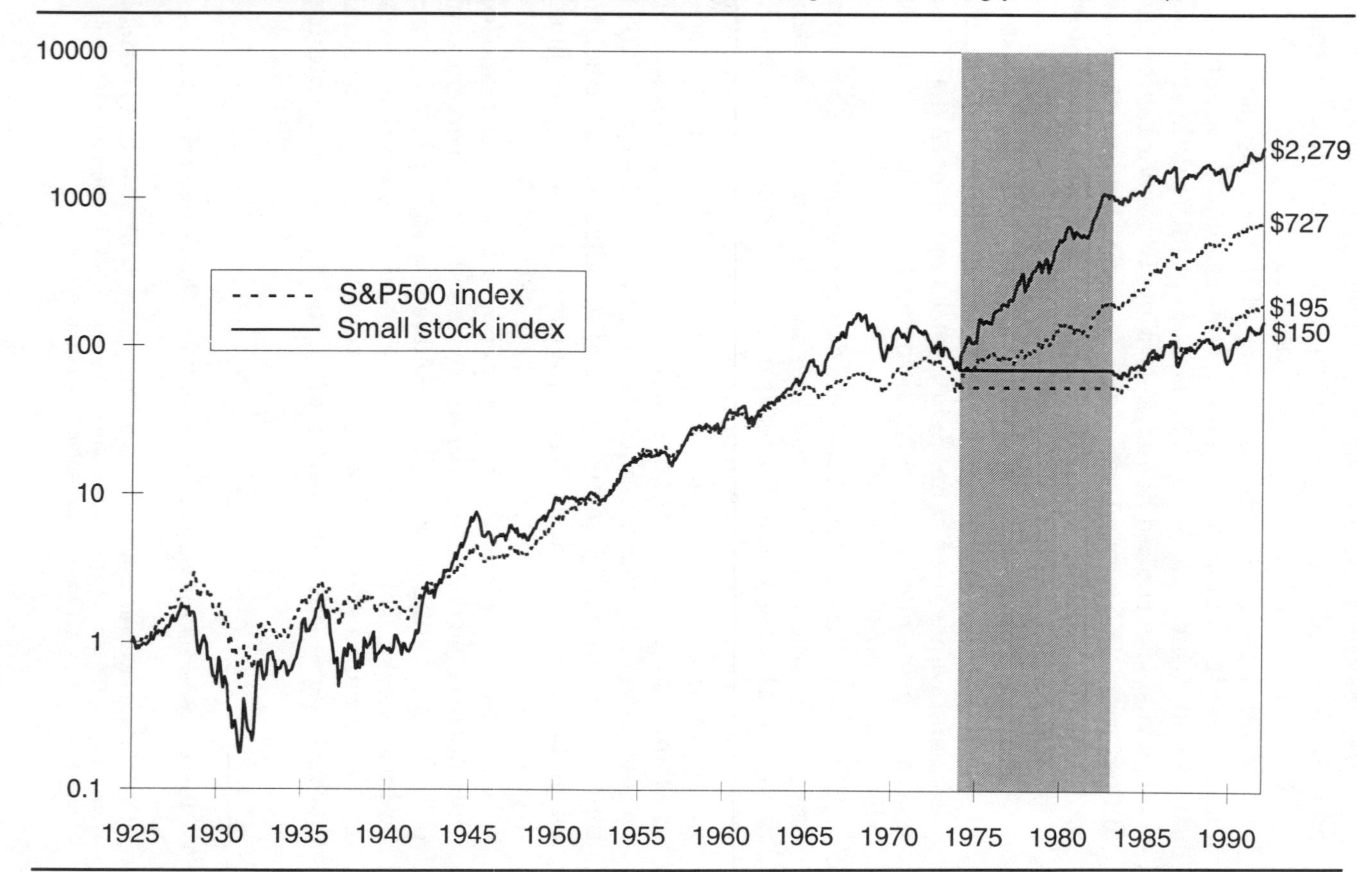

stocks again until 1991.[5] In fact, Figure 5–2 shows that if the nine-year period from 1975 through 1983 is eliminated, the total accumulation in small stocks over the entire period from 1926 through 1992 falls nearly 25 percent *below* that in large stocks. Even for the long-term investor, it is clear that if you don't catch the small-stock wave, you miss the boat!

Look at Table 5–1, which lists the percent of time small stocks beat large stocks over various holding periods from 1926. Over one- to five-year holding periods, small-stock returns have beaten large-stock returns, but just barely. In fact, over four-year holding periods, small stocks beat large stocks only one half the time. Excluding the 1975–83 period, it takes almost eight years on average for small-stock returns to match those of large stocks and even for 10-year holding periods, small stocks beat large stocks only 55 percent of the time.

But an even more surprising result from Table 5–1 is that the percent of time that large stocks beat bonds, over almost all holding periods, is larger than that for small stocks. It may seem paradoxical that although small stocks generally beat large stocks, large stocks give investors greater assurance of beating bonds. One reason is that when small stocks underperform, they often underperform all financial assets, while large stocks, even in bad years, will more often beat bonds.

The above data only consider returns. Investors should not forget that small stocks are riskier than large stocks. If your portfolio is fully invested in small stocks, you are exposing yourself to substantial additional risk. Diversifiable risk can only be ignored when an asset becomes part of a larger portfolio. If small stocks *are* the portfolio, the risk rises dramatically. In that case, the superior returns on small stocks are overwhelmed by the extra risk. In fact, on the basis of all the data, including the spectacular 1975–83 period, an investor could have created a leveraged portfolio of large stocks and have achieved virtually

---

[5] One factor which caused small stocks to underperform large stocks in the mid-and late 1980s was the rise of indexing, or the passive linkage of portfolios to broad-based market averages. Virtually all of the indexing was based on the large stocks found in the S&P 500 Index. Indexing tends to raise the price of stocks in the index relative to the smaller stocks not in the index.

TABLE 5–1
Holding Period Comparisons (1926–92)

	Entire Period			Excluding 1975 - 83		
Holding Period	Small Stocks Outperform Large Stocks	Large Stocks Outperform Bonds	Small Stocks Outperform Bonds	Small Stocks Outperform Large Stocks	Large Stocks Outperform Bonds	Small Stocks Outperform Bonds
1 year	56.7%	61.2%	58.2%	50.0%	60.3%	53.4%
2 years	53.0	69.7	68.2	43.9	68.4	61.4
4 years	50.0	75.0	64.1	41.8	74.5	58.2
6 years	58.1	77.4	71.0	47.2	73.6	64.2
8 years	60.0	78.3	75.0	51.0	68.6	68.6
10 years	70.7	87.9	86.2	55.1	71.4	73.5
20 years	93.8	97.9	100.0	76.9	97.4	92.3
30 years	94.7	100.0	100.0	65.5	100.0	100.0

the same return with the same risk as investing only in small stocks.

OTHER VALUE CRITERIA

Market capitalization is not the only factor influencing returns. In the late 1970s, Sanjoy Basu, building on the work of S. F. Nicholson in 1960, discovered that price-to-earnings ratios were significant factors for explaining returns on stocks.[6]

Figure 5–3 ranks stocks from the lowest to the highest price-to-earnings ratios over the period from April 1962 through December 1989 and reports the annual compound returns. The results are striking. Stocks with high price-to-earnings ratios do not do nearly as well as those with low P/E ratios, although there is no significant difference in risk between the high- and low-P/E-ratio stocks.

It may seem reasonable to investors that stocks with strong earnings should have superior returns. After all, earnings are the stuff from which future cash flows, and hence value, arise. Benjamin Graham and David Dodd in their classic 1940 text, *Security Analysis: Principles and Technique,* argued that a necessary condition for investing in common stock was a reasonable ratio of market price to average earnings. In it they stated:

> Hence we may submit, as a corollary of no small practical importance, *that people who habitually purchase common stocks at more than about 20 times their average earnings are likely to lose considerable money in the long run.*[7]

This advice is based on *historical* earnings. But if historical earnings are good predictors of future returns, and investments based on these earnings "beat the market" so handily, why should anyone spend time and effort forecasting *future* earnings? If mar-

---

[6] S. F. Nicholson, "Price–Earnings Ratios," *Financial Analysts Journal,* July/August 1960, pp. 43–50; and S. Basu, "Investment Performance of Common Stocks in Relation to their Price–Earnings Ratio: A Test of the Efficient Market Hypothesis," *Journal of Finance* 32 (June 1977), pp. 663–82.

[7] Graham and Dodd, *Security Analysis,* p. 533. Emphasis theirs.

FIGURE 5–3
Returns to Valuation Factors (April 1962–December 1989)

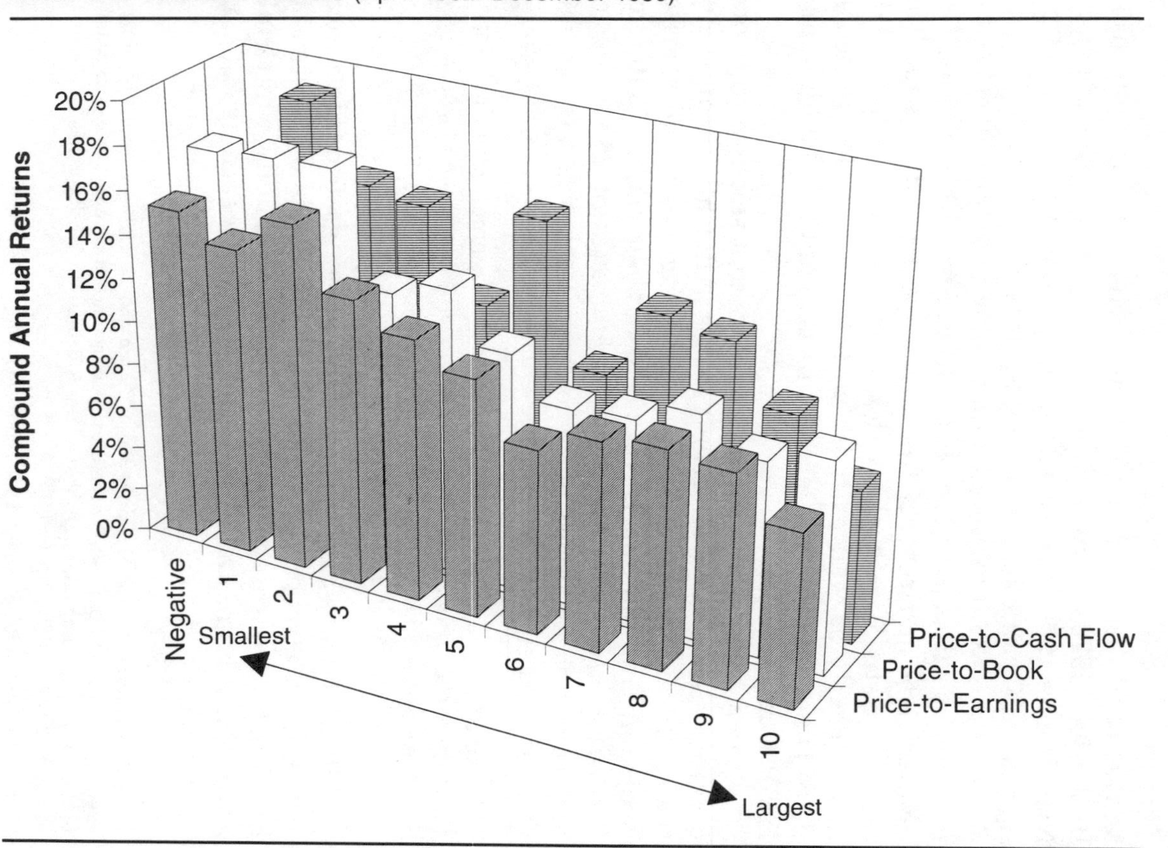

kets were efficient, information from the past should be well discounted in the current price and should have no influence on future returns.

One theory about why the high-P/E-ratio stocks underperform low-P/E stocks is that investors get overexcited about the growth prospects of firms with rapidly rising earnings and bid them up excessively. Researchers find that the future earnings of high P/E stocks do grow faster for about one year, but nowhere near long enough to justify their lofty ratios.[8]

Investors often project recent earnings trends too far into the future, failing to realize how quickly circumstances can—and do—change. When earnings growth slows, as it invariably does, this deflates the price/earnings multiple and causes a dramatic drop in the price of the stock. In the next chapter we explore the history of some of the premier growth stocks of the early 1970s, dubbed the "nifty fifty," to determine whether investors have indeed overpriced these high-flying stocks.

Not only do low P/E stocks show high subsequent returns, but even more surprising is that firms with losses, and hence negative P/E ratios, have nearly the *highest* returns. So a strange discontinuity is found in the relation between historical earnings yield and future returns. The lower the earnings per share, the poorer the future return on a stock until the earnings turn negative, at which point future returns skyrocket!

One clue to this paradox is that firms with negative earnings are generally small stocks that have not yet achieved profitability or larger firms which have fallen in value because of poor earnings. The market capitalization of the high-flying, high price-to-earnings-ratio stocks are more than six times that of stocks with negative earnings. So the P/E factor is linked to the small-stock premium.

It is interesting that although we have maintained that the overall superior returns for stocks means that investors tend to overdiscount future earnings and dividends of the market, they often become too optimistic about the prospects of "growth"

---

[8] Josef Lakonishok, Andrei Shleifer, and Robert W. Vishny, "Contrarian Investment, Extrapolation, and Risk," March 1993, unpublished.

stocks. "Story stocks" such as Intel, Microsoft, or Wal-Mart, which in the past provided fantastic returns, capture the fancy of investors, while those firms providing solid earnings and average growth suffer relative neglect.

But the price-to-earnings ratio is not the only valuation factor that is related to future returns. Researchers have found that the ratio of the market value of a firm to its book value is even more important. This ratio measures the value investors put on a company relative to the cost of acquiring and building the capital needed to produce its output. Figure 5–3 shows that stocks where the price-to-book ratio is high have low subsequent returns. The high price-to-book-ratio firms are often growth companies which have a very high market value.

Like the case with earnings, firms with a negative book ratio have among the subsequent highest returns. These are companies whose losses are so severe that their capital funds and retained earnings are completely exhausted. Clearly these are distressed companies, but historically they have offered investors tremendous returns.

Dividend Yields

Dividend yields have long been a favorite criterion of investors for choosing stocks. Research has shown that the higher the dividend yield, the higher the subsequent return, except that firms that pay *no* dividend at all—often small firms—do very well. Like the previous cases, the firms that pay no dividend are often small in size and/or financially distressed.

The relation between the dividend yield and return on stocks which do pay dividends can be explained with taxes. Dividends receive no tax preference, while capital gains offer investors favorable tax treatment. Stockholders should prefer firms that withhold dividends and either reinvest them in productive assets (reducing loan and bond indebtedness) or distribute the cash through repurchasing shares in the open market.[9] Hence stock

[9] See Robert Litzenberger and Krishna Ramaswamy, "The Effects of Personal Taxes and Dividends on Capital Asset Prices: Theory and Empirical Evidence," *Journal of Financial Economics*, 1979, pp. 163–95.

with higher dividends may offer investors a higher before-tax return, but may not have higher returns on an after-tax basis.

The superior returns to non-dividend paying stocks were first recognized in a book entitled, *Investing in Purchasing Power,* by Kenneth S. Van Strum, a financial writer of the 1920s. Van Strum set out to confirm Edgar Smith's study of a year earlier which proclaimed the superiority of stocks as long-term investments. Expecting only to find such superior performance in "investment grade" stocks, he was surprised to find quite the opposite. In one of his studies, Van Strum analyzed what would happen if the common-stock investor only purchased stocks of companies which had no dividends and which were priced under $50 per share, which at that time were viewed as low-priced speculative stocks. He concluded,

> This group [no dividends and price under $50 per share] of low-priced common stocks not only permitted the stock investor to maintain his purchasing power intact, but also showed the best results of any investment made in the entire group of studies.[10]

In fact, Irving Fisher, the greatest American monetary economist of the first half of this century, stated in the forward of Van Strum's book, "This result [the best performance of non-dividend-paying stocks] is as surprising as any among the many surprising results of this investigation."[11]

Price-to-earnings ratios, price-to-book ratios, and dividend yield are not the only factors predicting future returns. Recently, some researchers have found that cash flow per share is the best predictor of future returns.[12] Even the price of the stock alone, which is solely a function of the number of shares outstanding, appears to be a predictor of future returns, as low-priced stocks have outperformed high-priced stocks. And these findings have persisted over time. As Van Strum noted 70 years ago, non-dividend-paying, low-priced stocks outperformed investment-grade issues at the turn of the century.

---

[10] Kenneth S. Van Strum, *Investing in Purchasing Power* (New York: Barron's, 1925), p. 232.

[11] *Ibid.*, p. vii.

[12] Lakonishok, et al., "Contrarian Investment."

Most stocks which have low prices, negative cash flows, negative earnings, or negative book values have experienced very adverse financial developments and have become severely depressed. Many investors are quick to dump these stocks when the news gets bad. This often drives the price down below the value justified by their circumstances, as their subsequent superior returns indicate. Few investors seem able to see the light at the end of the tunnel, or are able to justify—to themselves or to their clients—the purchase of such stocks under such adverse circumstances. The rewards go to those able to see a future for such distressed firms.

VALUE AND GROWTH STOCKS

Stocks which display high dividend yields and low price-to-book and price-to-earnings ratios are often called *value* stocks, while those with low dividend yields, high P/E and market-to-book ratios are called *growth* stocks. Although some investors believe that small stocks represent growth stocks, this is not necessarily the case. Value and growth stocks are found in all sizes.

Of the 10 largest US corporations in the summer of 1993, seven can be regarded as growth stocks (GE, AT&T, Wal-Mart, Coca-Cola, Merck, Philip Morris, and GTE), while three (Exxon, Royal Dutch, and DuPont) are value stocks. Value stocks are concentrated in the oils, motors, and most utilities, while growth stocks are concentrated in the high-technology industries such as drugs, telecommunications, and computers. But the biggest factor pegging a stock as growth or value is its past and future projected earnings growth, not its industry: IBM is now classified as a value stock, while Microsoft and Intel are growth; General Electric is a growth stock, while Westinghouse falls in the value category.

There are few sound economic reasons why value stocks should outperform growth stocks even after adjustment for risk. Yet there is evidence that this is so not only in the United States, but also internationally.[13] Most value stocks do have higher divi-

---

[13] See Carlo Capaul, Ian Rowley, and William F. Sharpe, "International Value and Growth Stock Returns," *Financial Analysts Journal,* January–February 1993, pp. 27–36.

dend yields, so on an after-tax basis the difference between their returns and those on growth stocks is not as great. Nevertheless, on a before-tax basis, there seems a tendency for investors to overreward glamour stocks with high past growth and overdiscount those with poor current prospects.

While many investors recall the story stocks, such as Intel, Microsoft, and Wal-Mart, which have made investors rich, most forget about the many new firms that fail to fulfill their promise when they are issued. A study by Tim Loughran and Jay Ritter followed every operating company (almost 5,000) that went public between 1970 and 1990.[14] Those who bought at the market price on the first day of trading and held the stock for five years, reaped an average annual return of only 5 percent. Those who invested in companies *of the same size* on the same days that the initial public offerings (IPOs) were purchased, gave investors a 12 percent annual return.

Other studies have come up with similar results. One of the major reasons for the underperformance of IPOs is that they are growth stocks, often issued at huge price earnings multipliers. The lessons are clear. If you can get an IPO at the offering price, it is often a great buy. But don't hold on! The subsequent performance almost always disappoints.

INVESTMENT STRATEGY

The data in this chapter seem to imply that investors should hold primarily small, non-dividend-paying stocks with negative earnings and book value. Such junk stocks, as these might be called, are often shunned by investors and offer superior future returns.

But such a conclusion would be premature. First of all, we have shown that the superior performance of small stocks is quite dependent on the period analyzed, and secondly, small stocks are substantially riskier than large stocks. Furthermore, as we shall show in Chapter 17, strangely enough, most of the

---

[14] Tim Loughran and Jay Ritter, "The Timing and Subsequent Performance of New Issues," University of Illinois manuscript, 1993.

superior performance of small stocks occurs in the month of January, so that most of the year small stocks do not outperform large stocks.

Nevertheless, small stocks *do* belong in one's portfolio. Remember that the market value of the S&P 500 Index is just over 70 percent of the entire market. And the dividend yield on small stocks is substantially lower than that on large stocks, meaning that a much larger fraction of their return comes from favorably taxed capital gains. With marginal tax rates rising again, this form of wealth building is to be encouraged.

The stocks that pay no dividends or have negative earnings or book value are generally either small stocks or large stocks which have fallen on hard times. To the extent that the market overreacts to adverse developments, these stocks may be candidates for significant accumulation. But be careful. Investors are often attracted far too soon to *falling* angels rather than *fallen* angels, the name applied to once-stellar stocks which have crashed. Many investors bought IBM too early as it fell nearly 75 percent from a high of $160 and paid the consequences. Catching a falling star may well burn a hole in your pocket.

CHAPTER 6

THE NIFTY FIFTY REVISITED

> It was so easy to forget that probably no sizable company could possibly be worth over 50 times normal earnings. As the late Burton Crane once observed about Xerox, its multiple discounted not only the future but also the hereafter.[1]

In the last chapter we saw that the returns of stocks with high price-to-earnings or price-to-book ratios lagged behind those which sell for lower multiples. In this chapter we look at a group of high-flying growth stocks which soared in the early 1970s, only to come crashing to earth in the vicious 1973–74 bear market. These stocks were often held up as examples of speculation based on unwarranted optimism about the ability of growth stocks to continue to generate rapid and sustained earnings growth. And it was not just the public, but large institutions as well who poured tens of billions of dollars into these stocks. The 1973–74 bear market so slashed the value of many of these firms that many investors vowed never again to pay upwards of 30 times earnings for a stock.

But was the conventional wisdom that these stocks were markedly overvalued by the bull market of the early 1970s justified, or were investors eventually vindicated for having paid paying 40, 50, or sometimes even more times earnings for the leading growth stocks of the time? This chapter addresses this question.

---

1 "The Nifty Fifty Revisited," *Forbes,* December 15, 1977, p. 72.

THE NIFTY FIFTY

The nifty fifty were a group of premier growth stocks, such as Xerox, IBM, Polaroid, and Coca-Cola, which became institutional darlings in the early 1970s. All of these stocks had proven growth records, continual increases in dividends (virtually none had cut its dividend since World War II), and high market capitalization. This last characteristic enabled institutions to load up on these stocks without significantly influencing the price of their shares.

The nifty fifty were often called *one-decision* stocks: buy and never sell. Because their prospects were so bright, the only direction they could go was up, so money managers claimed. Since they had made so many rich, few, if any, investors could fault a money manager for buying them.

At the time, however, many investors did not seem to find 70, 80, even 100 times earnings at all an unreasonable price to pay for the world's preeminent growth companies. *Forbes* magazine retrospectively commented on the phenomenon as follows:

> What held the Nifty Fifty up? The same thing that held up tulip-bulb prices in long-ago Holland—popular delusions and the madness of crowds. The delusion was that these companies were so good it didn't matter what you paid for them; their inexorable growth would bail you out.
>
> Obviously the problem was not with the companies but with the temporary insanity of institutional money managers—proving again that stupidity well-packaged can sound like wisdom. It was so easy to forget that probably no sizable company could possibly be worth over 50 times normal earnings.[2]

WHAT IS THE RECORD?

Let's trace the performance of the nifty fifty stocks as identified by Morgan Guaranty Trust, one of the largest managers of equity trust assets.[3] These stocks are listed in Table 6–1, along with

---

[2] *Ibid.*

[3] Noted by M. S. Forbes, Jr., in "When Wall Street Becomes Enamored," *Forbes,* December 15, 1977, p. 72.

their 1972 price/earnings (P/E) ratios and dividend yields. They are ranked according to their annual compound returns from January 1972 through May 1993.[4] Corporate changes in the nifty fifty since the early 1970s are described in the appendix at the end of the chapter. The product lines of these stocks range from drugs, computers and electronics, photography, food and tobacco, to retailing, among others. Notably absent are the cyclical industries: autos, steels, transportation, capital goods, as well as the oils.

Many of the original nifty fifty stocks are still giants today. In 1993, 15 occupy the top 40 US stocks in terms of market capitalization, and four, General Electric, Coca-Cola, Merck, and Philip Morris, are among the top 10.

The nifty fifty did sell at hefty multiples. The average P/E ratio of the nifty fifty in 1972 was 37.3, more than double that of the S&P 500 Index, while their average dividend yield at 1.1 percent was less than one half that of other large stocks. Nearly one fifth of these firms sported price/earnings ratios in excess of 50, and Polaroid was selling at over 90 times earnings.

The drug stocks were clearly star performers. Merck, Bristol-Myers (which absorbed Squibb), Schering, Pfizer, Upjohn, and Johnson & Johnson all outperformed the S&P 500 Index over most of the period. But the biggest winner was Philip Morris, which has a 20.5 percent return since January 1971, and easily outperformed the S&P 500 Index over the time periods analyzed. The next five leaders were McDonald's, PepsiCo, Disney, Schlumberger, and Coca-Cola.

Of course there were also some big losers. MGIC Investment Corp., a mortgage investment firm, was the worst. It merged with Baldwin United, which went bankrupt and emerged as PHL Corp. From 1971, investors lost about 70 percent of their original stake, but over 90 percent since 1973 (including reinvested dividends). From the market peak on January 1, 1973, five stocks showed negative total returns.

---

[4] I used the following procedure to compute total returns to the nifty fifty stocks over the entire period. If a stock merged with, or was acquired by another firm, I combined the returns on the two stocks at the appropriate date of change. If the company went private, I spliced the return on the S&P 500 Index from that date forward.

TABLE 6–1
Nifty Fifty Returns, Dividends, and Earnings (January 1, 1972 through May 31, 1993)

			1972			
				P/E		
		Comp	Dividend	Actual	Hindsight	
		Return (%)	Yield	Ratio	*Before tax*	*After tax*
Philip Morris Cos. Inc.	MO	19.48%	1.3%	21.0	89.1	94.2
Gillette Co.	GS	16.23	2.8	19.7	46.3	43.0
PepsiCo Inc.	PEP	16.20	1.2	27.0	63.1	68.9
Heublein Inc.	HBL	14.81	1.7	26.7	48.3	47.5
Merck	MRK	14.47	2.2	25.9	43.9	50.8
The Coca Cola Co.	KO	14.25	1.2	42.3	68.8	70.1
McDonald's Corp.	MCD	13.96	0.0	59.8	92.2	126.3
Bristol-Myers Co.	BMY	13.95	1.9	24.4	37.5	40.7
Schlumberger Ltd.	SLB	13.40	0.7	35.7	49.5	62.5
Disney Walt Co.	DIS	13.10	0.1	55.3	72.5	99.0
General Electric Co.	GE	12.77	2.1	22.6	27.8	28.7
Pfizer Inc.	PFE	12.60	1.6	27.9	33.2	37.1
Squibb Corp.	SQB	12.54	1.6	30.2	41.4	46.4
Chesebrough-Pond's Inc.	CBM	12.13	1.4	34.0	37.1	39.2
Schering Plough Corp.	SGP	11.94	0.8	39.3	41.3	46.5
AMP Inc.	AMP	11.77	0.7	36.4	37.1	48.0
Am. Home Prod. Corp.	AHP	11.69	1.7	32.9	32.9	33.7
Revlon Inc.	REV	11.62	1.4	25.5	25.2	28.4
Dow Chemical Co.	DOW	11.52	2.0	22.3	21.6	22.2
Procter & Gamble	PG	11.32	1.9	24.0	22.4	24.5
Anheuser-Busch, Inc.	BUD	11.02	0.9	36.7	32.3	38.5
Upjohn Co.	UPJ	10.87	1.6	32.8	28.1	32.2
Intern'l Flavors & Frag	IFF	10.40	0.6	57.9	45.3	53.4
Am. Hospital Supply Corp.	AHS	10.34	0.6	47.9	37.0	46.7
Johnson & Johnson	JNJ	10.18	0.4	55.5	41.5	52.9
3M	MMM	9.65	1.2	35.7	24.1	27.0

Table 6–2 summarizes the returns on the nifty fifty stocks and the benchmark indexes for stocks, bonds, and bills. In order to analyze the returns on the nifty fifty, an equally weighted

[5] A "frozen" portfolio which did not rebalance was also analyzed. The return was similar to, but slightly lower than, the rebalanced portfolio.

TABLE 6–1 (*concluded*)

			1972			
				P/E		
		Comp	Dividend	Actual	Hindsight	
		Return (%)	Yield	Ratio	*Before tax*	*After tax*
LA Land & Exploration Co.	LLX	9.21	2.1	27.0	6.3	8.2
Citicorp	CCI	8.94	2.1	17.5	10.3	10.8
J. C. Penney Company, Inc.	JCP	8.93	1.3	28.7	16.8	18.3
American Express Company	AXP	8.77	0.9	28.4	16.1	18.9
Halliburton Co.	HAL	8.77	1.0	27.7	15.7	19.3
Baxter Intern'l Inc.	BAX	7.89	0.3	59.5	28.4	39.9
Lubrizol Corp.	LZ	7.66	0.9	34.9	15.9	19.0
Texas Instruments Inc.	TXN	7.43	0.5	36.8	16.0	22.1
I T T	ITT	7.01	2.1	14.8	5.9	6.0
Kmart Corp.	KM	6.66	0.4	42.5	15.9	20.2
Jos. Schlitz Brewing Co.	SLZ	6.08	1.1	32.2	10.7	13.9
Digital Equip. Corp.	DEC	5.87	0.0	53.2	16.9	27.7
Sears, Roebuck & Co.	S	4.97	1.4	28.6	7.6	9.1
Eastman Kodak Co.	EK	4.89	1.1	37.7	9.8	12.5
Eli Lilly & Co.	LLY	4.38	1.0	37.7	23.4	27.4
IBM	IBM	2.86	1.4	35.5	6.1	8.7
Avon Products, Inc.	AVP	2.85	1.1	55.4	9.5	12.5
Xerox Corp.	XRX	2.06	0.6	46.9	6.8	10.3
Black & Decker Mfg.	BDK	1.69	1.1	40.9	5.5	8.9
Polaroid Corp.	PRD	1.24	0.3	93.5	11.4	19.5
Simplicity Pattern	SYP	0.20	0.6	45.0	4.4	7.9
Burroughs Inc.	BGH	-0.82	0.3	41.0	3.2	6.5
Emery Air Fght. Corp.	EAF	-4.41	1.0	49.6	1.8	5.3
M G I C Investment Corp.	MGI	-8.72	0.1	53.0	0.7	4.1
Average			1.1	37.3	28.1	33.3
S&P 500			2.8	18.2		

Companies ranked according to the 1972 geometric return

portfolio was constructed which "rebalanced" every year so that each stock maintained its 2 percent allocation.[5]

Figure 6–1 displays the cumulative returns. From January 1972 to May 1993, the return on the nifty fifty beats the S&P 500 Index, but falls behind if measured from January 1973 and 1974. However, from the depth of the bear market in October 1974, the rebalanced portfolio again beats the S&P 500 Index.

TABLE 6–2
Nifty Fifty and Benchmark Returns (January 1972–May 1993)

Real Taxable Income	S&P 500	Nifty 50 Equal Weight	Bonds	Bills
$0	11.68%	12.02%	9.15%	7.43%
$50,000	8.39	9.00	5.38	4.26
$150,000	7.88	8.61	4.72	3.55
Maximum	7.74	8.54	4.50	3.35

Did the nifty fifty stocks become overvalued during the buying spree of 1972? Yes—but not by much, and by some criteria not at all! From January 1973, *on an after-tax basis,* the returns on the nifty fifty would have exceeded that of the S&P 500 Index except in the very lowest tax bracket. This is because the average dividend yield on the nifty fifty was about 2½ percentage points below the yield on the S&P 500 Index and the higher capital gains on the nifty fifty are lightly taxed.

WHAT IS THE RIGHT P/E RATIO?

Once we know the subsequent performance of the nifty fifty, we can determine what price investors should have paid for the earnings of these glamour stocks. Table 6–1 reports the price that investors should have paid for the nifty fifty stocks in January 1972 so that their return, given their May 1993 prices, would equal that of the S&P 500 Index. The table shows that the average multiple of the nifty fifty stocks in 1972 was 37.3. Given their subsequent performance, their average multiple should have been 30.4 on a before-tax basis, and 35.1 on an after-tax basis (at $150,000 real taxable income) in order to match the return on the S&P 500 Index. The average price-to-earnings

FIGURE 6–1
Nifty Fifty Returns and Benchmarks (January 1971–May 1993)

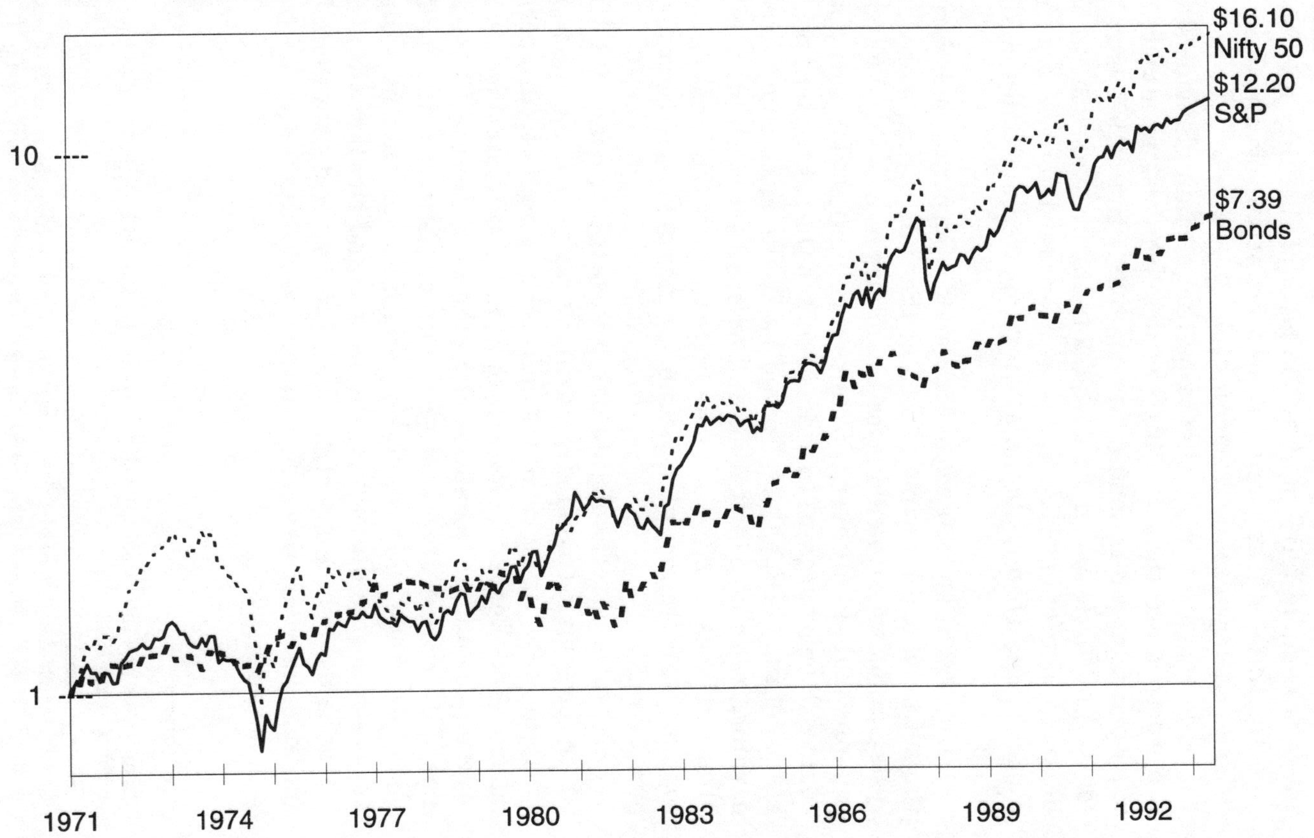

ratio of the stocks is very close to what high-income taxable investors should have paid at the peak of the nifty fifty boom. In 1972 these stocks were not significantly overvalued on the basis of their subsequent earnings.

It is very clear from this table that certain glamour stocks are worth more than the high multiple investors attached to their price. Investors should have paid 89.1 times 1972 earnings for Philip Morris (94 on an after-tax basis) instead of the 21 they did pay, undervaluing the stock by over four-to-one.[6] Coca-Cola, PepsiCo, and Disney should all have sported multiples of 70 or more.

But the real prize goes to McDonald's Corporation. It carried the astronomical multiple of 59.8 at the time, which many analysts claimed was ridiculous for a hamburger drive-in. Who could imagine that paying over 100 times earnings for a large company could still be a bargain? In order to match the subsequent performance of the S&P 500, McDonald's actually justified a price-to-earnings ratio of nearly 100, and over 120 if calculated on an after-tax basis![7] And who would have thought McDonald's could so thoroughly trounce such technology giants as IBM, Burroughs, and Xerox?

But trounce technology stocks this fast-food chain did. IBM, which commanded a 35 P/E ratio in the early 1970s, was actually worth only *6.1* times earnings on the basis on its future performance. And Xerox was worth only 6.8 times earnings, while investors should have paid no more than 3 times the 1972 earnings of Burroughs Corp. Burton Crane, a financial writer for *The New York Times,* did not know how right he was when he claimed Xerox's multiple discounted the future and the hereafter. But had he said the same of McDonald's, which carried an even higher multiple, he would have learned that profits can really fall from hamburger heaven.

---

[6] This takes into the account the stock's recent fall, which brought its price down 40 percent in early 1993.

[7] Since McDonald's Corp. is riskier than the market, an investor may have demanded a rate of return higher than the S&P 500. From 1972 through 1992, the beta of McDonald's was about 1.3 while the average beta for the nifty fifty stocks was very close to 1.0.

CONCLUSION

Many of the nifty fifty stocks did warrant price-to-earnings ratios of 40 and 50 in the early 1970s, far in excess of the average for the period. Interestingly, the group that was the most undervalued, and subsequently most successful both domestic and worldwide, is involved in "snack" foods, including McDonald's, Pepsico, and Coca-Cola. The technology stocks flunked badly.

A review of these stocks emphasizes an important lesson first noted in Chapter 3: Putting all your eggs in one basket can be very dangerous. Several of the nifty fifty stocks had negative total returns and one resulted in almost a total loss of capital. And a perennial investor favorite, IBM, offered virtually no return over the past 20 years. But the danger of being caught with bad apples is simple to avoid—diversify your stock portfolio and in the long run you are virtually guaranteed to outperform other assets.

APPENDIX

CORPORATE CHANGES IN THE NIFTY FIFTY STOCKS

There were nine corporate changes to the nifty fifty over the period.

American Hospital Supply merged with Baxter Travenol (later *Baxter International*) in November 1985.

Burroughs changed its name to *Unisys* (UIS) in 1987.

Chesebrough Ponds was merged in *Unilever NV* in February 1987.

Emery Air Freight merged with *Consolidated Freightways* in April 1989.

Heublein was merged into RJR Nabisco in October 1982, which became *RJR Industries* and was taken private on April 28, 1989.

MGIC Investment merged with Baldwin United in March of 1982, which went bankrupt, and emerged from bankruptcy in November 1986 under the name PHL Corp. PHL was absorbed by *Leucadia Corp.* in January 1993.

Revlon was subject to a leveraged buyout in July 1987.

Schlitz merged with Stroh Brewing, which was a privately held firm in June 1982.
Simplicity Pattern became Maxxam in May 1984 and then *Maxxam Group* in May 1988.
Squibb was purchased on October 4, 1989 by *Bristol-Myers*.

CHAPTER 7

TAXES AND STOCK RETURNS

In this world nothing is certain but death and taxes.

Benjamin Franklin[1]

The power to tax involves the power to destroy.

John Marshall[2]

For all long-term investors, there is only one objective—*maximum total real return after taxes.*

John Templeton[3]

John Templeton's objective, to maximize total real return after taxes must be considered in all investment strategies. For this purpose stocks are very well suited. We have already demonstrated that, in the long run, stocks overwhelmingly offer superior returns to bonds. And, in contrast to fixed-income investments, a significant portion of the return from stocks comes from capital appreciation, which is treated favorably by the tax code. Taxes are not paid until a gain is realized, and such gains have almost always been subject to a lower tax rate than that on dividend income. As in addition to having a superior before-tax return, stocks have a tax advantage over bonds.

---

[1] Letter to M. Leroy, 1789.

[2] *McCulloch* v. *Maryland,* 1819.

[3] Excerpts from *The Templeton Touch* by William Proctor, quoted in *Classics,* ed. Charles D. Ellis (Homewood, Ill.: Dow Jones-Irwin, 1989), p. 738.

HISTORY OF THE TAX CODE

Figure 7–1A plots the marginal tax rate on dividend and interest income for investors at three income levels: the highest tax bracket of those with the highest income, the tax rate for an individual investor with a real income of $150,000 in today's dollars, and the tax rate for an individual with a real income of $50,000. Figure 7–1B plots the tax rate on capital gains for the same levels of income. One can see the dramatic rise and fall in marginal tax rates, especially for the high-income investor, while the tax on gains has remained far more stable. A history of the tax code applicable to stock investors is provided in Appendix A at the end of this chapter.

THE TAX BENEFITS OF CAPITAL GAINS

Many investors assume that capital gains are beneficial solely because of the favorable rates at which such gains have been taxed. But lower capital gains tax rates are not the only advantage of investing in appreciating assets. Taxes on capital gains are paid only when the asset is sold, not when the capital gain is accrued. The advantage of this tax deferral is that assets accumulate at before-tax, rather than after-tax, rates of return.

Table 7–1 documents the increase in the effective rate of return resulting from the deferral of the capital gains tax using tax rates and projected returns prevailing in 1992. A 10 percent nominal return is assumed, consisting of a 3.5 percent dividend yield and a 6.5 percent capital gain. The table assumes a 28 percent capital gains rate and a 36 percent tax rate on dividend income. We assume that these tax brackets and return parameters are in effect over the entire holding period. Appendix B compares the tax consequences of stocks paying dividends against capital gain income.

Holding period yields are calculated for four cases: (1) taxes are paid yearly on dividends and capital gains; (2) taxes are paid yearly on dividends but capital gains tax is paid at the end of the holding period; (3) a sum is contributed tax-free to a pension plan and dividend and capital gains income are sheltered during

FIGURE 7–1
Federal Income Tax Rates 1913–92

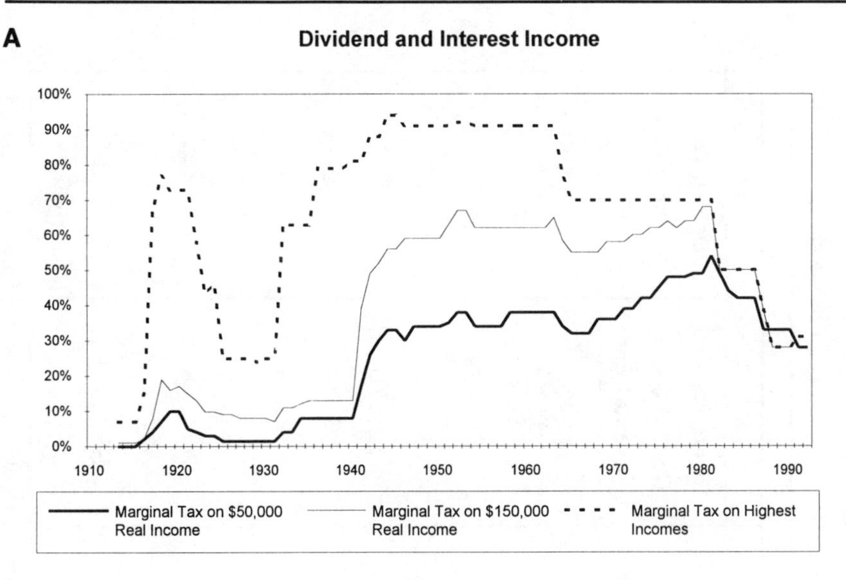

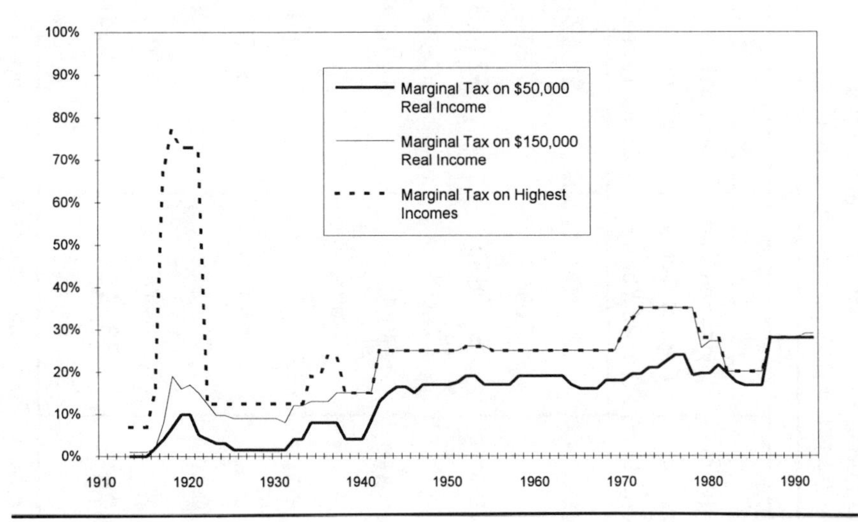

TABLE 7–1

Holding Period Accumulations and Returns ($1,000 Initial Investment)

3.5% Dividend Yield, 6.5% Capital Appreciation, 28% Tax on Capital Gains, 31% Tax on Dividends

	I	II	III*	IV
Length of Holding Period	Dividends and Capital Gains Taxed Yearly	Dividends Taxed Yearly, Capital Gains Taxed at End	Dividends and Capital Gains Taxed at End	Before-Tax Accumulation
5 years	$1,409	$1,424	$1,466	$1,611
	7.09%	7.32%	7.96%	10.00%
10 years	$1,985	$2,073	$2,197	$2,594
	7.09%	7.56%	8.19%	10.00%
20 years	$3,939	$4,592	$5,176	$6,727
	7.09%	7.92%	8.57%	10.00%
30 years	$7,818	$10,508	$12,742	$17,449
	7.09%	8.16%	8.85%	10.00%
40 years	$15,516	$24,399	$32,150	$45,259
	7.09%	8.31%	9.06%	10.00%
50 years	$30,794	$57,016	$82,209	$117,391
	7.09%	8.42%	9.22%	10.00%

*Accumulation taxed at the end of the holding period at dividend income tax rate and initial tax credit is invested at 4% taxable rate.

the holding period, but the entire amount is taxed at the ordinary income tax rate at the end of the period (this case corresponds to the accumulation that would take place with tax-deductible pension plans such as IRA's, Keoghs, 401(k) plans, etc.); and (4) all taxes are deferred. If an investor drops into a lower tax bracket at the end of the holding period, then the effect of deferral is magnified in cases (2) and (3), and approaches the accumulation in case (4) if the final-year tax bracket is zero or the estate is passed, tax-free, to heirs.

The impact of capital gains deferral increases dramatically as the number of years increases. After 10 years, the effect of capital gains deferral adds 47/100 of a percentage point (called *basis points*) to the return; after 30 years, 107 basis points. In fact, after 10 years, deferral of taxes at the current 28 percent rate is equivalent to a capital gains tax at a 20.8 percent rate if taxes are paid when gains are accrued. After 30 years, the effect of deferral is equivalent to a nondeferred capital gains tax of 11.6 percent, less than half the current rate.

From a tax standpoint, there should be a clear preference for investors to receive capital gains over dividend income. But dividend income is still preferred by many investors. Many investors believe that if management is committed to paying cash to shareholders, they may also be less likely to squander such money on nonproductive acquisitions or perks.[4] Furthermore, some investors prefer dividend income because they find it less worrisome simply to receive a steady, predictable cash flow rather than to be constantly calculating how much stock to sell. A final reason for preferring dividends over capital gains involves the relative simplicity of tax reporting.[5]

---

[4] Committed share repurchases also eliminate the possibility that management will waste the money, but many believe that maintaining a dividend commits management to a greater extent than share repurchases.

[5] The above reasons for why some investors prefer dividend income over capital gains do not imply that firms, in their choice of dividend payout ratios, are insensitive to tax incentives. We noted in Chapter 4 that prior to World War II the average payout ratio of corporations fell to 52 percent from 71 percent in reaction to the sharp increase in marginal tax rates.

A TOTAL AFTER-TAX RETURNS INDEX

In Chapter 1, we presented a total returns index for stocks, bonds, bills, and gold. In this chapter we calculate a range of after-tax returns on these assets under various tax rates. The upper line of the stock cone in Figure 7–2 represents the before-tax return, as shown in Figure 2–1 of Chapter 2. This accumulation would be applicable to tax-exempt individuals or institutions.

The lower line of the cone in Figure 7–2 assumes investors pay the highest tax rate on dividend, interest, and capital gains income, with no deferral of capital gains taxes.[6] The lower line assumes that dividends, interest income, and capital gains are taxed at the highest marginal tax rate prevailing in the year they were earned. The shaded cone shows the range of total after-tax accumulations. The difference in accumulated wealth is striking, with pre-tax stock returns accumulating to $3.05 million while after-tax accumulations at the highest tax rates amount to $166,000, only 5.4 percent of the pre-tax sum. A tax cone is also displayed for the accumulations on Treasury bonds. Naturally, the effect of taxes on investment returns is much greater in the third subperiod, when federal income taxes become important. In the period from 1926 to 1992, the average real return on stock is reduced from 6.6 percent to only 2.4 percent, or nearly two thirds, for those in the top bracket. (See Table 7–2.)

Despite the debilitating effect of taxes on equity accumulation, taxes cause the greatest damage to fixed-income investments. In the third subperiod, the real return on bonds is reduced from a positive 1.5 percent to a negative 1.4 percent for an investor in the top bracket and from a positive 0.5 percent to a negative 1.6 percent for Treasury bills. This means that on an after-tax basis, an investor in the top tax bracket who put $1,000 in Treasury bills at the beginning of 1926 would have $345 after inflation today, a real loss of 65 percent! During the period, the real return

[6] Since no state or local taxes have been considered, tax rates are set at zero before 1913, when the federal income tax was instituted.

FIGURE 7–2
Total Nominal Return Indexes (Before and After Federal Tax 1802–1992)

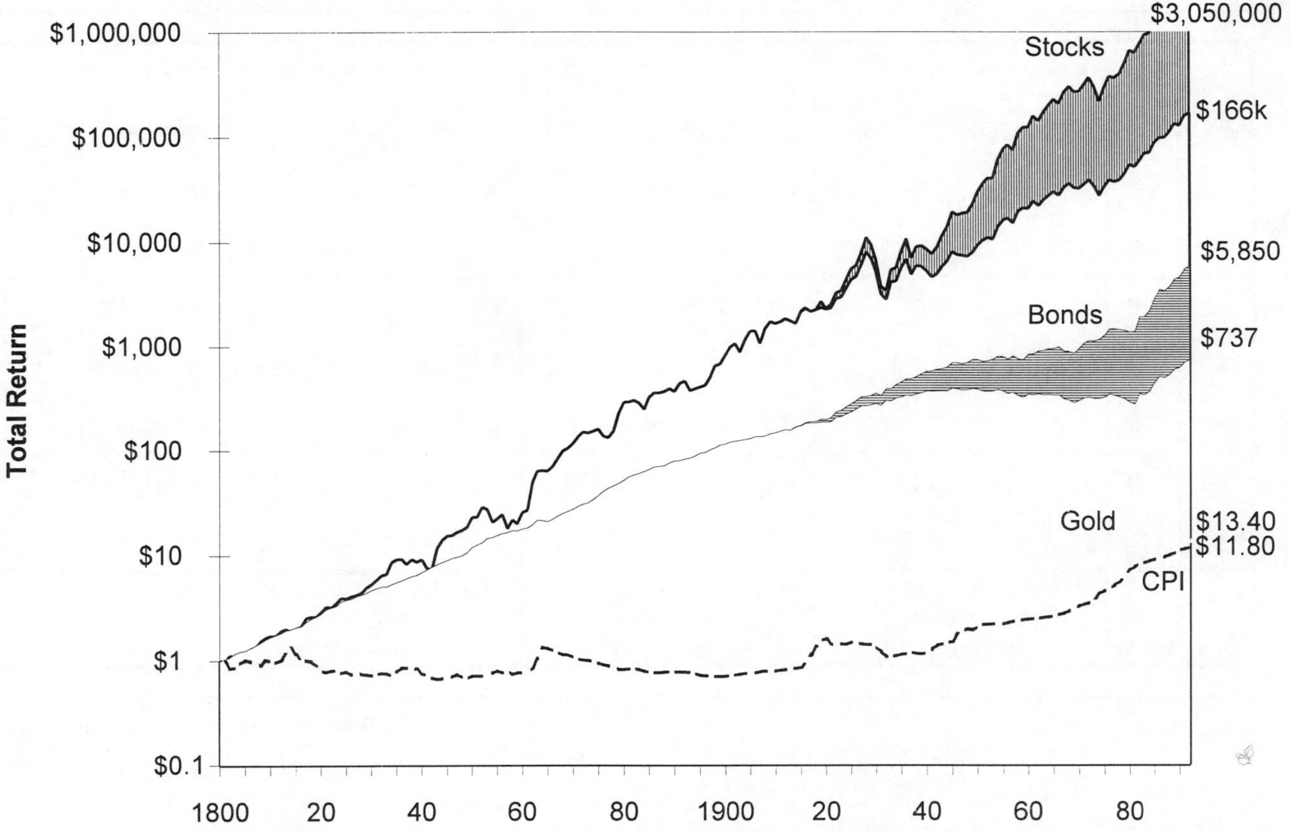

Total Return

$1,000,000
$100,000
$10,000
$1,000
$100
$10
$1
$0.1

1800 20 40 60 80 1900 20 40 60 80

Stocks
$3,050,000
$166k
Bonds
$5,850
$737
Gold
$13.40
$11.80
CPI

TABLE 7–2
Historical Asset Real Returns and Taxes

		Stock Returns Tax Bracket				Bond Returns Tax Bracket				T-Bill Returns Tax Bracket				Gold	CPI
		$0	$50k	$150k	Max	$0	$50k	$150k	Max	$0	$50k	$150k	Max		
Period	1802-1992	6.7%	6.0%	5.7%	5.1%	3.3%	2.7%	2.5%	2.2%	2.9%	2.4%	2.3%	2.0%	0.1%	1.3%
	1871-1992	6.6	5.5	4.9	4.1	2.5	1.6	1.2	0.8	1.7	1.0	0.7	0.3	0.0	2.0
Major Sub-Periods	I 1802-1870	6.8	6.8	6.8	6.8	4.6	4.6	4.6	4.6	4.9	4.9	4.9	4.9	0.2	0.0
	II 1871-1925	6.6	6.6	6.4	6.2	3.7	3.7	3.6	3.4	3.2	3.1	3.1	2.7	-0.8	0.6
	III 1926-1992	6.6	4.6	3.7	2.4	1.5	-0.1	-0.7	-1.4	0.5	-0.8	-1.3	-1.6	0.7	3.1
Post-War Periods	1946-1992	6.6	4.1	3.1	2.1	0.2	-1.9	-2.6	-3.0	0.4	-1.5	-2.2	-2.6	-0.1	4.5
	1966-1981	-0.4	-2.1	-2.9	-3.3	-4.3	-6.6	-7.5	-7.7	-0.2	-3.0	-4.1	-4.6	8.8	7.0
	1966-1992	4.2	1.8	1.3	0.8	1.2	-1.7	-2.4	-2.6	1.3	-1.5	-2.3	-2.6	1.9	5.7
	1982-1992	11.1	7.8	7.6	7.1	9.8	5.8	5.5	5.3	3.3	0.6	0.5	0.5	-7.4	3.8

on gold has been a positive 0.7 percent, exceeding that in bonds or bills, but still far less than stocks.[7]

In fact, for someone in the highest tax bracket, short-term fixed-income assets have yielded no after-tax real return since 1874, and even longer if state and local taxes are taken into account. However, a high-income investor would have increased her stake in stocks by 90-fold, even if she paid all capital gains and dividend taxes.

SUMMARY

Tax planning must be a significant factor in maximizing effective returns from financial assets. Because of favorable capital gains rates and deferral potential, stocks hold a significant tax advantage over fixed-income assets. Nevertheless, it definitely pays to shelter stock investment income from taxes as much as possible, because returns on stocks are so much more favorable than those on bonds.

The best way to shelter stock returns from taxes, other than placing them in a pension account, is to defer capital gains as long as possible. Fortunately, for the long-term stockholder this is not difficult. By holding a diversified list of common stocks and not buying and selling individual stocks searching for higher returns, gains will accumulate tax-free. In the last chapter we will discuss how best to accomplish this goal.

APPENDIX A

HISTORY OF THE TAX CODE

The federal income tax was first collected under the Revenue Act of 1913, when the 16th Amendment to the US Constitution was ratified. Until 1921 there was no tax preference given to capital gains income.

---

[7] Legally, individuals must pay taxes on the capital gain from buying gold, but in the case of gold coins or bullion this tax is very difficult to collect.

When tax rates were increased sharply during World War I, investors refrained from realizing gains and complained to Congress about the tax consequences of selling their assets. Congress was persuaded that such frozen portfolios were detrimental to the efficient allocation of capital, and so in 1922 a maximum tax rate of 12.5 percent was established on capital gains income. This rate became effective at a taxable income of $30,000, which at that time was equivalent to about $240,000 in today's dollars.

In 1934, a new tax code was enacted which, for the first time, excluded a portion of capital gains from taxable income. This exclusion allowed middle income groups, and not just the rich, to enjoy the tax benefits of capital gains income. The excluded portion of the gain depended on the length of time that the asset was held: there was no exclusion if the asset was held one year or less, but the exclusion was increased to 70 percent if the asset was held more than 10 years. Since marginal tax rates ranged up to 79 percent in 1936, the effective maximum tax on very-long-term gains was reduced to about 24 percent.

In 1938, the tax code was amended again to provide for a 50 percent exclusion of capital gains income if an asset was held more than 18 months, but in no case would the tax exceed 15 percent on such capital gains. The maximum rate on capital gains income was raised to 25 percent in 1942, but the holding period was reduced to six months. Except for a 1 percent surtax which raised the maximum rate to 26 percent during the Korean war, the 25 percent rate held until 1969.

In 1969, the maximum tax rate on capital gains in excess of $50,000 was phased out over a number of years, so that ultimately the 50 percent exclusion applied to all tax rates. Since the maximum rate on ordinary income was 70 percent, this meant the maximum tax rate on capital gains rose to 35 percent by 1973. In 1978, the exclusion was raised to 60 percent, which lowered the effective maximum tax rate on capital gains to 28 percent. When, in 1982, the maximum tax rate on ordinary income was reduced to 50 percent, the maximum tax rate on capital gains was again reduced to 20 percent.

In 1986, the tax code was extensively altered to reduce and simplify the tax structure and ultimately eliminate the distinction between capital gains and ordinary income. By 1988, the tax rate on both the capital gains and ordinary income was identical at 33 percent. For the first time since 1922, there was no preference on capital gains income. In 1990, the top rate was lowered to 28 percent on both ordinary and capital gain income. In 1991, a slight wedge was reopened between capital gains and ordinary income—the top rate on the latter was raised to 31 percent, while the former remained at 28 percent. In 1993,

President Clinton raised tax rates again, increasing the top rate on ordinary income to 39.6 percent while keeping the capital gains tax unchanged.*

APPENDIX B

GAIN FROM DEFERRING TAXES

Assume we have two firms, DIV and CAP, which realize identical returns on their stocks. DIV pays a 10 percent annual dividend, but realizes no capital gain. CAP realizes a 10 percent capital gain per year, but pays no dividend. Assume that the tax rate on both dividend income and realized capital gains is 40 percent, so there is no preference given to capital gains over ordinary income.

Each year an investor holding DIV will have to pay taxes, which amount to 40 percent on the income received as dividends. The after-tax rate of return on DIV is 6 percent.

In contrast, an investor in CAP does not pay tax until he sells his shares. Until the tax is paid, the return to an investor in CAP is compounded at 10 percent per year instead of 6 percent. Although 40 percent of the profits from holding CAP are paid when the stock is sold, the deferral of tax paid benefits the investor and increases his after-tax return.

If CAP stock is sold after only one year, investors in both DIV and CAP experience an identical 6 percent after-tax return (assuming the dividend is paid at the end of the year). But if CAP is held for five years, the after-tax compound rate of return on CAP increases to 6.44 percent. After 10 years, the return rises to 6.94 percent, after 20 years to 7.73 percent, and after 30 years to 8.28 percent. If CAP is never sold, the return to the investor is 10 percent per year. In contrast, the return on DIV remains at 6 percent per year, no matter how long the stock is held.

* Because of the phaseout of exemptions and certain itemized deductions, the marginal tax rate is higher at certain income levels.

CHAPTER 8

GLOBAL INVESTING

> Today let's talk about a growth industry.
> Because investing worldwide is a growth industry.
> The great growth industry is
> international portfolio investing.
>
> *John Templeton*[1]

In chapter 1, we showed that the superior returns to equity were not unique to the United States. Investors in Britain, Japan, and even Germany also accumulated substantial wealth through investing in stocks. But for many years, foreign markets were almost exclusively the domain of native investors, considered too remote and risky to be entertained by foreigners.

But no longer. *Globalization* is the financial buzzword of the decade. The United States, once the unchallenged giant of capital markets, has become only one of many countries in which investors can accumulate wealth. At the end of World War II, US stocks comprised almost 90 percent of the world's equity capitalization; by 1970 they still comprised two thirds. But today they constitute barely one third of the world's stock values. To invest only in the United States is to ignore most of the world's capital.

---

[1] Transcript of address delivered to Annual Conference of the Financial Analysts Federation, May 2, 1984.

FOREIGN STOCK RETURNS

Although over long periods of time equities yield a 6 or 7 percent rate of return after inflation, returns can very widely over periods as long as 10 or 15 years. The period from 1970 onward, which is often taken as the benchmark for measuring foreign returns, is not sufficiently long to draw any definitive conclusions about the expected return from foreign investing. For example, US stock returns averaged negative 0.7 percent for the 15 years between 1966 and 1981, while since 1982 the average real return has been almost 13 percent.

The problem with projecting short-term historical returns into the future is best illustrated with the Japanese market. In the 1970s and 1980s, Japanese stocks experienced dollar returns which were more than 10 percentage points above the US market's. During this time, the dollar returns in the Japanese market dominated those from every other industrialized country. In 1989, for the first time since the early part of this century, the American equity market was no longer the world's largest. Japan, a country whose economic base was totally destroyed by US military action 44 years earlier and which possesses only one half the population and 4 percent of the land mass of the United States, became the home to a stock market which exceeded the valuation of America or all of Europe.

The superior returns on the Japanese market attracted billions of dollars of foreign investment. Valuations on many Japanese stocks reached stratospheric levels. Nippon Telephone and Telegraph, or NTT, the Japanese version of America's AT&T, was priced at a P/E ratio above 300 and a market valuation of hundreds of billions of dollars. This was a value which dwarfed the aggregate stock values of all but a handful of countries around the world.

While traveling in Japan in 1989, Leo Melamed, president of the Chicago Mercantile Exchange, questioned his Japanese hosts on how such high valuations could be placed on Japanese stocks. "You don't understand," they responded, "We've moved to an entirely new way of valuing stocks here in Japan." At that moment Melamed recalls feeling certain that the Japanese market must be near the end of its great bull market.[2] For it is when investors cast aside the lessons of history that those lessons come back to haunt the market.

The Nikkei Dow-Jones, which had surpassed 39,000 at the end of 1989, fell to nearly 14,000 by August of 1992—a fall worse than any experienced by the US Dow Industrials since the great 1929–32 crash. The shares of NTT fell from 3.2 million yen to under 500,000 by August 1992. The mystique of the Japanese market was broken.

After the collapse of the Japanese market, the emphasis of the global enthusiasts switched to emerging markets. An *emerging market* is a market of a developing or newly developed country. Investors had already witnessed the stock booms of Taiwan, Korea, and Thailand. Now India, Indonesia, and even China were set to join the fray.

But Asian countries were not the only players. Latin America, long a backwater of authoritarian, anti-free-market regimes (of both the right and left) turned full circle and aggressively sought foreign investment. Equity gains were extremely impressive in such countries as Argentina and Mexico.

Even China, the last major country ruled by "communist" leaders, founded stock markets. The opening of the first Chinese stock market in Shenzhen was met with a riot as thousands stood days in lines waiting to be allocated shares in firms in the world's most populated country. And who would have imagined five years ago that one of the world's best performing stock markets would be Hong Kong, destined in a couple of years to be taken over by the communists, the sworn enemy of capitalism.

The term *emerging,* as applied to these markets, is evocative of a beautiful butterfly rising from its chrysalis, ready to soar to the heavens. But the enthusiasm which greeted these markets often far exceeded their ability to perform. Just as most butter-

---

[2] Martin Mayer, *Markets* (New York: W. W. Norton, 1988), p. 60.

flies are eaten by birds after they take their first flight, many of these newly emerging markets crash soon after reaching a peak.

Taiwan is a case in point. In 1986, the Taiwanese stock index stood at 848. By February 1990, less than four years later, it soared to 12,424, sporting an average price/earnings ratio in excess of 100. The market capitalization in Taiwan exceeded $300 billion, larger than Britain in 1985 and the entire world market outside the United States in 1969.

Financial analyst John S. Bolsover, chief executive officer of the London firm Baring Investment, believed that Taiwan was symptomatic of the overoptimistic attitudes towards emerging economies. In a speech delivered at the market peak, entitled "Alice in Taiwanderland," Bolsover warned, "Beware of the temptation to say, 'This time is different.' " He ended his speech with Santayana's famous words, "Those who ignore history are doomed to relive it."[3] By October 1990, the Taiwan stock market had collapsed nearly 80 percent.

SUMMARY DATA ON GLOBAL MARKETS

Most financial advisers recommend foreign investments by projecting superior returns beyond our borders. And most foreign stock markets have indeed offered higher returns to dollar investors than US stocks.

Table 8–1 displays the total returns in some of the world's stock markets from 1970 to the present,[4] while Table 8–2 shows

---

[3] Quoted in *Classics II*, ed. Charles D. Ellis (Homewood, Ill.: Business One Irwin, 1991), pp. 520–22.

[4] These summary data are taken from the Morgan Stanley Capital International data base. These indexes cover about 60 percent of the capitalization in each country. In the United States, this amounts to 334 stocks.

TABLE 8–1
World Stock Returns (Annualized Geometric Returns from January 1970 through May 1993. Standard deviations in parenthesis)

Country or Region	Local Return	Exchange Rate Change	US Dollar Returns
Non-USA			
World Index	10.8% (20.4)	2.4% (10.9)	13.4% (23.7)
Value Weighted			
World Index	10.4 (17.1)	1.2 (5.6)	11.7 (17.7)
Equal Weighted			
World Index	13.3 (22.5)	1.0 (9.2)	13.7 (22.3)
USA	10.8 (16.4)	----	10.8 (16.4)
Europe	11.5 (20.7)	0.5 (12.2)	12.1 (22.6)
Japan	12.1 (31.6)	5.3 (13.6)	18.0 (38.2)

the considerable variation in these returns over time. The dollar return from investing in foreign markets is the sum of the *local return,* which is calculated in terms of the local currency, and the change in the exchange rate between the local currency and the dollar. Changes in the exchange rate can either enhance or diminish the local returns for the dollar investor.

The average annual compound capitalization-weighted dollar return on all foreign markets has been 13.4 percent per year between 1970 and May 1993. Over the same time, the annual

TABLE 8–2

Dollar Returns in World Stock Markets (Annualized Geometric Returns by Decades. Standard deviations in parenthesis)

Country or Region	1970 - 1979	1980 - 1989	1990 - 1993*
Non-USA World Index	**10.1%**	**22.6%**	**-1.3%**
	(22.4)	(23.0)	(21.6)
Value Weighted World Index	**7.0**	**19.9**	**2.9**
	(18.1)	(14.6)	(16.2)
Equal Weighted World Index	**12.7**	**17.4**	**6.3**
	(24.1)	(22.6)	(15.9)
USA	**4.6**	**17.1**	**11.4**
	(19.0)	(12.5)	(13.7)
Europe	**8.6**	**18.5**	**4.4**
	(21.0)	(25.9)	(16.8)
Japan	**17.4**	**28.7**	**-6.7**
	(45.4)	(28.6)	(32.9)

* Through May 1993

return from US stocks has averaged only 10.8 percent.[5] It is of interest that the local stock returns in Europe, Japan, and the United States are quite similar. The superior dollar returns from

[5] Since the Morgan Stanley indexes contain even larger stocks than the S&P 500 Index, and smaller stocks have outperformed larger stocks over this period, the returns reported here are less than those of broader-based indexes. This bias, however, is uniform across countries, since small stocks have outperformed larger stocks abroad as in the United States.

FIGURE 8–1
Total Dollar Returns in Major Markets (January 1970 through May 1993)

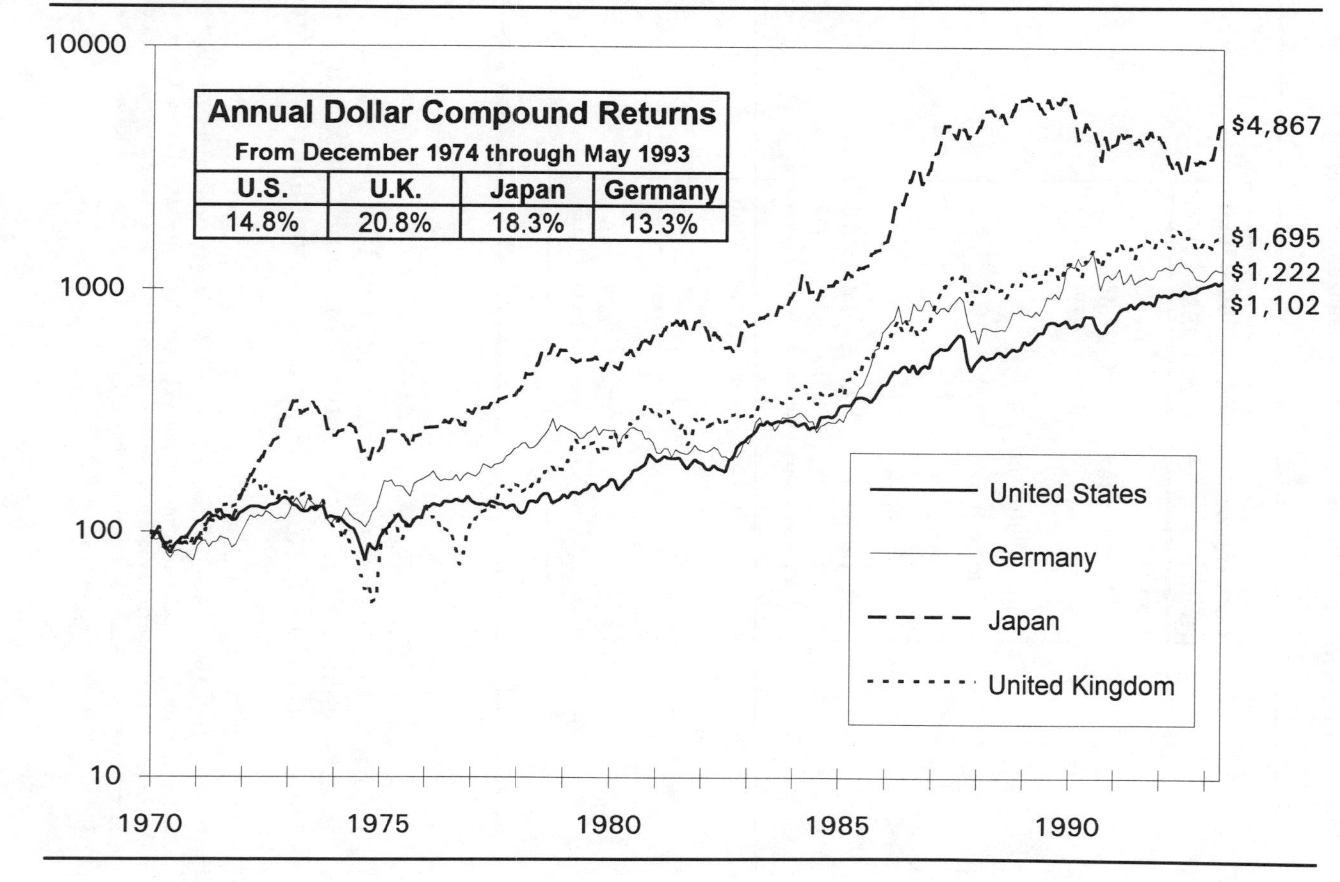

investing abroad have arisen mostly from the appreciation of foreign currencies against the dollar.

Figure 8–1 displays the monthly dollar return index for the United States, the United Kingdom, Japan, and Germany since January 1970. Over the entire period, Japan has outperformed all other major markets, despite its horrible performance since 1989. A $100 investment in January 1970 would have grown to $4,867 in Japan by May 1993, but only $1,695 in the United Kingdom, $1,222 in Germany, and $1,102 in the US. But, contrary to popular opinion, Japan's superior stock returns had virtually all been achieved by the early 1970s. From April 1973 onward, the average compound annual return in Japan exceeded the return in the United States by less than 2 percent and bettered the United Kingdom by less than one percentage point.

Few realize how profitable it has been to invest in the British market in the postwar period, especially after its severe decline in 1973–74. From December 1973 onward, a dollar investor in Britain would have handily beaten investors in every other market, including Japan. This has occurred despite the fact that since 1974 the GDP of Japan has grown at 4.2 percent per year, while GDP in the United Kingdom has grown at less than one half that rate. This shows that economic growth alone is no guarantee of superior stock market returns.

SOURCES OF DOLLAR RISK IN INTERNATIONAL STOCKS

Exchange-Rate Risk

Movements of exchange rates are a source of risk for foreign investors, since dollar returns are the sum of local returns and changes in the exchange rate. In the long run, there is wide agreement that the primary source of exchange-rate changes between countries centers around differing rates of inflation. Countries with higher rates of inflation will find their currencies depreciate relative to countries with lower rates of inflation.

TABLE 8–3
Sources of Dollar Risk in Stocks (from January 1970 through December 1992, Annual)

Country or Region	Domestic Risk	Exchange Risk	Total Risk	Correlation Coefficient*
Non-USA World Index	**20.44%**	**10.86%**	**23.74%**	**56%**
Value Weighted World Index	**17.15**	**5.59**	**17.68**	**83**
USA	**16.40**	**----**	**16.40**	**100**
Europe	**20.71**	**12.23**	**22.57**	**64**
Japan	**31.56**	**13.62**	**38.25**	**33**

* Correlation between US dollar returns and foreign dollar returns.

But in the short run, inflation is a very minor factor in exchange-rate movements. Expectations of changing interest rates and central bank policy, trade balances, capital movements, and particularly the relative growth rates of demand and output in each economy also influence the exchange rate. The short-run foreign exchange market is very speculative and the movements of exchange rates on a daily basis can often exceed that of stock prices themselves.

Dollar Risk

Table 8–3 analyzes the stock market risk for dollar investors in foreign stocks over the period from January 1970 through December 1992. The *local risk* is the risk calculated from stock returns denominated in the local currencies. The *exchange risk* reflects the fluctuations of the dollar against the country's currency. The total risk of the dollar return of a foreign market reflects both the local risk and the exchange-rate risk.

It is very important to note that the total risk of holding foreign equities is substantially *less than* the sum of the local and exchange risks. This is because these risks are not perfectly correlated, so that movements in the exchange rate and the local stock market frequently offset each other. In fact, for some countries, such as the United Kingdom, the exchange risk offsets the local risk so much that a US holder of British equities since 1970 has experienced less volatility in dollar returns than a British investor does in pounds sterling!

Table 8–3 also indicates that the local risks in foreign markets, even before the exchange rate is taken into account, are higher than those in the US market. The local risk of a diversified European portfolio is over 21 percent, while the risks in some individual countries range to 50 percent and more. The Japanese market is nearly twice as volatile as the US market. The total risk to dollar holders of a fully diversified foreign portfolio is 23.7 percent, over seven percentage points higher than that of a US portfolio, while returns have been nearly three percentage points higher.

It is instructive to compare the case of US stocks and Treasury bills. Since 1970, US stocks have a 3 percent higher return than bills, yet this 3 percent is earned at the cost of 17 percent greater risk. Seen in this context, 7 extra percentage points of risk in foreign markets is not an unreasonable price to pay for 2 percentage points extra return. These trade-offs will be explored in more detail in Chapter 19.[6]

Although exchange-rate risk does not add much to the dollar risk of holding stocks, it is substantial for dollar holders of foreign money market assets. Historically, exchange risk has been over 12 percent for Europe and nearly 14 percent for Japan. This is

---

[6] Furthermore, the risks calculated in Table 8–3 use the volatility of annual returns, a risk measure which emphasizes the short run. We do not have reliable data on the risks of foreign investments over longer holding periods since for most markets the data being comprehensively in 1970. On an annual basis, foreign stocks may appear riskier than domestic stocks, but it is not clear that this is the case over longer periods of time.

not much less than the 16.8 percent risk from investing in US stocks! The extra return in foreign money market assets is not nearly sufficient in my opinion to compensate the foreign holder for the risks involved.

THE RATIONALE FOR INVESTING ABROAD

A superficially persuasive reason for foreign investing is the expectation that countries abroad will grow faster than the United States. But expectations—and even realizations—of superior economic growth abroad do not necessarily provide a rationale for investing in foreign markets. We have already noted that since 1974 Japan has grown at nearly twice the rate as the United Kingdom, yet investors in the British market have experienced higher dollar returns than those investing in Japan.

Just as in the United States, stock prices in foreign markets take into account the consensus of future growth expectations. If the market expects superior growth, the price of shares will be bid to levels reflecting these expectations. Foreign investing will be rewarded with abnormally high returns only if subsequent earnings growth exceeds that already priced into the market.

If the market already prices growth into share values, is there then a rationale for investing in foreign markets? Yes, and for the same reason that it pays to invest in a broad portfolio of domestic stocks: *diversification*. Diversification will increase investors' expected compound returns while reducing risk *even if* expected returns on foreign equities do not exceed those for US stocks. In fact, a substantial portion of a dollar investor's portfolio should be placed in foreign stocks even if foreign returns are not expected to exceed those in the United States since the diversification of risk increases expected compound returns. The fraction of your portfolio that should be invested in foreign equities is discussed in the last chapter.

HEDGING FOREIGN EXCHANGE RISKS

Since foreign exchange risk does add to the dollar risk of holding foreign securities, it appears to pay for an investor in foreign markets to hedge against currency movements. *Hedging* means to take a position in a market which offsets the changes in the value of the currency relative to the dollar. After all, stock market fluctuations can cause enough anxiety without the extra concern of whether the dollar exchange rate will rise, thereby reducing the value of one's foreign portfolio.

In recent years there has been an explosion of markets in which you can hedge movements of foreign currencies. But many investors need to seek the help of a professional to operate in these markets as hedging foreign portfolio risk is not at all straightforward. And, as we shall see, currency hedging is not that important for the equity holder, particularly those looking to the long run.

Costs of Hedging Foreign Markets

There are two considerations involved in hedging exchange risk. The first is the transaction costs—brokerage fees, bid-ask spreads, margin requirements—of dealing in currency markets. Although these are small for large investors, they might be substantial for the small investor. A second consideration is the price at which you can hedge the foreign currency. This price can be either greater or less than the current exchange rate and depends on whether domestic interest rates are higher or lower than the interest rates in the hedged currency.

Hedging currency risks essentially involves borrowing and lending funds in different countries, so the spread between the interest rates is the critical factor in determining the cost of the hedge. If interest rates are higher in the United States than abroad, hedging your currency risk will actually *increase* your expected dollar return (ignoring transactions costs) over your local expected return. This is because hedging involves borrowing the local currency and investing in US dollars, which will lead to a profit. However, if interest rates are higher abroad, a currency hedge will lower the dollar returns of your foreign portfolio.

Do Currency Hedges Pay Off for Stock Investors?

Although hedging seems like an attractive way to offset exchange risk, there are many situations when it is unnecessary. In the United Kingdom from 1910 onward, the pound depreciated from $4.80 to about $1.50. It might seem obvious that an investor who hedged the fall of the pound would be better off than one who had not. But this is not the case. Since the interest rate was, on average, substantially higher in the United Kingdom than in the United States, the cost of hedging was high. The unhedged returns for British stocks in US dollars actually exceeded the hedged accumulation, despite the fall of the British pound.

For investors with long-term horizons, hedging currency risk in foreign stock markets is not beneficial. In fact, there is recent evidence that in the long run currency hedges might actually increase the volatility of dollar returns.[7] In the long run, exchange rate movements are determined primarily by changes in local prices. Equities are claims on real assets which compensate the stockholder for changes in the price level. To hedge such a long-run investment would be self-defeating since by buying a real asset one automatically hedges a depreciating currency.

Hedging Rapidly Depreciating Currencies

It might appear that an investor achieves superior dollar returns by hedging currencies prone to rapid inflation, since one can capture the rising local returns and offset the depreciating cur-

---

[7] Kenneth A. Froot, "Currency Hedging over Long Horizons," N.B.E.R. Working Paper no. 4355, May 1993.

rency. This, however, is not usually the case. There are two difficulties to hedging rapidly depreciating currencies. First, in many of these countries hedging is very expensive, if it is even possible. Since the market knows that inflation will cheapen the future value of the currency, the cost of offsetting exchange-rate movements—selling the currency in the futures market against the dollar or buying options to protect against a dollar loss—is extremely expensive. Secondly, hedging, as always, is a two-way street. If inflation in the foreign country turns out to be lower than expected—even if it remains substantial—then a currency hedge will result in a lower expected dollar return than an unhedged position.

Hedging currency movements is particularly counterproductive if there is a change in monetary policy. In that case, hedges may actually increase the volatility of your dollar returns. For example, if the Bundesbank, Germany's central bank, tightens credit and raises interest rates, this will cause the deutsche mark to rise. But German stock prices will fall, as rising interest rates lower the value of stocks.

If an investor does not hedge, the downward movement in the stock market will be offset by the upward movement of the deutsche mark, thereby reducing fluctuations in the dollar returns on German stocks. On the other hand, if the investor hedges, he forgoes the appreciation of the deutsche mark which offsets the decline in the value of German stocks.

Although changes in exchange rates and stock prices often move in the opposite direction, this is not always so. An increase in optimism about the growth prospects in a country often increases both stock prices and currency values. When vice president Al Gore won the debate with Ross Perot supporting NAFTA in November 1993, both the Mexican peso and Mexican stocks rose. Optimism about economic growth drives up both the exchange rate and stock prices.

In the above circumstance, hedging will decrease the volatility of your dollar returns. However, since both monetary and real factors drive exchange rate and stock movements, it is not surprising that the stock and currency markets often move independently of one another. The inability to identify in advance

FIGURE 8–2A

British Currency and Stocks during September 1992 ERM Crisis (British Pounds Sterling)

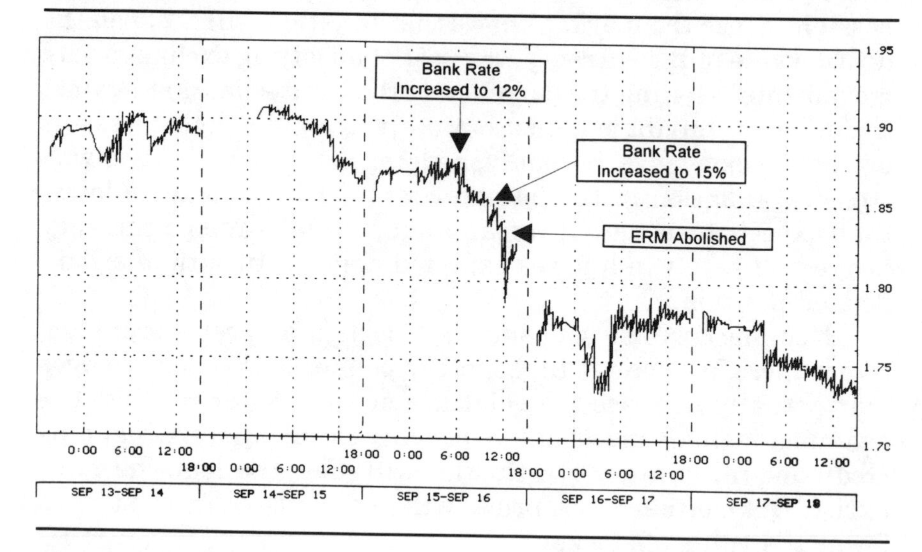

Source: Bloomberg LP

FIGURE 8–2B

(FT–SE 100 Stock Index)

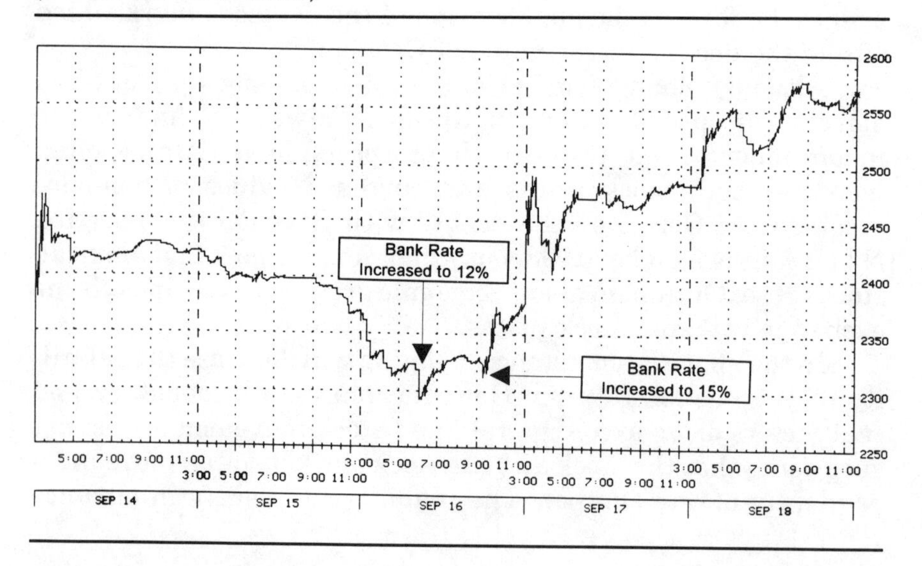

Source: Bloomberg LP

the source of movement in these markets reduces the attractiveness of hedging foreign stock risk.

STOCKS AND THE BREAKDOWN OF THE EUROPEAN EXCHANGE-RATE MECHANISM

A dramatic example of the offsetting movements of currency and equity markets occurred during the September 1992 breakdown of the European exchange-rate mechanism. The exchange-rate mechanism dictated that member countries must keep their currencies within a narrow band of each other. For some months, many investors had felt that the British pound and the Italian lira were overvalued relative to the deutsche mark. On Sunday night, September 12, the Italian government devalued the lira. Speculators felt it was only a matter of time before the British pound would also be forced to devalue.

Britain's conservative prime minister, John Major, and his Chancellor of the Exchequer, Norman Lamont, were determined to hold out and defend the pound against the speculative attack. At 11:00 A.M. on Wednesday, September 16, Lamont announced a 2 point increase in the Bank of England base lending rate, a key short-term rate of great significance to UK banks. The Financial Times Stock Exchange Index (FT–SE, called the *footsie*) immediately fell almost 30 points, or 1.5 percent, after the Bank's announcement. The movements of the British markets are depicted in Figures 8–2A and 8–2B, where the times listed represent eastern standard time, five hours earlier than the London times quoted above.

But the British pound barely budged on the foreign exchange market when the lending rate was increased. Normally an increase in this key rate would cause the pound to soar due to foreign investors flocking to the higher interest rate on sterling balances. But on this day the pound continued to push against the lower limit allowed by European Monetary System, and the Bank of England was forced to accelerate the buying of pounds against the deutsche mark.

Why did the rise in the bank rate prompt more selling in sterling? Perhaps speculators sensed that the Bank would have to do far more than raise interest rates by 2 percent to save the pound from devaluation.

At 2:15 in the afternoon, the Bank of England made its final, desperate move. It raised the rate to 15 percent—the first time in the 300-year history of the Bank that the rate had been raised twice in one day. There was a brief fall in the stock market as investors contemplated the meaning of this dramatic action. But within minutes, stocks began rallying furiously. The market knew that there was no way the British government could hold a 15 percent interest rate in the face of one of its deepest recessions since World War II. Stockholders believed that maintaining such punishing rates in such a bad economy was politically untenable.

Britain abandoned support of the pound that evening. The FT–SE 100 stock index rose over 100 points on the following day and continued to rally on Friday while the pound sank lower against both the dollar and the deutsche mark. From the market bottom on Wednesday, September 16 to the top on Friday, the FT–SE index had rallied almost 300 points, or about 13 percent. Over the same time, the pound fell from $1.83 to $1.74, a drop of only 5 percent. Hence British stocks were up about 8 percent in dollar terms during this turbulent period. Despite the continued depreciation of the pound, British stock in dollar terms continued to outpace the US and German markets through the next year.

It is true that a US investor who had hedged his sterling stock investments during the ERM crisis would have done even better than an unhedged investor. But this is not always the case during monetary turmoil. When the French franc came under attack the following week, French interest rates—and hence the cost of covering franc investments—skyrocketed. Yet the Bank of France held firm. The franc was not devalued for nearly a year, and speculators who hedged were faced with substantial losses.[8]

---

[8] Even after the ERM bands were widened in August 1993, the fall in the franc was not nearly sufficient to cover the losses of having continually speculated against the franc.

The lesson for a dollar investor is that hedging is unnecessary during exchange-rate turbulence. The British stock market rallied as the pound fell. Investors bid stocks up as the prospect of a lower pound and lower interest rates stimulated equity prices. And indeed the Bank of England lowered the base lending rate to 9 percent the following week, a prelude to further cuts.

Despite the stock market surge, leaving the exchange-rate mechanism did have some ominous implications for Britain. Since the pound sterling was no longer linked to the deutsche mark, there was no sure anchor to the British price level and British anti-inflationary policy was in doubt. But the inflationary implications of leaving the ERM were of more concern to the bondholder than to those investing in stocks. Stocks in the long run ride easily with inflation, especially when it is generated by monetary expansion.

SUMMARY

Global investment is best viewed as an extension of domestic diversification. An investor can achieve a substantial reduction in risk by investing in foreign equities since foreign markets do not move in tandem with the domestic market. As the United States becomes a smaller and smaller part of the world equity market, sticking only to US equities is akin to restricting one's investments to a single industry, a strategy far too risky for the long-term investor.

As the world moves toward free markets, equity markets will spring up and grow in foreign countries. The currency risks of foreign investing add little to the total dollar risk, so that foreign equity holders need not worry about appreciation or depreciation of currencies. Hedging currency risk is unnecessary for the long-term equity investor.

The correlation between country markets will probably increase in the future as world economies become increasingly interdependent. Under these circumstances, the diversification gains from foreign investment will be reduced. But the stock markets of individual countries may become more stable as product markets expand worldwide, so that the earnings of global firms will not be held hostage to the state of the economy in one country or in one region. In fact, worldwide integration may lead to a lower total risk to holding equities and an increase in global stock prices.

PART 3

ECONOMIC ENVIRONMENT OF INVESTING

CHAPTER 9

MONEY, GOLD, AND INFLATION

In the stock market, as with horse racing, money makes the mare go. Monetary conditions exert an enormous influence on stock prices.

Martin Zweig[1]

Irredeemable paper money has almost invariably proved a curse to the country employing it.

Irving Fisher[2]

On September 20, 1931, the British government announced that England was going off the gold standard. It would no longer exchange gold for balances at the Bank of England nor for British currency, the pound sterling. The government insisted that this action was only "temporary," that it had no intention to abolish forever its commitment to exchange its money for gold. Nevertheless, this action was to mark the beginning of the end of both Britain's and the world's gold standard, a standard that had existed for over 200 years.

Fearing chaos in the currency market, the British government ordered the London Stock Exchange closed. New York Stock Exchange officials decided to keep the US exchange open, but braced themselves for panic selling. The suspension of gold payments by Britain, the second-greatest industrial power, raised fears that other industrial countries might be forced to abandon gold. For the first time ever, the New York Exchange banned short selling to moderate the expected collapse in share

[1] *Winning on Wall Street* (New York: Warner Books, 1990), p. 43.

[2] *The Purchasing Power of Money*, 1929 ed. (New York: Macmillan, 1911), p. 131.

prices. Central bankers called the suspension "a world financial crisis of unprecedented dimensions."[3]

But much to New York's surprise, stocks rallied sharply after an early sinking spell, and many issues ended the day higher. Clearly, British suspension was not seen as negative for American equities.

Nor was this "unprecedented financial crisis" a problem for the British stock market. When England reopened the exchange on September 23, prices soared. The AP wire gave the following colorful description of the reopening of the exchange:

> Swarms of stock brokers, laughing and cheering like schoolboys, invaded the Stock Exchange today for the resumption of trading after the two-day compulsory close-down—and their buoyancy was reflected in the prices of many securities.[4]

Despite the dire predictions of government officials, shareholders viewed casting off the gold standard as good for the economy and even better for stocks. As a result of the gold suspension, the British government could expand credit and the fall in the value of the British pound would increase the demand for British exports. The stock market gave a ringing endorsement to the actions which shocked conservative world financiers. In fact, September 1931 marked the low point of the British stock market, while the United States and other countries which stayed on the gold standard continued to sink into depression. The lesson from history: money feeds the stock market and shareholders regard inflation as a secondary concern.

MONEY AND PRICES

In 1950, President Truman startled the nation in his State of the Union address with a prediction that the typical American family income would reach $12,000 by the year 2000. Consider-

---

[3] "World Crisis Seen by Vienna Bankers," *The New York Times,* September 21, 1931, p. 2.

[4] "British Stocks Rise, Pound Goes Lower," *The New York Times,* September 24, 1931, p. 2.

ing that median family income was about $3,300 at that time, $12,000 seemed like a kingly sum and implied that America was going to make unprecedented economic progress in the next half century. In fact, President Truman's prediction has proved quite modest. Median family income in 1993 is already $40,000. Yet that $40,000 buys less than $7,000 in 1950 prices, a testament to the persistent inflation of the last half century.

Rising and falling prices have characterized economic history as far back as economists have gathered data. However, steady inflation is unique to the second half of this century. What has changed over the past 50 years that makes steady inflation the norm rather than the exception? The answer is simple: the control of money has shifted from gold to the government, and with it a whole new system relating money, government deficits, and inflation has come into being.

Take a look at Figure 9–1, which displays the price levels in both Great Britain and the United States from 1800. It is striking how similar the general trends are: virtually no overall inflation until World War II and then protracted inflation after. Until the last 50 years, inflation occurred only because of war, crop failures, or other crises. But the behavior of prices in the postwar period has been entirely different. The price level almost never declined: the only question was the *rate* at which prices rose.

Economists have long known that one variable is paramount in determining the price level: the amount of money in circulation. The robust relation between money and inflation is strongly supported by the evidence. Take a look at Figure 9–2, which displays money and prices per unit output in the United States since 1830 (we shall look at government debt later). The overall trend of the price level has closely tracked that of the money supply.

The strong relation between money and prices is a worldwide phenomenon. No sustained inflation is possible without continuous money creation, and every hyperinflation in history has been associated with an explosion of the money supply. Figure 9–3 plots the rates of inflation and the increase in the money supply for 60 countries in the post–World War II period. One can see that most countries fall very close to the 45-degree line where

FIGURE 9–1
US and UK Price Indexes (1800–1992)

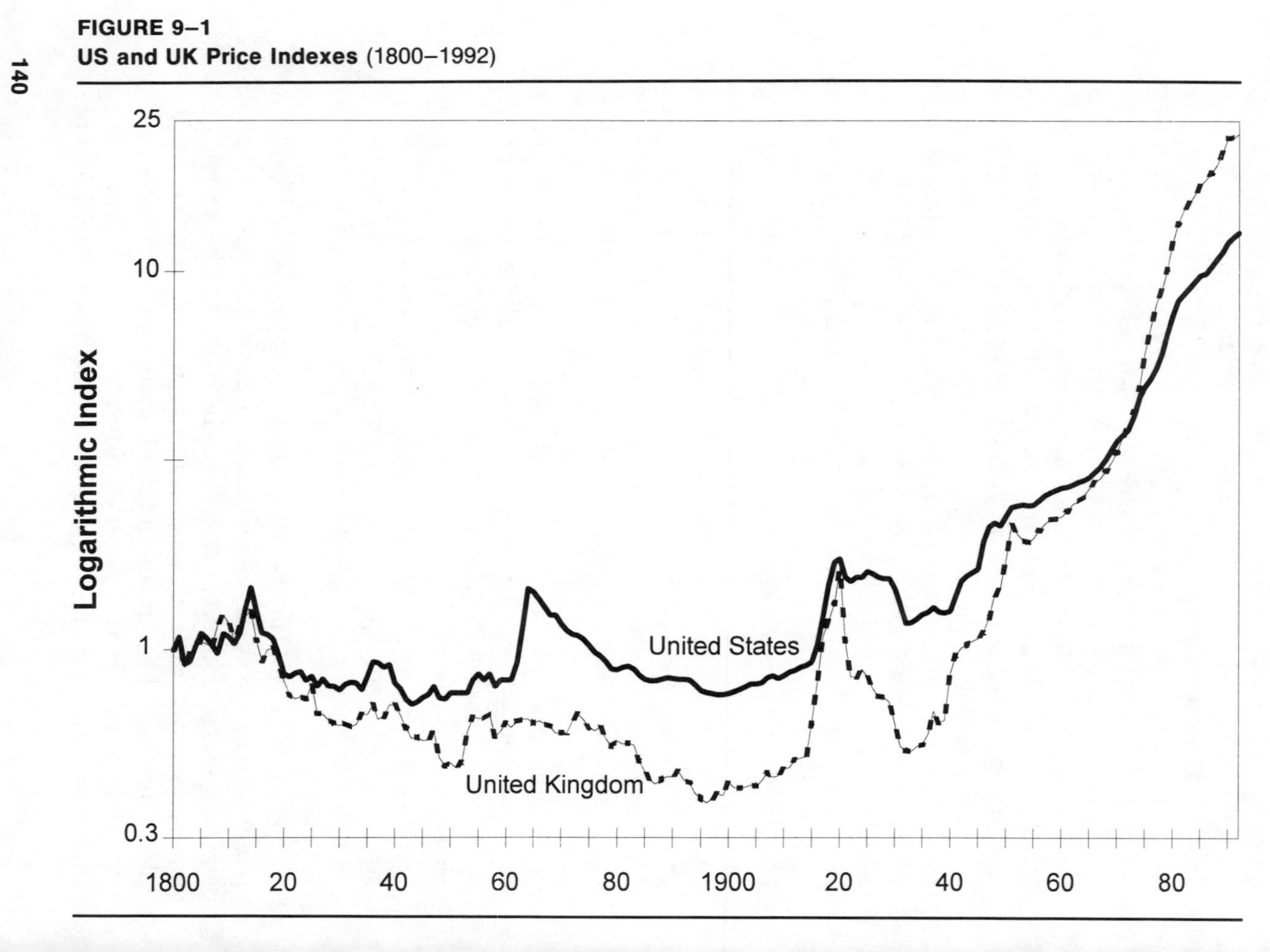

FIGURE 9–2
Money, Debt, and Price Indexes for the US (1830–1992) (1992 = 100)

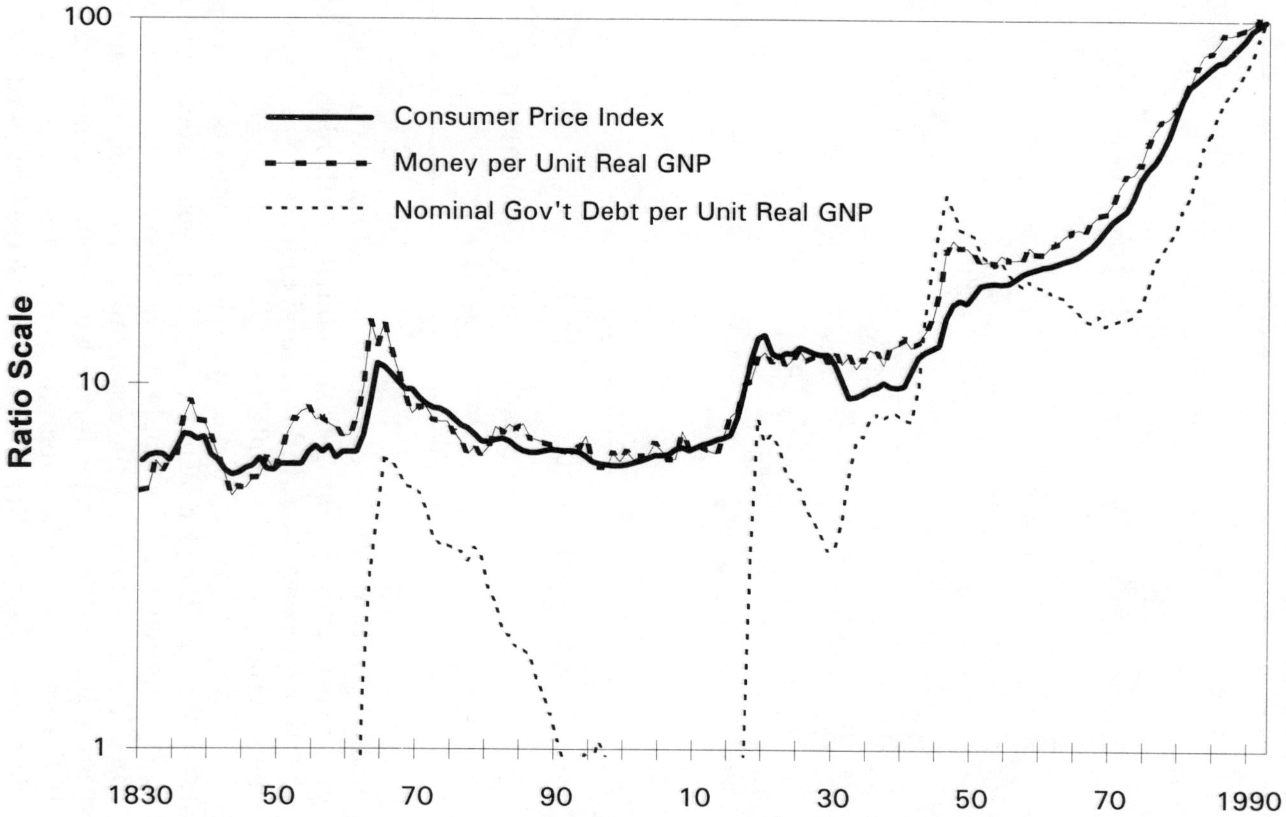

FIGURE 9–3
Money Growth and Inflation (60 Countries 1960–1990)

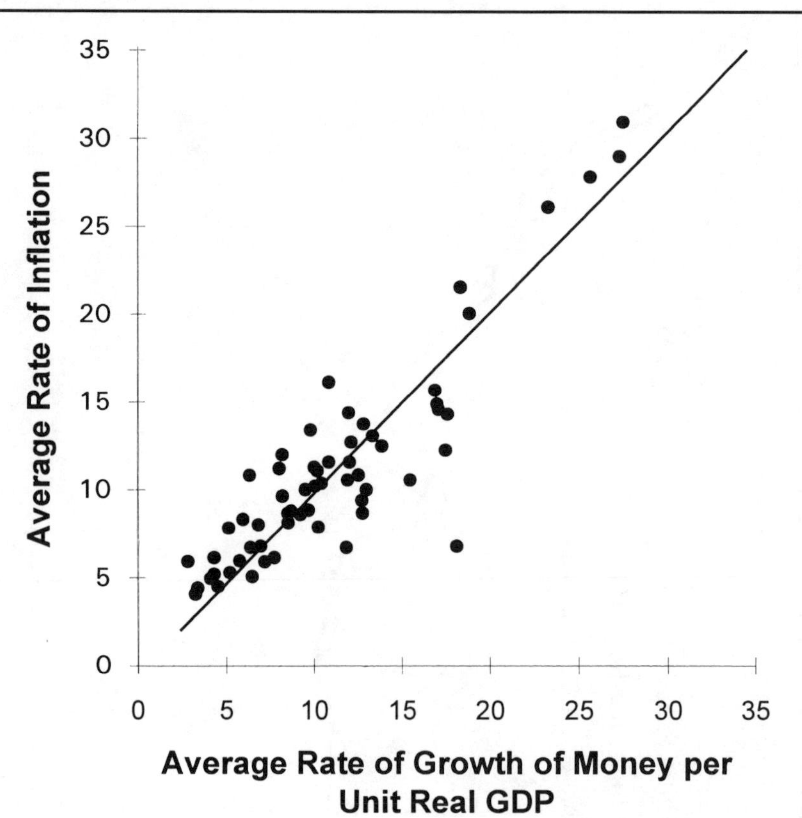

money growth (relative to output) and inflation are equal. The evidence is overwhelming that countries with high monetary growth experience high inflation and countries with restrained money growth have low inflation.

Why is the quantity of money so closely connected to the price level? Because the price of money, like any good, is determined by supply and demand. The supply of dollars is printed by the central bank. The demand for dollars is created by households and firms transacting millions of goods and services in a complex economy. If the supply of dollars increases when there is not an equal increase in the quantity of goods transacted, this leads to inflation. The classic description of the inflationary process, "too many dollars chasing too few goods," is as apt today as ever.

THE GOLD STANDARD

For the nearly 200 years prior to the Great Depression, most of the industrialized world was on a gold standard. A *gold standard* meant that the government obligated itself to exchange its own money for a fixed amount of gold. To do this, the government had to keep gold reserves in sufficient quantity to assure money holders that it would always be able to make this exchange. Since the total quantity of gold in the world was fixed (except for new gold finds which were a small fraction of the total outstanding), prices of goods in terms of either gold or government money held either relatively constant or declined.

The gold standard was adopted by Great Britain in 1717, setting the price of gold at 3.8938 pounds per ounce. Adherence to the gold standard was considered a sine qua non among policy makers. Sir Robert Peel called "the ancient standard of 3.8938 pounds per ounce a magic price for gold from which England ought never to stray and to which, if she did, she must always return as soon as possible."

The only times when the gold standard was suspended were during crises, such as wars. Britain suspended the gold standard during both the Napoleonic and First World Wars, but in both cases returned to original parity with gold after each war.

The United States had also temporarily suspended the gold standard, but, like Britain, returned to the standard after the war. When the government issued non-gold-backed money during the Civil War, this money was called *greenbacks* because the only backing was the green ink printed on the note. Yet just 20 years later, the government redeemed each and every one of those notes in gold, completely reversing the inflation of the Civil War period.

The adherence to the gold standard is the reason why the world experienced no overall inflation during the 19th and early 20th centuries. But overall price stability was not achieved without a cost. By setting the amount of money equal to the quantity of gold, the government essentially relinquished discretionary monetary control. This meant the inability to provide extra money during times of depression or financial crisis, or expand money to stabilize falling prices or accommodate rising output. Adherence to gold turned from being a symbol of government restraint and responsibility to a straitjacket from which the government sought to escape.

THE ESTABLISHMENT OF THE FEDERAL RESERVE

The problems of liquidity crises caused by strict adherence to the gold standard prompted Congress in 1913 to create the Federal Reserve System. The responsibilities of the Fed were to provide an elastic currency, which meant that in times of banking crises the Fed would become the lender of last resort. This meant that the central bank would provide currency to enable depositors to withdraw their deposits without forcing banks to liquidate loans and other assets.

In the long run, the money creation by the Fed was constrained by the gold standard, since Federal Reserve notes promised to pay a fixed amount of gold. But in the short run, the Federal Reserve was free to create money as long as that did not threaten the convertibility. In fact, the Fed was never given any guidance or criteria by which to determine the right quantity of money. This confusion was aptly described by Milton Friedman in his *Monetary History of the United States:*

> The Federal Reserve System therefore began operations with no effective legislative criterion for determining the total stock of money. The discretionary judgment of a group of men was inevitably substituted for the quasi-automatic discipline of the gold standard. Those men were not even guided by a legislative mandate of intent. . . . Little wonder, perhaps, that the subsequent years saw so much backing and filling, so much confusion about purpose and power, and so erratic an exercise of power.[5]

---

[5] *Monetary History of the United States* (Princeton N.J.: Princeton University Press, 1963), p. 193.

FALL OF THE GOLD STANDARD

The lack of guidance on how to keep money stable had disastrous consequences just two decades later. In the wake of the stock crash of 1929, the world economies entered a severe recession. Falling asset prices and failing businesses made banks subject to increased suspicion. Depositors withdrew billions of dollars of deposits and placed the banks at peril. In an astounding show of institutional ineptitude, the Fed failed to provide extra reserves needed to stem the currency drainage of the banks. Investors then sought even greater safety, turning their government notes into gold, a process which put extreme pressure on the gold reserves of the gold-standard countries.

The first step towards the abandonment of the gold standard occurred on September 20, 1931, when Britain suspended all payments of gold for sterling. Eighteen months later, on April 19, 1933, as the depression worsened in the United States, the United States also suspended the gold standard.

The reaction of the US stock market to suspension was even more enthusiastic than that of the British. Stocks soared over 9 percent on that day and almost 6 percent the next. This was the greatest two-day rally in stock market history. Stockholders felt the government could now provide extra liquidity to raise prices and stimulate the economy, which they regarded as a boon for stocks. Bonds, however, fell as investors feared the inflationary consequences of leaving the gold standard.

Business Week, in a positive editorial on the suspension, asserted:

> With one decisive gesture, [President Roosevelt] throws out of the window all the elaborate hocus-pocus of "defending the dollar." He defies an ancient superstition and takes his stand with the advocates of managed money. . . . The job now is to manage our money effectively, wisely, with self-restraint. It can be done.[6]

---

[6] "We Start," *Business Week,* April 26, 1933, p. 32.

Postdevaluation Policy

Ironically, while the right to redeem dollars for gold was denied US citizens, it was soon reinstated for foreign central banks at the devalued rate of $35.00 per ounce. As part of the Bretton Woods agreement which set up the rules of international exchange rates after the close of World War II, the US government promised to redeem for gold all dollars held by foreign central banks at a rate of $35 per ounce as long as they fixed their currency to the dollar.

But postwar inflation made gold seem more and more attractive to foreigners at that price. US gold reserves began to dwindle, despite official claims that the United States had no plans to change its gold exchange policy. As late as 1965, President Johnson stated unequivocally in the *Economic Report of the President:*

> There can be no question of our capacity and determination to maintain the gold value of the dollar at $35.00 per ounce. The full resources of the Nation are pledged to that end.[7]

Yet four years later, in the 1969 *Economic Report,* President Johnson declared:

> Myths about gold die slowly. But progress can be made—as we have demonstrated. In 1968, the Congress ended the obsolete gold-backing requirement for our currency.[8]

"Myths about gold?" "Obsolete gold-backing requirement?" The government finally admitted that monetary policy would not be subject to the discipline of gold, and that the guiding principle of international finance and monetary policy for almost two centuries was summarily dismissed as a relic of incorrect thinking.

The United States continued to redeem gold at $35 an ounce, although private investors were paying over $40 in the private

---

[7] *Economic Report of the President* (Washington: Government Printing Office, 1965), p. 7.

[8] *Economic Report of the President* (Washington: Government Printing Office, 1969), p. 16.

markets. Foreign central banks rushed to turn in their dollars for gold. The United States, which held almost $30 billion dollars of gold at the end of World War II, was left with $11 billion by the summer of 1971, and hundreds of millions of dollars were being withdrawn each month.

Something dramatic had to happen. On August 15, 1971, President Nixon, in one of the most extraordinary economic acts since Roosevelt's 1933 Bank Holiday, startled the world financial community by freezing wages and prices and forever closing the "gold window." The link of gold to money was permanently—and probably irrevocably—broken.

But few shed a tear for the gold standard. The stock market responded enthusiastically to Nixon's announcement (which was also associated with wage and price controls and higher tariffs), jumping almost 4 percent on record volume. But this was not surprising. Suspensions of the gold standard or devaluations of currencies have witnessed some of the most dramatic stock market rallies in history.

Post-Gold Monetary Policy

With the complete dismantling of the gold standard, there was no longer any constraint on monetary expansion, either in the United States or in foreign countries. The first inflationary oil shock from 1973–74 caught most of the industrialized countries off guard, and all suffered significantly higher inflation as governments vainly attempted to stimulate the economy in the face of massive energy cost increases.

Because of the inflationary bent of monetary policy, Congress tried to control the monetary expansion by the Fed. In 1975, a congressional resolution obliged the Federal Reserve to announce monetary growth targets. Three years later, the Fed was forced to present targets before Congress twice annually, in February and July. It was the first time in over 60 years that Congress gave some guidance to the Fed as to the control of the stock of money in the economy.

But the Fed largely ignored the targets they set. The surge of inflation in 1979 brought increased pressure on the Federal Reserve to change its policy and seriously attempt to break inflation. On October 6, 1979, Paul Volcker, who had been appointed in April to succeed G. William Miller as Chairman of the Board of the Federal Reserve System, announced a radical change in the implementation of monetary policy. No longer would the Federal Reserve set interest rates to guide policy. Instead, the System would exercise control over the supply of money without regard to interest rate movements.

The prospect of restricted liquidity was a shock to the financial markets. Although the Saturday night announcement (later referred to as the "Saturday Night Massacre" by traders in the bond and stock markets) did not immediately capture the headlines like Nixon's New Economic Policy, which had frozen prices and closed the gold window earlier in the decade, the announcement roiled the financial markets. Stocks went into a tailspin, falling almost 8 percent on record volume in $2^1/_2$ days following the announcement. Stocks shuddered at the prospect that the Fed was suddenly going to take away the money that had fed inflation during the past decade. The tight monetary policy of the Volcker years eventually broke inflation. The experience of the United States, as well as that of Japan and Germany who also used monetary policy to stop inflation, proved that restricting money was the only real answer to controlling prices.

THE FEDERAL RESERVE AND MONETARY CREATION

The process by which the Fed changes the money supply and controls credit conditions is straightforward. When the Fed wants to increase the money supply, it buys a government bond in the open market—a market where billions of dollars in bonds are transacted every day. What is unique about the Federal Reserve is that when it buys government bonds it pays for them by crediting the reserve account of the bank of the customer from whom the Fed bought the bond. A *reserve account* is a deposit a bank maintains at the Federal Reserve to satisfy reserve requirements and facilitate check clearing.

If the Federal Reserve wishes to reduce the money supply, it sells government bonds from its portfolio. The buyer of these bonds instructs his bank to pay the Fed from his account. The Fed then debits the reserve account of the bank and that money disappears from circulation.

The buying and selling of government bonds are called *open market operations*. An *open market purchase* increases reserves of the banking system, while an *open market sale* reduces reserves.

How the Fed Affects Interest Rates

When the Federal Reserve buys and sells government securities, it influences the amount of reserves of the banking system. There is an active market for these reserves among banks, where billions of dollars are bought and sold each day. This market is called the *federal funds market* and the interest rate at which these funds are borrowed and lent is called the *federal funds rate*.

Although called the *federal funds market,* this market is not run by the government, nor does it trade government securities. The federal funds market is a private lending market among banks where rates are dictated by supply and demand. However, it is clear that the Federal Reserve has powerful influence over the federal funds market. If the Fed buys securities, then the supply of reserves is increased and the interest rate on federal funds goes down, as banks have ample reserves to lend. Conversely, if the Fed sells securities, the supply of reserves is reduced and the federal funds rate goes up as banks scramble for the remaining supply.

Although federal funds are only borrowed for one day, the interest rate on federal funds forms the anchor to all other short-term interest rates. These include the prime rate, Treasury bill rates, and Eurodollar lending rates, upon which literally *trillions* of dollars of loans and securities are based.

Who Makes the Decisions about Monetary Creation?

The Board of Governors, sitting in Washington, is the main policy-making arm of the Federal Reserve System. The seven Board members, including the chairman (there has not yet been a woman chair), are chosen by the President and confirmed by the Senate. The tenure of Board members is 14 years. The policy decisions of the Federal Reserve are final and not subject to review or veto by any congressional or executive body.

The Board of Governors has the power to set the *discount rate,* the interest rate at which our central bank lends funds to banking institutions. This rate receives wide notoriety, but in practice it is quite unimportant. This is because there are very few funds actually borrowed by banks from the Federal Reserve. In recent years, borrowings have run to far less than 1 percent of the banks' total reserve requirements, and constitute less than 0.01 percent of total banking assets. Over the years, the discount mechanism has evolved into a very-short-term lending facility for failing banks. This does not mean the market ignores the discount rate, since its level often indicates the future range where the Fed will set the federal funds rate, but it is the fed funds rate, not the discount rate, which influences the market.

The real power of the Fed lies in its ability to control the federal funds rate and supply reserves. The committee which carries on these operations is called the Federal Open Market Committee, or the FOMC. The FOMC consists of the seven board members and the presidents of the 12 regional or district Federal Reserve banks. All 12 bank presidents sit on the meetings of the Open Market Committee. But only five of them vote: four with a rotating one-year term, and one, the president of the New York Bank, designated as a permanent voting member. The presidents of the regional banks are not chosen by or even confirmed by the President or Congress. They are chosen by boards composed of private citizens from the individual district banks.

The FOMC meets formally eight times a year to determine interest rate policy. The basic decision of the committee is the determination of the federal funds rate. It is the job of the chairman to craft a policy which balances those who want the Fed to pay more attention to fighting inflation and those who wish to focus on the state of economic activity. Although a unanimous vote is desirable, this is not always achieved, and dissenting votes, which are duly reported in the minutes of the Fed, are not uncommon in the formulation of Fed policy.

The bond and stock markets watch the members of the open market committee like hawks. Since the direction of Federal

Reserve policy is of paramount importance to interest rates, anyone who can predict Fed actions has an enormous advantage in the markets. The actions of the Federal Open Market Committee are in many ways the most important taken by any government committee. Yet it is surprising that few Americans can name any member of the committee outside the chairman, and still fewer have any concept of how this committee determines money and credit in the economy. If you follow the stock market closely, it is necessary to understand the actions of this committee.

GOVERNMENT DEFICITS AND THE MONETARY PROCESS

When the government runs a deficit, it borrows money by issuing government bonds. The government outside the Fed has no control over the money supply; only the open market operations of the central bank can change the quantity of money. When the government issues bonds, it borrows money from the private sector, and immediately spends it to pay its bills.

Virtually all debt issued by the US government is denominated in dollars. Although individuals, corporations, and even state and local governments can default on their debt, it is absolutely impossible for the federal government to do so. Although the federal government does not issue money, it is inconceivable that the Federal Reserve, which is a creation of Congress, would not print the money to pay interest and principal on government bonds as a last resort. Since there is no restriction on the amount of money that can be printed, there is no theoretical limit on the ability of the central bank to finance government deficits.

This is both comforting and ominous. It is comforting for the millions of government bondholders to know that their federal debt is absolutely safe. The government will always pay the number of dollars promised on the coupons and principal of the bond. Yet, it is ominous because there is absolutely no certainty what these dollars will be worth, if anything. Although the government cannot default in a formal sense, the government can de facto default on its debt by paying it off with depreciated dollars. The effect on the bondholder is the same as a legal default: a smaller real return than has been expected.

Under the gold standard, default by inflation was impossible. Government bonds, like the money the government issued, were promises to pay interest and principal in gold. The government could default by running out of gold, but it could not print money that was not backed by gold and use that money to pay off the bonds. Under a fiat money standard, the prudent bondholder must assess the prospects for inflation and assess the probability that the central bank will resort to inflationary finance to pay off its debts.

Monetization of Government Debt

The separation of the monetary authority from the fiscal authority is deliberate. The "independence" of the central bank is designed so that it can resist entreaties from the government and safeguard the value of the currency for the public. Yet, as we noted, the monetary authority is ultimately a creature of Congress, established by the Federal Reserve Act, and would certainly help finance the government's debt in a crisis. The direct transformation of that debt into money is called the *monetization of the debt.*

The inflation caused by the monetization of the debt feeds on itself. Other sources of tax revenue, which are mostly denominated in money terms, decline dramatically in real terms when inflation increases quickly. Government workers and suppliers demand increased inflation protection, not to speak of bondholders who will refuse to refinance any government debt except at very high nominal interest rates or with inflation protection. And finally, as individuals spend their money balances as quickly as possible due to their loss of purchasing power, prices often increase even faster than money. The end result is ever-spiraling prices and hyperinflation.

This scenario has played itself out many times over in less-developed countries. But, fortunately, in modern times, hyperinflation has been absent in the world's industrialized economies. They have always come back from the brink of rapid inflation. On a year-over-year basis, inflation reached 26.5 percent in Britain in 1975, 26.2 percent in Japan in 1974, and 12.2 percent in the United States in 1974. Each time the monetary authority squeezed money sufficiently to stop the inflation—even at the cost of a recession.

Look again at Figure 9–2. It shows the government debt per unit GNP against money and the price level in the United States since the 1830s. There is no question that the price level is much more closely related to the money supply than to government debt. There can be long periods of time when government debt and money do not move in tandem. As long as the treasury has access to capital markets to borrow, increases in government debt are not necessarily associated with increases in money or prices.

Stocks and Bonds in a Deficit Economy

The rate of growth of government debt cannot forever exceed the rate of growth of money. In the 1980s, the increase of government debt far exceeded the growth of money, as the Federal Reserve increased money at a moderate rate to keep inflation low.

If the growth of government debt accelerates, either of two scenarios will follow. If the Fed refrains from supplying more liquidity to the market, lenders will have to be enticed with ever higher interest rates to hold US government obligations. This will eventually crush both the stock and bond market, precipitating a severe economic crisis. In the second scenario, the government pressures the Fed to supply sufficient liquidity to the market to absorb the government debt. This involves increasing bank reserves and the money supply.

In neither of these two scenarios would an investor want to be in the bond market. Higher interest rates caused by either a credit crunch or virulent inflation will crunch bond prices. But in the second scenario, stockholders will at least maintain their capital because equity, unlike bonds, hedges the inflation. Holding real assets is the ultimate hedge against fiscal irresponsibility. Furthermore, even if price increases do not become virulent, stocks in the long run protect the investor from the chronic inflation which is endemic to a world of paper money.

CONCLUSIONS

The Great Depression dethroned gold as the linchpin of the world's monetary system. The control of money was passed directly to the central bank under authority of the central government.

Release from the shackles of the gold standard has always been marked by celebration in world equity markets. Stocks thrive on the liquidity provided by the central bank and shareholders well tolerate the inflation that accompanies such monetary accommodations. On the other hand, monetary stringency designed to force commodity prices down to meet exchange-rate or inflation guidelines is always painful to the stock market. Volcker's move against inflation in 1979, the Bundesbank's tight money policies of 1992 and 1993, and the Bank of England's vain attempt to stay within the Exchange Rate Mechanism, as we detailed in the last chapter, are such examples. When the monetary tightness is released, the equity markets explode.

Despite the inflationary bias of managed money, no country is ever likely to return to the gold standard. The ability to control overall prices is sufficiently beneficial to compensate for the inflationary bias that a managed money standard entails. Inflation is one of the reasons why equity has outperformed bonds so handily since the end of World War II. Managed money is a success, but with the success comes inflation with which the equity holder is best able to cope.

CHAPTER 10

INFLATION AND STOCKS

> In steadiness of real income, or purchasing power, a list of diversified common stocks surpasses bonds.
>
> *Irving Fisher*[1]

A modern adaptation of a story that has been a perennial favorite among investors for many years tells of a youngish, well-to-do man who wanders off into the forest and falls into a deep sleep, much like Rip Van Winkle. He awakens many years later and his first thoughts turn to his portfolio. He searches out a pay phone and dials his broker's 800 number. The number is still operative and the computer-simulated voice responds to his account number: "Thank you for calling your Merrill Lynch/Dean Witter/Paine-Webber/Smith Barney-Shearson/Schwab Consolidated Account. The value of your stock portfolio is $50 billion . . . short-term bond portfolio $500 million . . . long-term bond portfolio $50,000."

Our now aged investor was ecstatic at his new-found wealth until he heard the automated operator come on with the request: "Toll-free calls are limited to 60 seconds, please deposit $1 million for the next 3 minutes, please!"

This story almost always elicits laughter from investors who hear it for the first time. Everyone understands that you cannot know what money will buy unless you know what will happen to inflation. Images of Germans 70 years ago carrying billions of near-worthless Reichsmarks to buy a pint of milk are cruel reminders of the ravages of inflation. And we need not go even that far back into history to find rampant inflation. Brazil, Argentina, and many other developing countries have suffered hyperin-

---

[1] From foreword by Irving Fisher in Kenneth S. Van Strum, *Investing in Purchasing Power* (New York: Barron's, 1925), p. vii.

flation as a result of excessive government monetary expansion. Nobody wants to end up with a $50 billion portfolio if a phone call costs a million bucks!

But the final values for the stock and bond portfolios in our story were not chosen at random. In the event of hyperinflation, stocks will be, by far, the best-performing financial asset. Over the past several decades, the currencies of Brazil and Argentina have depreciated by more than a billionfold against the dollar, yet their stock markets have appreciated by an even greater extent.

Holders of short-term bonds, such as Treasury bills, will try to keep up with rampant inflation—and will have moderate success in doing so. These investors can reset the interest rate frequently in an attempt to keep up with the rising prices. But long-term bond holders, locked into fixed coupon and principal payments, will see their capital wiped out—their bonds won't be worth enough to pay for a phone call!

STOCKS AS INFLATIONARY HEDGES

Despite the ever-present threat of inflation, it is surprising how many investors are pleased with an investment which makes only fixed monetary payments. When asked how much $100,000 will buy in 30 years, many realize it will be less than today, but few recognize how much less. At a 4 percent rate of inflation, $100,000 will be worth just over $30,000 in today's dollars. And 4 percent inflation is considered by many to be a good average rate for 30 years. At 6 percent inflation, $100,000 will command $17,000; at 8 percent less than $10,000; and if inflation averages 10 percent a year (which could mean quite a few good years of moderate price increases combined with a few bad years of double-digit inflation), the purchasing power of $100,000 drops by almost 95 percent to $5,700.

In contrast to the inflation risk of fixed-income assets, the historical evidence is convincing that the returns on stocks over time have kept pace with inflation. The period since World War II has been the most inflationary in our history, yet the real return on stocks has equaled that of the previous 1½ centuries.

The fact that stock returns have compensated for inflation should come as no surprise. Since stocks are claims on the earnings of real assets—assets whose value is intrinsically related to labor and capital—it is reasonable to expect that their return will not be influenced by inflation. This is particularly true since we have shown in the previous chapter that, in the long run, the rate of inflation is caused by monetary expansion, which influences input and output prices equally.

Despite the overwhelming evidence that the returns on stocks compensate the shareholder for increased inflation, investors' acceptance of stocks as inflation hedges has undergone significant changes. In the 1950s, stocks were praised as hedges against rising commodity prices. For that reason, many stock investors stayed with stocks, despite seeing the average dividend yield on equities fall below that available on fixed-income investments in 1958 for the first time in history. In the 1970s, however, stock prices were ravaged during the inflation triggered by OPEC oil price hikes and it became unfashionable to view equity as an effective hedge against inflation.

When we speak of stocks being a hedge against inflation, we mean that stocks will increase in value sufficiently to compensate the investor for any erosion in the purchasing power of money. Although stocks are excellent long-term hedges against inflation, they fail miserably in the short run.

Let us examine the evidence. Figure 10–1 plots the annual compound returns on stocks, bonds, and Treasury bills against the rate of inflation over 1- and 30-year holding periods from 1871–1991. The inflation rates are ranked from the lowest to the highest according to quintiles so that the first point plotted represents the returns associated with the lowest 20 percent of all inflation rates recorded over that holding period, the next point covers the returns over the next lowest inflation rates, and so on.

What do these figures tell us? First that neither stocks, bonds, nor bills are good *short-term* hedges against inflation. Real returns on these financial assets are highest when the inflation rates are low, and fall as inflation increases. But look how the returns on stocks are virtually immune to the inflation rate over longer horizons. Fixed-income assets, on the other hand,

FIGURE 10–1
Holding Period Returns and Inflation (1871–1991)

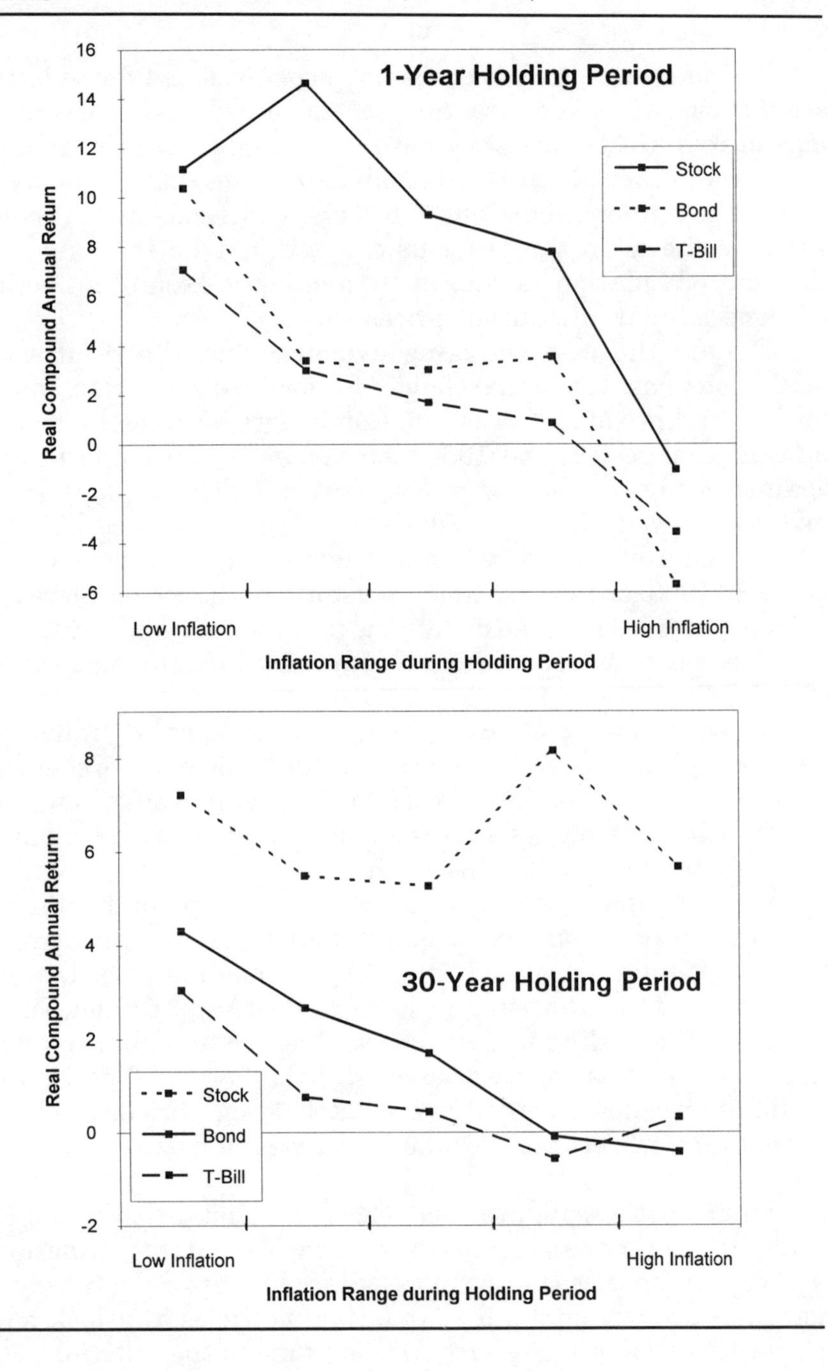

simply cannot compete with stocks over any holding period, even those that cover several decades.

This was the conclusion of Edgar Smith's book, *Common Stocks as Long-Term Investments*. He showed that stocks outperform bonds in time of falling as well as rising prices, taking the period after the Civil War and before the turn of the century as his test case. We have shown that Smith's results are quite robust, holding over the entire 120 year history of our data.

WHY STOCKS FAIL AS A SHORT-TERM INFLATION HEDGE

Higher Interest Rates

Although stocks survive inflation well over long periods of time, they are poor *short-term* hedges against inflation. A popular explanation for this fact notes that since inflation increases interest rates, and the interest rate on bonds competes with stock yields, inflation must be bad for stocks. In other words, inflation must send stock prices down sufficiently to increase their dividend yield to match the higher rates available on bonds.

Expectations of rising prices do indeed increase interest rates. It has long been recognized that lenders seek to protect themselves against inflation by adding a premium to the interest rate that they demand. Since the early part of this century, economists have understood that the interest rate is composed of two parts: the *real rate of interest*—the rate prevailing in an economy with no inflation, plus the *expected rate of inflation*—a premium compensating lenders for the depreciation of the value of money. This relation has been called the *Fisher Equation,* after Irving Fisher, the famous early-20th-century American economist who first popularized this way of looking at interest rates.[2]

[2] The exact Fisher Equation for the nominal rate of interest is the sum of the real rate plus the expected rate of inflation plus the cross product of the real rate and the expected rate of inflation. If inflation is not too high, this last term can often be ignored.

The Fisher Equation explains the broad trends of interest rates. Certainly the increase in interest rates in the postwar period has been directly related to the inflationary experience. The Fisher Equation, once regarded as an arcane bit of economics, is now widely acknowledged by investors as fundamental to understanding interest rates. Today, virtually every discussion of long-term interest rates begins with the inflation outlook.

Because expected inflation raises interest rates, it is seemingly easy to conclude that inflation would be bad for stocks. But this explanation ignores the fact that higher expected inflation, in addition to increasing the interest rate, also raises the expected future cash flows available to stockholders. Stocks are claims on the earnings of real assets, whether these assets are the production from machines, labor, land, or ideas. As the price level rises, the cost of the inputs will rise, but so will the price of the output. The difference between the two contributes to the earnings from which dividends will be paid, and these earnings and dividends will rise with the price level.

Expected inflation increases both the future earnings of the firms and the rate at which those earnings are discounted. When expected inflation is fully incorporated into interest rates and future dividends, these factors *exactly* offset each other and the current stock price should not be adversely affected. Over time, the price of stocks—as well as the level of dividends—will rise, at a rate equaling that of inflation. Stock returns will keep up with rising prices and act as complete hedges against inflation.

Supply-Induced Inflation

There are some circumstances when earnings cannot keep up with inflation. Stocks declined during the 1970s since inflation did not affect input and output prices equally. Because of the restriction in OPEC oil supplies, firms were not able to raise the prices of their output by as much as the soaring cost of their energy inputs.

Recall that inflation is the result of too much money chasing too few goods. Inflation can be caused by a reduction in goods supplied as well as an increase in money issued. A reduction in output can occur because of low productivity or a sharp rise in input prices. In these circumstances, it is not surprising that inflation caused by supply problems should impact negatively on the stock market. The inflationary 1970s were just such a period.

US manufacturers, who for years had thrived on low energy prices, were totally unprepared to deal with surging oil costs. The recession that followed the first OPEC oil squeeze destroyed the stock market. Productivity plummeted, and by the end of 1974 real stock prices, measured by the Dow-Jones average, had fallen 65 percent from the January 1966 high—the largest decline since the crash of '29. Pessimism ran so deep that nearly one half of all Americans in August 1974 believed the economy was heading towards a depression such as the one the nation had experienced in the 1930s.[3]

Fed Policy and Government Spending

Another important reason why stocks react poorly to inflation, especially in the short run, is the fear that the Federal Reserve will take restrictive action to curb rising prices. This invariably involves raising short-term interest rates through open market sales.

As we saw in the previous chapter, inflation, especially in less developed countries, is also closely linked with government budget deficits and excessive government spending. If the government becomes involved in a larger and larger part of the economy, inefficiency and overregulation may occur. In that case, increased government presence in the economy coupled with large budget deficits could lead to lower growth, lower corporate profits, and higher inflation.

---

[3] Gallup poll taken August 2–5, 1974.

INFLATION AND THE US TAX CODE

Another very important reason why stocks are poor short-term hedges against inflation is the US tax code. There are two significant areas in which the tax code works to the detriment of shareholders during inflationary times: corporate profits and nominal capital gains.

INFLATIONARY DISTORTIONS TO CORPORATE EARNINGS

When analyzing trends in the markets, analysts often point to the quality of earnings that firms report. But what is meant by the *quality of earnings*? Is not a dollar of profit a dollar of profit, as long as it is accurately determined by standard and accepted accounting practices?

The answer is no. Standard accounting practices, and those accepted by the tax authorities, do not properly take into account the distortionary effects of inflation on corporate profits. This distortion shows up primarily in the treatment of depreciation, inventory valuation, and interest costs.

Depreciation of plant, equipment, and other capital investments is based on historical costs. These depreciation schedules are not adjusted for any change in the price of capital which may occur during the life of the asset. During inflation, the cost of replacing capital rises, but reported corporate depreciation does not make any adjustment for this. Therefore, depreciation allowances are understated since firms do not make adequate allowances for the rising cost of replacing capital. As a result, inadequate depreciation causes reported earnings to be overstated.

But depreciation is not the only bias. In calculating the cost of goods sold, firms must use the historical cost of the inventory purchased. In an inflationary environment, the gap between historical costs and selling prices widens, producing inflationary profits for the firm. These "profits" do not represent an increase in the real earning power of the firm, but just record that part of the firm's capital—namely the inventory—which *turns over* and is realized as a monetary profit. This treatment of inventories differs from the firm's other capital, such as plant and equipment, which is not revalued on an ongoing basis for the purpose of calculating earnings.

The Department of Commerce, the government agency responsible for gathering economic statistics, is well aware of these distortions and has computed both a depreciation adjustment and an inventory valuation adjustment. These have been calculated back to 1929 and are currently reported on a quarterly basis along with the comprehensive figures on gross domestic product. But the Internal Revenue Service does not recognize any of these adjustments for tax purposes. Firms are required to pay taxes on *reported* profits, even if these profits are biased upwards. After-tax earnings, and therefore stock prices, are hurt by inflation because the tax law does not recognize these distortions.

These inflationary biases are often significant. In the inflationary 1970s, reported corporate profits were overstated by up to 50 percent, meaning that the quality of reported earnings during that period was very low. On the other hand, in the low inflation period of the late 1980s and 1990s, reported corporate profits were actually below adjusted profits, increasing the "quality" of reported earnings.

Inflation Biases in Interest Costs

There is another inflationary distortion, however, which is not reported in the government statistics. This adjustment is based on the inflationary component of interest costs and, in contrast to depreciation and inventory profits, may lead to a *downward* bias in reported corporate earnings during periods of inflation.

Most firms raise some of their capital by floating fixed-income assets such as bonds and bank loans. This borrowing *leverages* the firm's assets, since extra profits above and beyond the debt service go only to the stockholders.

In an inflationary environment, the *nominal* interest costs of leverage rise, even if the real interest costs remain unchanged. But corporate profits are calculated by deducting nominal interest costs, which overstates the real interest costs to the firm. Hence, reported corporate profits are depressed and less taxes are owed. But since the firm is paying back loans with depreciated dollars, the higher nominal interest expense is offset by the reduction in the real value of the bonds and loans owed by the firm, and the firm's real profits do not suffer. Unfortunately, it is not easy to quantify this earnings bias, since one cannot easily identify the share of interest due to inflation and that due to the real interest costs.

Inflation and the Capital Gains Tax

In the United States, capital gains taxes are paid on the difference between the cost of an asset and the sale price, with no adjustment made for inflation. If asset values rise with inflation, then the investor accrues a tax liability which must be paid at the time the asset is sold, whether or not the investor has realized a *real* gain, or gain after inflation is taken into account. This means that an asset which appreciates by less than the rate of inflation—so that the investor is worse off in real terms—will be taxed upon sale.

Higher inflation increases the effective tax on capital assets. Figure 10–2A displays the after-tax real rate of return for various inflation rates and various holding periods under the current tax system.[4]

One can see that the inflation tax has a more severe effect on annual compound returns the shorter the holding period. This is because the more an investor turns over an asset, the more the government can capture the nominal capital gains tax. For an investor with a one-year holding period, the real after-tax return with a moderate inflation of 4 percent is reduced by more than one percentage point over the return in a no-inflation environment. For 30-year holding periods, the effective after-tax annual compound real return for 4 percent inflation is reduced by 43 basis points. And if inflation increases to 8 percent, an investor

[4] The same parameters are used to calculate Figure 10–2 as Table 7–1 in Chapter 7: a real return of 2.4 percent, a dividend yield of 3.5 percent, and tax rates of 28 percent and 31 percent, respectively, on capital gains and dividend income. If inflation is 4 percent, the return on stocks will be 10 percent in nominal terms. There is an interaction between the inflation rate and real capital accumulation, so that the nominal return is slightly higher than the sum of the real return and the inflation rate.

FIGURE 10–2
Taxes and Inflation

A 3.5% Dividend Yield, 2.4% Real Capital Appreciation, 28% Capital Gains Tax, 31% Dividend Tax

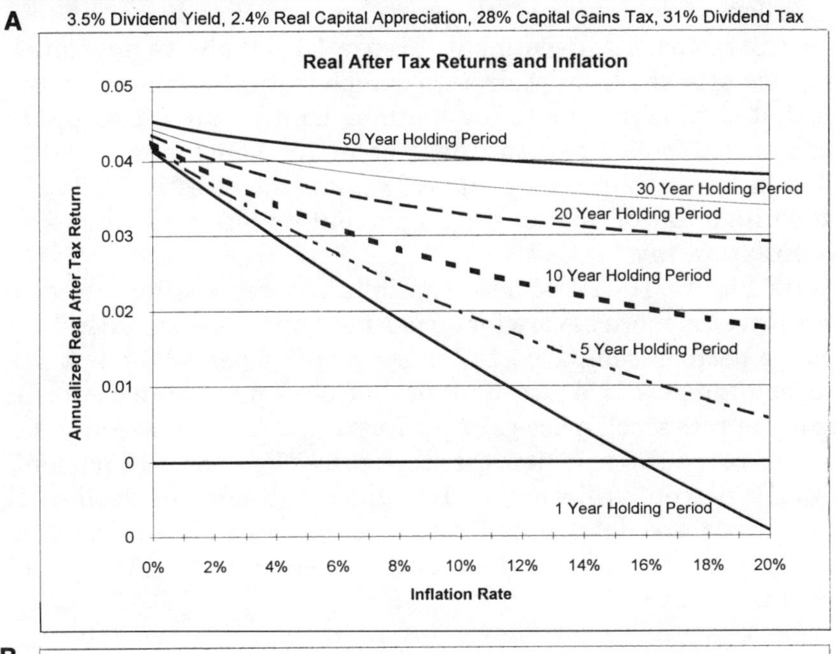

B

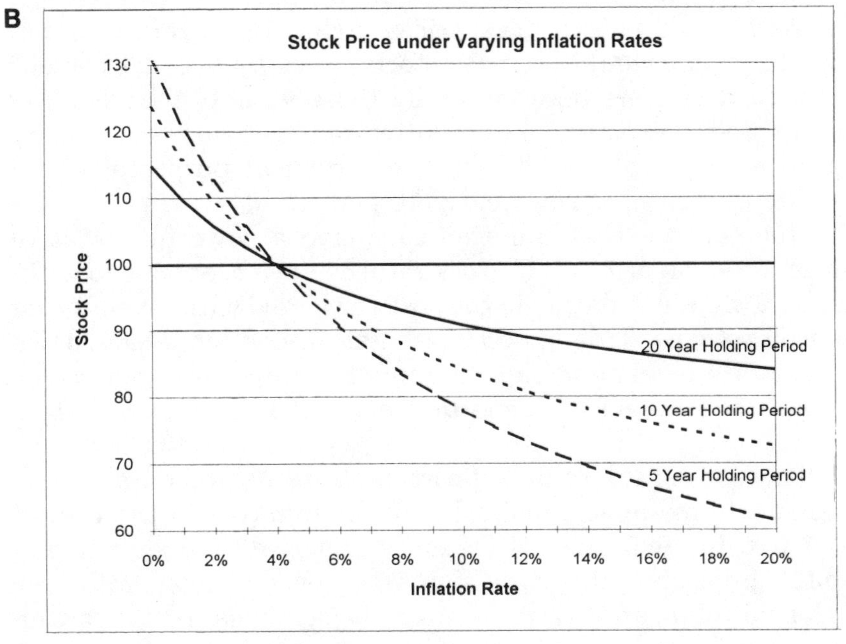

with a 30-year horizon suffers a 66 basis points reduction in average annual compound real return.

Inflation depresses stock prices because it reduces the real after-tax return on investment. Figure 10–2B shows how much the price of a stock must drop to compensate the holder for the fact that our tax system taxes nominal capital gains. This figure is calculated with 4 percent inflation as the benchmark, so that inflation lower than 4 percent will reduce the effective inflation tax, while inflation higher than 4 percent will increase the effective inflation tax.

As Figure 10–2A shows, the inflation-depressing effect on stock prices is more severe for stocks held by investors with short holding periods compared to longer holding periods. For a 10-year holding period, a rise of inflation from 4 percent to 6 percent would depress stock prices almost 7 percent. An increase of inflation to 8 percent would depress stock prices by nearly 12 percent, while 10 percent inflation would cause a 16 percent decline. If stock prices are determined by investors with shorter holding periods, the price of the stock declines even further to restore after-tax returns.

On the other hand, lower inflation improves the after-tax real return and boosts stock prices. Achieving a zero inflation from 4 percent would increase stock prices by over 23 percent if stock prices were determined by those with 10-year holding periods. Even a reduction of inflation to 2 percent, which many regard as a "stable price level" for practical purposes, would cause stock prices to rise nearly 10 percent.

One can see that inflation can have a powerful negative impact on stock prices. Yet stock returns have been able to withstand the higher inflation in the postwar period without suffering reduced returns. This is because inflation has come back down to moderate levels and capital gains tax rates were not raised as high as those on dividend and interest income since World War II.

There is considerable support, both inside and outside government, to make some adjustment for inflation in the capital gains tax. In 1986, the US Treasury proposed the indexation of capital gains, but this provision was never enacted into law. Under this plan, an investor would only pay taxes on that portion of the gain (if any) that exceeded the increase in the price level over the holding period of the asset.[5] Tax indexation would have a very positive effect on stock prices.

CONCLUSIONS

The message of this chapter is that in the short run, stocks are not good hedges against inflation—but no financial asset is. In the long run, stocks are extremely good hedges against inflation, while bonds are not. Stocks are also the best asset to buy if you fear rapid inflation, since many countries which have high inflation can still have quite viable, if not booming, stock markets. Fixed-income assets, on the other hand, cannot protect the investor from excessive monetary issuance.

Inflation, although kinder to stocks than bonds, does have some downsides, even for the equity holder. Fear that the Fed will tighten credit causes traders to avoid stocks, at least in the short run. Inflation also overstates corporate profits and increases the taxes firms have to pay. Furthermore, because the US capital gains tax is not indexed, inflation causes investors to pay higher taxes than would exist in a noninflationary environment. This chapter demonstrates that the distortions of our tax system, which cause both firms and investors to pay higher taxes in an inflationary environment, can be partially remedied by indexation of the capital gains tax.

---

[5] Some economic advisors felt so strongly on the measure that they urged President Bush to index capital gains by executive order in 1992, but the dubious legal status of such an order deterred any action.

CHAPTER 11

STOCKS AND THE BUSINESS CYCLE*

The stock market has predicted nine out of the last five recessions!

Paul Samuelson[1]

A well-respected economist is about to address a large group of financial analysts, investment advisers, and stock brokers. There is obvious concern in the audience. The stock market has been surging to new all-time highs almost daily, driving down dividend yields to record lows and price/earnings ratios skyward. Is this bullishness justified? The audience wants to know if the economy is really going to do well enough to support these high stock prices?

The economist's address is highly optimistic. He predicts that the real gross domestic product of the U.S. will increase over 4 percent during the next four quarters, a very healthy growth rate. And there will be no recession for at least three years, and even if one occurs after that it will be very brief. Corporate profits, one of the major factors driving stock prices, will increase at double-digit annual rates for at least the next three years. To boot, a Republican will easily win the White House in next year's presidential elections, a situation obviously comforting to the overwhelmingly conservative audience.

The crowd obviously likes what it hears. Their anxiety is quieted and many are ready to recommend that their clients increase their stake in stocks.

---

* This chapter is an adaptation of my paper "Does It Pay Stock Investors to Forecast the Business Cycle?" in *Journal of Portfolio Management,* Fall 1991, vol. 18, pp. 27–34. The material benefited significantly from discussions with Prof. Paul Samuelson.

[1] "Science and Stocks," *Newsweek,* September 19, 1966, p. 92.

The time of the address: the summer of 1987. The stock market is poised to take one of its sharpest falls in history, including the record-breaking 508-point decline on October 19, 1987. In just a few weeks most stocks can be bought for about one-half of the price paid when the address was given. But the biggest irony of all: The economist was dead right in each and every one of his predictions.

The lesson is that the markets and the economy are often out of sync. It is not surprising that many investors dismiss economic forecasts when planning their market strategy. The substance of Paul Samuelson's famous words, cited at the beginning of this chapter, still remains true almost 30 years after they were first uttered.

But do not dismiss the business cycle too quickly when choosing your portfolio. The stock market still responds quite powerfully to changes in economic activity. Figure 11–1 shows the reaction of the S&P 500 Index to the business cycle. Although there are many "false alarms" like 1987, when the market collapse was not followed by a recession, stocks almost always fall prior to a recession and rally rigorously on signs of an impending recovery. It is clear that if you can predict the business cycle, you can beat the buy-and-hold strategy that has been advocated throughout this book.

But this is no easy task as Figure 11–1 indicates. We will show that to make money by predicting the business cycle, you must be able to identify peaks and troughs of economic activity *before* they actually occur, a skill very few economists have been able to display. Yet business-cycle forecasting is a popular Wall Street endeavor not because it is successful—most of the time it is not—but because the potential gains from successfully calling business booms and busts are so large.

WHO DETERMINES THE BUSINESS CYCLE?

It is surprising to many that the dating of business cycles is not done by any of the myriad government agencies that collect data on the economy. Instead, the task falls to the National Bureau of Economic Research (the N.B.E.R.), a private research organi-

FIGURE 11–1

S&P 500, Earnings, and Dividends through the Business Cycle (1938–1992) (NBER Recessions Shaded)

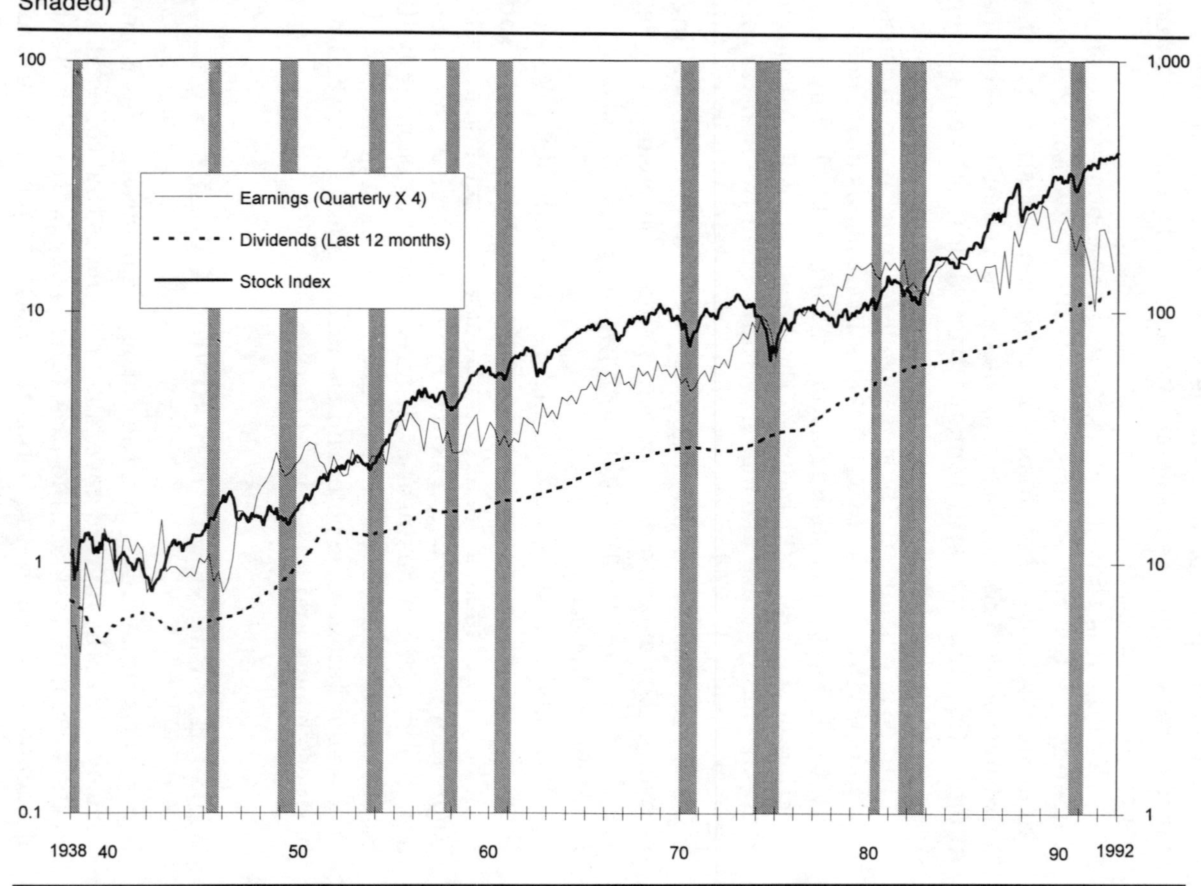

zation founded in 1920 for the purpose of documenting business cycles and developing a series of national income accounts. In the early years of its existence, the Bureau's staff compiled comprehensive chronological records of the changes in economic conditions in many of the industrialized economies. In particular, the Bureau developed monthly series of business activity for the United States and Britain back to 1854.

In a 1946 volume entitled *Measuring Business Cycles,* Wesley C. Mitchell, one of the founders of the Bureau, and Arthur Burns, a renowned business-cycle expert who later headed the Federal Reserve Board, gave the following definition of a business cycle:

> Business cycles are a type of fluctuation found in the aggregate economic activity of nations that organize their work mainly in business enterprises: a cycle consists of expansion occurring at about the same time in many economic activities, followed by similarly general recessions, or contractions, and revivals that merge into the expansion phase of the next cycle; this sequence of changes is recurrent but not periodic; in duration business cycles vary from more than one year to ten or twelve years and they are not divisible into shorter cycles of similar character.[2]

It is commonly assumed that a recession occurs when gross domestic product (or GDP), the most inclusive measure of economic output, declines for two consecutive quarters. But this is not necessarily so. Although this criterion is a reasonable rule of thumb for indicating a recession, it is not the rule used by the N.B.E.R. For example, the 1981 recession occurred when there was only a single quarter decline in GDP. The Bureau looks at many other indicators, including real personal income and sales, employment, and industrial production to date the peaks and troughs of the business cycle.

The business-cycle dates are confirmed by the Business Cycle Dating Committee of the National Bureau. The Dating Committee consists of academic economists who are associated with the Bureau and who meet to examine economic data whenever condi-

---

[2] Wesley C. Mitchell and Arthur Burns, "Measuring Business Cycles," *N.B.E.R. Reporter,* 1946, p. 3.

tions warrant. Over the entire period 1802–1993, the United States has experienced 41 recessions, averaging nearly 18 months in length, while the expansions have averaged almost 38 months. This means that over these 181 years, almost exactly one third of the time the economy has been in a recession. However, since World War II, there have been nine recessions, averaging 10 months in length, while the expansions have averaged 50 months. So in the postwar period, the economy has been in a recession only one sixth of the time.

The dating of the business cycle is of no small importance. The economy is often described as being in a recession or an expansion—a designation which has political as well as economic implications. For example, when the Bureau called the onset of the 1990 recession in July rather than August, it raised quite a few eyebrows in Washington. This is because the Bush administration had told the public that the Iraqi invasion of Kuwait and the surge in oil prices was responsible for the economic recession. This explanation was undermined when the Bureau actually dated the onset of the recession a month earlier.

The Business Cycle Dating Committee is in no rush to call the turning points in the cycle. Never has a call been reversed because of new or revised data which have become available—and the N.B.E.R. wants to keep it that way. As Robert E. Hall, current head of the seven-member Business Cycle Dating Committee indicated, "The N.B.E.R. has not made an announcement on a business cycle peak or trough until there was almost no doubt that the data would not be revised in light of subsequent availability of data."[3]

Recent examples of the N.B.E.R.'s dating makes the point. The July 1981 peak was not called until early January 1982, while the November trough was not dated until July 1983. The July 1990 peak of the last recession was not officially called until nine months later. And the March 1991 trough was not designated until December 1992, 21 months later. It is ironic that the N.B.E.R. officially called the peak of the 1990–91 business cycle a month after the trough had already been reached.

---

[3] Robert Hall, "Economic Fluctuations," *N.B.E.R. Reporter,* Summer 1991, p. 1.

Clearly, waiting for the Bureau to designate business cycles is far too late to be of any use in timing the market.

STOCK RETURNS AROUND BUSINESS-CYCLE TURNING POINTS

Almost without exception, the stock market turns down prior to recessions and rises before economic recoveries. In fact, out of the 41 recessions from 1802 through 1993, 38 of them, or 93 percent, have been preceded (or accompanied) by declines of 8 percent or more in the total stock returns index. The only three that were not were the 1829–30 recession, the recession that followed the economic reconversion immediately after World War II, and the 1953 recession, where stock declines fell just shy of our 8 percent criterion.

Table 11–1 summarizes the return behavior for the nine post–World War II recessions. One can see that the stock return index peaked anywhere from 0 to 13 months before the beginning of a recession. The recessions which began in January 1980 and July 1990 are among the very few in US history where the stock market gave no advance warning of the economic downturn.

During the postwar period, if one waits until the stock returns index has declined by 8 percent before signaling a business-cycle peak, then the stock market leads the business cycle by an average of only 1.3 months. This signal ranges from a lead of 10 months in the 1970 recession to a lag of three months in the 1990–91 recession. In all but two of the postwar recessions, an 8 percent decline in the returns index led the business-cycle peak by less than one month, giving little advance warning of an impending recession.

As the Samuelson quote at the head of this chapter indicates, the stock market is also prone to false alarms, and these have increased in the postwar period. Excluding the war years, where declining stock markets have coincided with expanding war economies, there have been 12 episodes since 1802 when the cumulative returns index for stocks has fallen by 8 percent or more, but the drop has not then been followed by a recession within the next 12 months. This happened five times in the 19th century

TABLE 11–1
Recessions and Stock Returns

Recession	Peak of Stock Index (1)	Peak of Business Cycle (2)	Lead Time between Peaks (3)	Decline in Stock Index from (1) to (2) (4)	Months Between 8% Stock Index Decline and (2) (5)	Maximum 12 Month Decline in Stock Index (6)
1948 - 49	May 1948	Nov 1948	6	-8.74%	0	-8.19%
1953 - 54	Dec 1952	Jul 1953	7	-3.91	*	-7.18
1957 - 58	Jul 1957	Aug 1957	1	-5.05	-1	-13.90
1960 - 61	Dec 1959	Apr 1960	4	-8.28	0	-8.20
1970	Nov 1968	Dec 1969	13	-12.19	10	-25.50
1973 - 75	Dec 1972	Nov 1973	11	-16.20	7	-40.10
1980	Jan 1980	Jan 1980	0	0.00	-2	-8.90
1981 - 82	Nov 1980	Jul 1981	8	-4.08	-1	-14.20
1990 - 91	Jul 1990	Jul 1990	0	0.00	-3	-13.92
		Average	**5.6**	**-6.49%**	**1.3**	**-15.56%**
		Standard Deviation	4.4	5.10%	4.4	10.17%

* Market never declined 8%.

and seven times in the 20th century. All the occasions in this century have occurred since World War II.

Table 11–2 lists declines greater than 8 percent in the stock returns index during the postwar period that were not followed by recessions. The 1987 decline of 29 percent, from August through November, is the largest decline in the nearly two-century history of stock returns data after which the economy did not fall into a recession. Chapter 15 will discuss the 1987 stock crash and explain why it did not lead to an economic downturn.

Table 11–3 compares the trough in the stock return index and the trough in the N.B.E.R. business cycle. The average lead time between a market upturn and an economic recovery has been 5.1 months, and the range has been quite narrow. This compares to an average 5.6-month lead time between the peak in the market and the peak in the business cycle, with a much greater variability in these figures. As we shall see, stock returns actually rise more in a recession in anticipation of an economic recovery than they fall before an economic downturn.

GAINS THROUGH TIMING THE BUSINESS CYCLE

Table 11–4 displays the excess returns to investors who can time their investment strategy in relation to the peaks and troughs in economic activity. Since stocks fall prior to a recession, an investor would want to switch out of stocks and into bills, returning to stocks when prospects for economic recovery look good. Excess returns are calculated by assuming that an investor who leads the business cycle switches out of stocks and into bills some months before the peak of business expansions and switches back into stocks some months before the trough of recessions. In contrast, an investor who lags the business cycle switches out of stocks and into bills after the cycle peak and back into stocks after the cycle trough. The excess returns are measured relative to a buy-and-hold stock strategy of the same risk as the timing strategies employed above.

In the postwar period, the excess return is minimal over a buy-and-hold strategy if one switches into bills at the peak and into stocks at the trough of the business cycle. In fact, an investor

TABLE 11–2
False Alarms by Stock Market (Postwar Declines of 8% or More When No Recession Followed within 12 Months; Ranked by Severity of Decline)

Year of False Alarm	Peak Month Stock Index	Low Month Stock Index	Decline in Market (%)
1987	Aug 1987	Nov 1987	-29.10%
1946	May 1946	May 1947	-24.00
1962	Dec 1961	Jun 1962	-23.10
1966	Jan 1966	Sep 1966	-15.50
1978	Aug 1978	Oct 1978	-10.80
1956 - 57	Jul 1956	Feb 1957	-8.30
1984	Nov 1983	May 1984	-8.20

switching into bills just one month *after* the business cycle peak and back into stocks just one month after the business cycle trough would have lost 0.6 percent per year compared to the benchmark buy-and-hold strategy.

Interestingly, it is more important to be able to forecast troughs of the business cycle than peaks. An investor who buys stocks before the trough of the business cycle gains more than an investor who sells stocks an equal number of months before the business-cycle peak.

The maximum excess return of 4.8 percent per year is obtained by investing in bonds four months before the business-cycle peak and in stocks four months before the business-cycle troughs. The strategy of switching between bills and stock gains almost 30 basis points (30/100 of a percentage point) in average annual return for each *week* during that four-month period in which the investor is able to predict the business-cycle turning point.

The extra returns from successfully forecasting the business cycle are impressive. An increase of 1.8 percent per year in returns, achieved by predicting the business-cycle peak and trough only one month before it occurs, will increase your wealth by over 60 percent over any buy-and-hold strategy over 30 years.

TABLE 11–3
Expansions and Stock Returns

Recession	Trough of Stock Index (1)	Trough of Business Cycle (2)	Lead Time between Troughs (3)	Rise in Stock Index from (1) to (2) (4)	Months between 8% Stock Index Rise and (2) (5)
1948 - 49	May 1949	Oct 1949	5	15.59%	3
1953 - 54	Aug 1953	May 1954	9	29.13	5
1957 - 58	Dec 1957	April 1958	4	10.27	1
1960 - 61	Oct 1960	Feb 1961	4	21.25	2
1970	Jun 1970	Nov 1970	5	21.86	3
1973 - 75	Sep 1974	Mar 1975	6	35.60	5
1980	Mar 1980	Jul 1980	4	22.60	2
1981 - 82	Jul 1982	Nov 1982	4	33.13	3
1990 - 91	Oct 1990	Mar 1991	5	25.28	3
		Average	**5.1**	**23.86%**	**3.0**
		Standard Deviation	1.73	8.59%	1.41

TABLE 11–4
Excess Returns around Business-Cycle Turning Points

		Lead					Lag			
		4 month	3 month	2 month	1 month	Peak	1 month	2 month	3 month	4 month
Lead	4 month	**4.8%**	4.0%	4.2%	4.1%	3.3%	2.7%	2.1%	2.2%	1.9%
	3 month	4.0	**3.3**	3.5	3.3	2.6	1.9	1.4	1.5	1.3
	2 month	3.3	2.6	**2.8**	2.6	1.9	1.2	0.7	0.8	0.7
	1 month	2.5	1.8	2.0	**1.8**	1.1	0.5	0.0	0.1	0.0
	Trough	1.9	1.2	1.4	1.2	**0.5**	-0.2	-0.7	-0.6	-0.7
Lag	1 month	1.5	0.8	1.0	0.8	0.1	**-0.6**	-1.1	-1.0	-1.1
	2 month	0.9	0.2	0.4	0.2	-0.5	-1.1	**-1.7**	-1.6	-1.7
	3 month	0.5	-0.2	0.0	-0.2	-0.9	-1.5	-2.1	**-2.0**	-2.1
	4 month	0.3	-0.4	-0.2	-0.3	-1.1	-1.7	-2.2	-2.1	**-2.2**

If you can predict four months in advance, the annual increase of 4.8 percent in your returns will more than triple your wealth over the same time period compared to a buy-and-hold strategy.

HOW HARD IS IT TO PREDICT THE BUSINESS CYCLE?

Billions of dollars of resources are spent forecasting the business cycle. It is not surprising that Wall Street employs so many economists desperately trying to predict the next recession or upturn. But the record at being able to predict exact business-cycle turning points is extremely poor.

Stephen McNees, vice president of the Federal Reserve Bank of Boston, has done extensive research into the accuracy of economic forecasters' predictions. He claims that a major factor in forecast accuracy is the time period over which the forecast was made. He concludes, "Errors were enormous in the severe 1973–75 and 1981–82 recessions, much smaller in the 1980 and 1990 recessions, and generally quite minimal apart from business-cycle turning points."[4] But it is precisely these business-cycle turning points that turn a forecaster into a successful market timer.

The 1974–75 recession was particularly tough for economists. Almost every one of the nearly two dozen of the nation's top economists invited to President Ford's anti-inflation conference in Washington in September 1974 was unaware that the US economy was in the midst of its most severe postwar recession to date. McNees, studying the forecasts issued by five prominent forecasters in 1974, found that the median forecast overestimated GNP growth by six percentage points and underestimated inflation by four percentage points. Early recognition of the 1974 recession was so poor that many economists "jumped the gun" on the next recession, which didn't strike until 1980, but most economists thought had begun early in 1979.

---

[4] Stephen K. McNees, "How Large Are Economic Forecast Errors?" *New England Economic Review,* July/August 1992, p. 33.

For over 15 years, Robert J. Eggert has been documenting and summarizing economic forecasts of a noted panel of economic and business experts. These forecasts are compiled and published in a monthly publication entitled *Blue Chip Economic Indicators*.

In July 1979, the *Blue Chip Economic Indicators* indicated that a strong majority of forecasters believed that a recession had already started—forecasting negative GNP growth in the second, third, and fourth quarters of 1979. However, the N.B.E.R. declared that the peak of the business cycle did not occur until January 1980 and that the economy expanded throughout 1979.

By the middle of the next year, forecasters were convinced a recession had begun. But as late as June 1980 the forecasters believed that the recession had started in February or March and would last about a year, or about one month longer than the average recession. This prediction was reaffirmed in August, when the forecasters indicated that the US economy was about halfway through the recession. In fact, the recession had ended the month before, in July, and the 1980 recession turned out to be the shortest in the postwar period.

Forecasters' ability to predict the severe 1981–82 recession, when unemployment reached a postwar high of 10.8 percent, was no better. The headline of the July 1981 *Blue Chip Economic Indicators* read "Economic Exuberance Envisioned for 1982." Instead, 1982 was a disaster. By November 1981 the forecasters realized that the economy had faltered, and optimism turned to pessimism. Most thought that the economy had entered a recession (which it had done four months earlier), nearly 70 percent thought that it would end by the first quarter of 1982 (which it would not, instead tying the record for the longest postwar recession, ending in November), and 90 percent thought that it would be mild like the 1971 recession rather than severe—wrong again!

In April 1985, with the expansion well underway, forecasters were queried as to how long the economy would continue in recovery. The average response was 49 months, which would put the peak at December 1986, more than 3½ years before the cycle actually ended. Even the most optimistic forecasters picked spring 1988 as the latest date for the next recession to begin. This question was asked repeatedly throughout 1985 and 1986 and no forecaster imagined that the 1980s expansion would last as long as it did.

Following the stock crash of October 1987, forecasters reduced their GNP growth estimates of 1988 over 1987 from 2.8 percent to 1.9 percent, the largest drop in the 11-year history of the survey. Instead, economic growth in 1988 was nearly 4 percent, as the economy failed to respond to the stock market collapse.

As the expansion continued, belief that a recession was imminent turned into the belief that prosperity was here to stay. The continuing expansion fostered a growing conviction that perhaps the business cycle had been conquered—by either government policy or the "recession-proof" nature of our service-oriented economy. Ed Yardeni, senior economist at Prudential-Bache securities, wrote a "New Wave Manifesto" in late 1988 concluding that self-repairing, growing economies were likely through the rest of the decade.[5] On the eve of one of the worst worldwide recessions in the postwar era, Leonard Silk, senior economics editor of *The New York Times* stated in May of 1990 in an article entitled "Is There Really a Business Cycle?":

> Most economists foresee no recession in 1990 or 1991, and 1992 will be another presidential year, when the odds tip strongly against recession. Japan, West Germany and most of the other capitalist countries of Europe and Asia are also on a long upward roll, with no end in sight.[6]

By November 1990, *Blue Chip Economic Indicators* reported that the majority of the panel believed the US economy had already, or was about to, slip into a recession. But by then, not only had the economy been in recession for four months, but the stock market had already hit its bottom and was headed upward! Had an investor given in to the prevailing pessimism at the time when the recession seemed confirmed, he would have sold after the low was reached and stocks were headed for a strong three-year rally.

---

[5] "New Wave Economist," *Los Angeles Times,* March 18, 1990, Business Section p. 22.

[6] Leonard Silk, "Is There Really a Business Cycle?" *The New York Times,* May 22, 1992, p. D2.

As Robert Eggert, the editor of the *Blue Chip Economic Indicators,* rightly points out, the October consensus forecasts of next year's growth in gross domestic product is twice as accurate as blindly assuming that next year will be the same as this year. Yet this does not mean that forecasters can pick the turning points in the economy with any accuracy. And, as our research has shown, investors must be able to predict business-cycle turning points in advance in order to give them an edge in playing the market.

CONCLUDING COMMENTS

Stock values are based on corporate earnings and the business cycle is a prime determinant of these earnings. The gains to being able to predict the turning points of the economic cycle are enormous. Yet doing so with any precision has eluded economists of all persuasions. And despite the growing body of economic statistics, predictions are not getting much better over time.

The lessons to investors are clear. Beating the stock market by analyzing real economic activity requires a degree of prescience that forecasters do not yet have. Turning points are rarely identified until several months after the peak or trough has been reached. By then, it is far too late to act in the market.

The worst course an investor can take is to follow the prevailing sentiment about economic activity. This will often leave him buying at the high when times are good and everyone is optimistic and selling at the low when the recession nears its trough and pessimism prevails.

The inability to predict the business cycle does not mean that an investor will lose in the market. One does not have to beat the market to accumulate wealth. The superior returns to stocks can be obtained by riding out the periods of boom and bust which have always been part of our economy.

CHAPTER 12

EVENTS WHICH MOVE FINANCIAL MARKETS

I can predict the motion of heavenly bodies, but not the madness of crowds.

Isaac Newton

In October 1962, during the height of the cold war, the US government had determined that the Soviet Union was installing missile launchers with nuclear strike capability in Cuba, just 90 miles off the coast of Florida. President Kennedy ordered Soviet Premier Nikita Khrushchev to remove all such missiles and, to prevent any further installations, erected a naval blockade preventing any ships from approaching the island nation.

The financial markets were extremely tense over this confrontation. The Dow Industrials fell 3 percent in the two days following the news of the Russian installations and Kennedy's hard-line response. It was the first face-to-face confrontation between the nuclear superpowers, an incident without precedent.

A young stock trader sought advice from his mentor, a veteran with long experience trading stocks.

"What should I do, Mike," the young trader inquired, "if we get a report across the broad tape that the Soviet Union has launched on all-out nuclear attack on the United States? Obviously everyone will be selling and stock prices will plummet."

The veteran replied, "That's the easiest question you've ever asked. Buy! Buy stocks with all the money and credit you can muster!"

"How can you be so sure," the younger trader inquired, "that the report will turn out false?"

"Oh, I'm not sure at all," Mike shot back. "Certainly if the report is false, stock prices will rebound and you'll make a bundle. And if the report's true," the old-timer hesitated a moment, "your trades will never clear!"

With the end of the Cold War, stock investors will hopefully never again worry that a nuclear blast might vaporize their trading tickets. Yet there will be no shortage of crises impacting the market. Politics—and, unfortunately, military encounters—are as unpredictable today as they have been throughout history.

WHAT MOVES THE MARKET

Although one might think that economic and political news should be the major source of market movements, it is surprising how much volatility occurs in the absence of any clearly defined news event. There have been 120 days since 1885, when Dow Jones averages were first formulated, when the Industrial average has changed by 5.00 percent or more. Of these, only 28, or less than one in four, can be identified with a specific world political or economic event, such as war, political changes, and policy shifts. Table 12–1A ranks the 40 largest changes and Table 12–1B identifies those changes greater than 5.00 percent associated with specific events.[1]

Of the 10 largest changes, only two can be attributed to news. The record one-day move in the stock market, the October 19, 1987 drop of 22.63 percent in the Dow Industrials, is not associated with a readily identifiable news event. Since 1940, there have been only two days of big moves where the cause is identified: the 6.62 percent drop on September 26, 1955, when President Eisenhower suffered a heart attack, and the 6.12 percent drop on Friday, October 13, 1989. This latter decline has often been attributed to the collapse of the leveraged buyout of United Air Lines, although the market was already down substantially before this news was announced late in the day. It is of interest that there has been no 5 percent drop during US involvement in any war during this century.

---

[1] This expands the research originally published in David M. Cutler, James M. Poterba, and Lawrence H. Summers, "What Moves Stock Prices," *Journal of Portfolio Management,* Spring 1989, pp. 4–12.

Despite the difficulty in attributing market changes to clearly identifiable events, it is not unusual for financial writers to find all sorts of reasons why the market moves up or down. Since the level of the market represents a resolution of a struggle between the bulls, who are armed with reasons why the market should go higher, and bears, who believe they have good cause for it to go lower, it is easy to tap into one group or the other to explain the market movement.

Even then, there can be sharp disagreement over the cause of the market change. On November 15, 1991, when the Dow fell over 120 points, or nearly 4 percent, *Investors Business Daily* titled the article about the market: "Dow Plunges 120 in a Scary Stock Sell-off: Biotechs, Programs, Expiration and Congress Get the Blame."[2] In contrast, the New York writer for the London *Financial Times* titled the front-page article "Wall Street Drops 120 Points on Concern at Russian Moves." What is interesting is that such news, specifically that the Russian government had suspended oil licenses and taken over the gold supplies, was not even mentioned once in the US article! That one major newspaper can highlight "reasons" which another does not even report illustrates the difficulty of finding explanations for the movements of markets.

UNCERTAINTY AND THE MARKET

The market fears uncertainty or any event which jars investors from their customary framework for analyzing the world. President Eisenhower's heart attack on September 26, 1955, caused a 6.54 percent decline in the Dow Industrials, the sixth largest in the postwar period. The fall was a clear sign of Eisenhower's popularity with the market. President Kennedy's assassination on November 22, 1963, caused the Dow Industrials to drop 2.9 percent and persuaded the New York Stock Exchange to close two hours early to prevent more panic selling. Yet, when the market reopened the following Tuesday and Lyndon Johnson,

---

[2] Virginia Munger Kahn, *Investors Business Daily*, November 16, 1991, p. 1.

TABLE 12–1A

Largest Movements in the Dow Jones Industrials

(Daily Changes over 5 Percent in the Dow Jones Industrial Average)

Rank	Date	Change	Rank	Date	Change	Rank	Date	Change
_1_	_Oct 19, 1987_	_-22.61%_	_16_	_Dec 18, 1899_	_-8.72%_	_31_	_Jul 20, 1933_	_-7.07%_
2*	Oct 6, 1931	14.87	17	Oct 8, 1931	8.70	_32*_	_Oct 13, 1989_	_-6.91_
_3_	_Oct 28, 1929_	_-12.82_	_18_	_Dec 20, 1895_	_-8.51_	_33*_	_Jul 30, 1914_	_-6.90_
4	Oct 30, 1929	12.34	_19_	_Mar 14, 1907_	_-8.29_	_34_	_Jan 8, 1988_	_-6.85_
_5_	_Oct 29, 1929_	_-11.73_	_20_	_Oct 26, 1987_	_-8.04_	35	Oct 14, 1932	6.83
6	Sep 21, 1932	11.36	21	Jun 10, 1932	7.99	_36_	_Nov 11, 1929_	_-6.82_
7	Oct 21, 1987	10.15	_22_	_Jul 21, 1933_	_-7.84_	_37*_	_May 14, 1940_	_-6.80_
_8_	_Nov 6, 1929_	_-9.92_	_23_	_Oct 18, 1937_	_-7.75_	_38_	_Oct 5, 1931_	_-6.78_
9	Aug 3, 1932	9.52	_24*_	_Jul 26, 1893_	_-7.39_	_39*_	_May 21, 1940_	_-6.78_
10*	Feb 11, 1932	9.47	25*	Sep 5, 1939	7.26	40	Mar 15, 1907	6.69
11*	Nov 14, 1929	9.36	_26*_	_Feb 1, 1917_	_-7.24_	41*	Jun 20, 1931	6.64
12	Dec 18, 1931	9.35	_27_	_Oct 5, 1932_	_-7.15_	42	Jul 24, 1933	6.63
13	Feb 13, 1932	9.19	28	Jun 3, 1931	7.12	43	Jul 27, 1893	6.63
14*	May 6, 1932	9.08	29	Jan 6, 1932	7.11	_44*_	_Jul 26, 1934_	_-6.62_
15*	Apr 19, 1933	9.03	_30_	_Sep 24, 1931_	_-7.07_	_45_	_Aug 12, 1932_	_-6.61_

(Negative changes are italicized. *—Changes associated with news items.) (Excludes 15.34% change from March 3 through 15, 1933 for US bank holiday.)

TABLE 12–1B
Largest News-Related Movements in the Dow Jones Industrial Average

Rank	Date	Change	News Headline
2	Oct 6, 1931	14.87%	Hoover Urges $500M Pool to Help Banks
10	Feb 11, 1932	9.47	Liberalization of Fed Discount Policy
11	Nov 14, 1929	9.36	Fed Lowers Discount Rate/Tax Cut Proposed
14	May 6, 1932	9.08	U.S. Steel Negotiates 15% Wage Cut
15	Apr 19, 1933	9.03	U.S. Drops Gold Standard
24	*Jul 26, 1893*	*-7.39*	*Erie Railroad Bankrupt*
25	Sep 5, 1939	7.26	World War II Begins in Europe
26	*Feb 1, 1917*	*-7.24*	*Germ. announces unrestricted sub. warfare*
32	*Oct 13, 1989*	*-6.91*	*United Airline Buy-out Collapses*
33	*Jul 30, 1914*	*-6.90*	*Outbreak of World War I*
37	*May 14, 1940*	*-6.80*	*Germans Invade Holland*
39	*May 21, 1940*	*-6.78*	*Allied Reverses in France*
41	Jun 20, 1931	6.64	Hoover Advocates Foreign Debt Moratorium
44	*Jul 26, 1934*	*-6.62*	*Fighting in Austria; Italy mobilizes*
46	*Sep 26, 1955*	*-6.54*	*Eisenhower Suffers Heart Attack*
64	Oct 31, 1929	5.82	Fed Lowers Discount Rate
65	*Jun 16, 1930*	*-5.81*	*Hoover to Sign Tariff Bill*
66	Apr 20, 1933	5.80	Continued Rally on Dropping of Gold Standard
71	May 2, 1898	5.65	Dewey Defeats Spanish
73	Mar 28, 1898	5.56	Dispatches of Armistice with Spain
81	Dec 22, 1916	5.47	Lansing Denies U.S. Near War
84	*Feb 25, 1933*	*-5.40*	*Maryland Bank Holiday*
88	Oct 23, 1933	5.37	Roosevelt Devalues Dollar
90	*Dec 21, 1916*	*-5.35*	*Sec. of State Lansing implies U.S. Near War*
99	*Dec 18, 1896*	*-5.25*	*Senate votes for Free Cuba*
100	Apr 9, 1938	5.25	Congress Passes Bill Taxing U.S. Govt Bond Int
119	Oct 20, 1931	5.03	ICC Raises Rail Rates
120	*Mar 31, 1932*	*-5.02*	*House Proposes Stock Sales Tax*

(Negative changes are italicized.)

as was expected, took over the reins of government, the market soared 4.5 percent, representing one of the best days in the post-war period.

The market almost always declines in reaction to sudden, unexpected changes related to the presidency. When William McKinley was shot on September 14, 1901, the market dropped by more than 4 percent. But stocks regained all of their losses on the following trading day. The death of Warren Harding caused a milder setback which was soon erased. Sell-offs such as these provide good opportunities for investors to step up and buy stocks because the market usually reverses itself quickly following the change in leadership.[3]

DEMOCRATS AND REPUBLICANS

It is well known that the stock market prefers Republicans to Democrats. Most corporate executives and stock traders are Republicans and many Republican policies are perceived to be favorable to stock prices and capital formation. Democrats are perceived to be less amenable to favorable tax treatment of capital gains and more in favor of regulation and income redistribution. Yet the markets do no worse under Democrats than Republicans.

Figure 12–1 shows the performance of the Dow Jones Industrials during every administration since Grover Cleveland was elected in 1888. The greatest bear market in history occurred during the Hoover administration, while stocks did quite well under Franklin Roosevelt, despite the fact that he was frequently reviled in boardrooms and brokerage houses around the country.

Table 12–2 lists the performance of the Dow Industrials before and after each presidential election since 1888. The immediate reaction of the market does indeed conform to the fact that investors like Republicans better than Democrats. Since 1888, the market has fallen an average of 0.75 percent on the day following Democratic victories, but risen by 0.81 percent on the day following a Republican victory. Since World War II, the market has fallen over 1 percent when a Democrat has won, and has risen only slightly on Republican victories.

---

[3] But there are some whom the market never forgives. Stocks rallied over 4 percent in the week following the news of the death of Franklin Roosevelt, who was never a favorite on Wall Street.

FIGURE 12–1

The Dow Jones Industrial Average and Presidential Terms

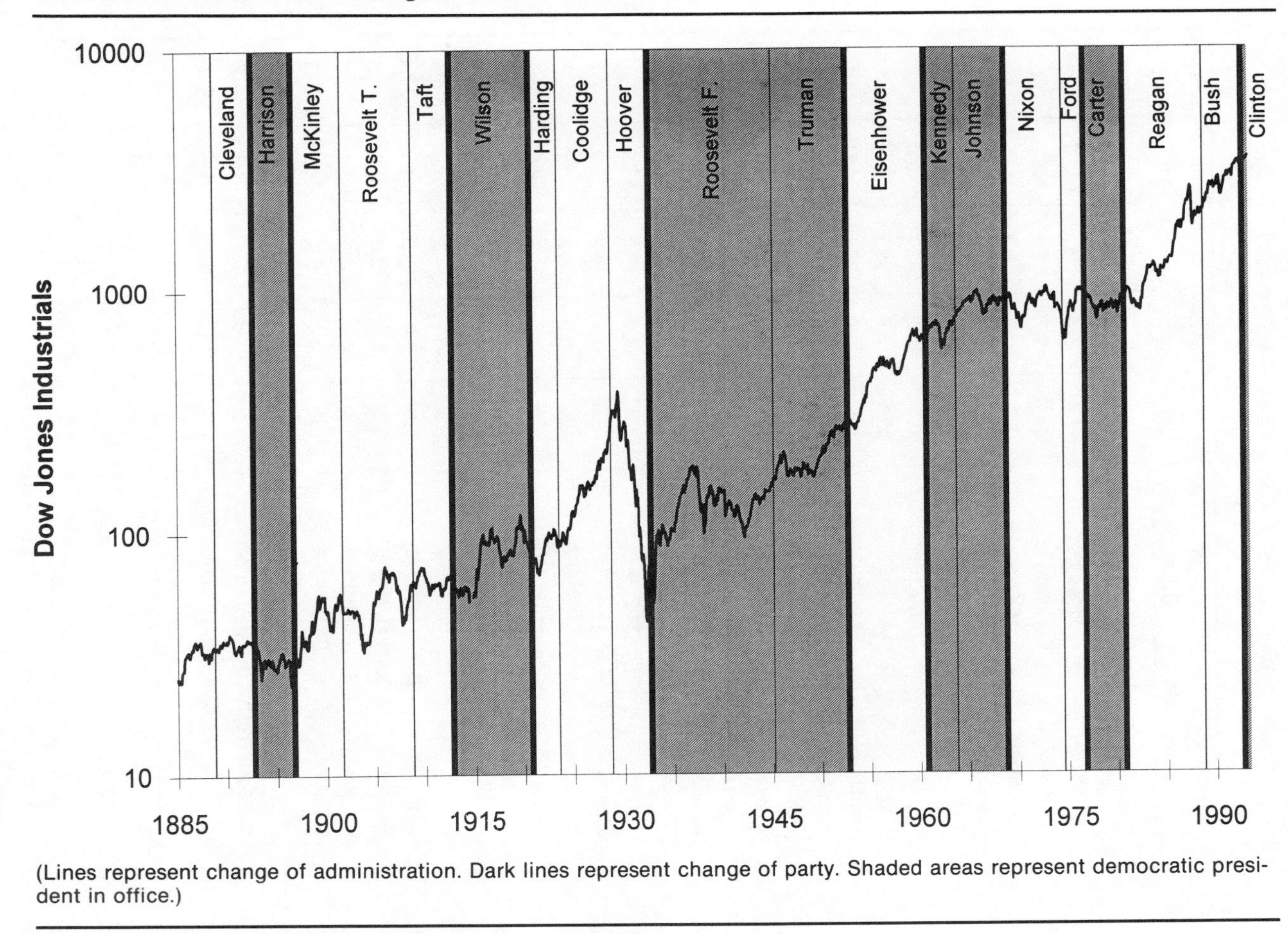

(Lines represent change of administration. Dark lines represent change of party. Shaded areas represent democratic president in office.)

TABLE 12–2
Stock Returns around Presidential Elections
(Measured in percent by Dow Jones Industrial Average)

President's Name	Party	Election Date	From: / To:	3 mon b/f / 1 day b/f	1 day b/f / 1 day aft	1 day b/f / 1 mon aft	1 day b/f / 3 mon aft	1 day b/f / 1 year aft
Harrison	R	11/6/1888		1.3	0.4	-4.2	1.0	5.9
Cleveland	*D*	*11/8/1892*		*-1.6*	*-0.5*	*-4.2*	*-2.8*	*-21.1*
McKinley	R	11/3/1896		14.8	2.7	2.1	0.2	12.3
McKinley	R	11/6/1900		5.7	3.3	6.9	14.8	6.1
Roosevelt T.	R	11/8/1904		25.6	1.3	2.7	9.6	24.1
Taft	R	11/3/1908		2.3	2.4	4.4	2.1	20.9
Wilson	*D*	*11/5/1912*		*0.3*	*1.8*	*-2.7*	*-8.0*	*-13.5*
Wilson	*D*	*11/7/1916*		*20.6*	*-0.4*	*-0.7*	*-14.0*	*-33.3*
Harding	R	11/2/1920		0.6	-0.6	-9.6	-12.3	-14.0
Coolidge	R	11/4/1924		0.6	1.2	7.4	16.0	52.1
Hoover	R	11/6/1928		18.1	1.2	8.6	23.1	-9.9
Roosevelt F.	*D*	*11/8/1932*		*-4.6*	*-4.5*	*-7.0*	*-8.8*	*47.9*
Roosevelt F.	*D*	*11/3/1936*		*6.9*	*2.3*	*2.6*	*6.8*	*-26.3*
Roosevelt F.	*D*	*11/5/1940*		*6.9*	*-2.4*	*-3.9*	*-8.2*	*-11.4*
Roosevelt F.	*D*	*11/7/1944*		*1.8*	*-0.3*	*0.9*	*5.3*	*29.8*
Truman	*D*	*11/2/1948*		*4.8*	*-3.8*	*-8.5*	*-5.0*	*1.7*
Eisenhower	R	11/4/1952		-3.4	0.4	4.2	7.0	2.4
Eisenhower	R	11/6/1956		-3.6	-0.9	-0.5	-5.0	-12.0
Kennedy	*D*	*11/8/1960*		*-2.8*	*0.8*	*1.3*	*8.6*	*21.1*
Johnson	*D*	*11/3/1964*		*4.2*	*-0.2*	*-0.5*	*3.5*	*9.8*
Nixon	R	11/5/1968		8.4	0.3	3.3	0.0	-9.7
Nixon	R	11/7/1972		3.3	-0.1	4.9	-1.7	-6.6
Carter	*D*	*11/2/1976*		*-1.6*	*-1.0*	*-2.0*	*-1.4*	*-17.1*
Reagan	R	11/4/1980		0.7	1.7	3.6	0.5	-7.5
Reagan	R	11/6/1984		3.4	-0.9	-5.9	2.9	12.8
Bush	R	11/8/1988		1.0	-0.4	0.7	10.1	23.3
Clinton	*D*	*11/3/1992*		*-4.2*	*-0.9*	*0.8*	*3.7*	---
Average from 1888 to 1992		Democratic		2.5	-0.8	-2.0	-1.7	-1.1
		Republican		5.3	0.8	1.9	4.6	6.7
		Overall		4.1	0.1	0.2	1.8	3.4
Average from 1948 to 1992		Democratic		0.1	-1.0	-1.8	1.9	3.9
		Republican		1.4	0.0	1.5	2.0	0.4
		Overall		0.8	-0.4	0.1	1.9	1.7

(Italics represent Democratic administrations.)

But the negative reaction to a Democratic victory is not justified by the postwar data. Since 1948, within one year of the election, the market has gained, on average, far more under a Democratic administration than under a Republican.

The superior performance under the Democrats in recent years can be documented even if we include dividends and inflation in our calculations. Table 12–3 records the total real and nominal returns under Democratic and Republican administrations. Since 1888, the market has fared equally well under Democrats and Republicans, but inflation has been lower when the Republicans have held office. But since 1948, the market has fared better under the Democrats whether or not inflation is factored in.

STOCKS AND WAR

Since 1885, the US economy has been at war or on the sidelines of a world war about one fifth of the time. The stock market does equally well in *nominal* returns whether there is war or peace, but inflation has averaged nearly 6 percent during wartime and less than 2 percent during peacetime, so that the real returns on stocks during peacetime greatly outstrips those during wars.

It is of interest that the volatility of the market, measured as the monthly range of the Dow Industrials, has actually been *greater,* on average, during peacetime than during war. The greatest volatility in US markets occurred in the late 1920s and early 1930s, well before the United States was engaged in a worldwide conflict. Only during World War I and the short Gulf War did wartime stocks have higher volatility than average.

In theory, war should have a profound influence on stock prices. Tremendous resources are commandeered by governments, while high taxes and huge government borrowings compete with investors' demand for stock. Whole industries are nationalized to further the war effort. Moreover, if loss of war is deemed a possibility, then stocks could well decline as the victors impose sanctions on the vanquished. However, as we have seen in Chapter 1, the economies of Germany and Japan were quickly restored to health and stocks boomed following World War II.

TABLE 12–3
Presidential Administrations and Stock Returns

President's Name	Party	Date	Months in Office	Annualized Nominal Stock Return	Annualized Inflation	Annualized Real Return
Harrison	R	11/88 - 10/92	48	5.7	0.0	5.7
Cleveland	*D*	*11/92 - 10/96*	*48*	*-3.3*	*-1.9*	*-1.4*
McKinley	R	11/96 - 8/01	58	20.7	0.0	20.7
Roosevelt T	R	9/01 - 10/08	86	4.8	1.4	3.4
Taft	R	11/08 - 10/12	48	7.5	0.8	6.7
Wilson	*D*	*11/12 - 10/20*	*96*	*4.7*	*9.4*	*-4.3*
Harding	R	11/20 - 7/23	33	5.5	-4.0	9.9
Coolidge	R	8/23 - 10/28	63	28.0	0.1	27.9
Hoover	R	11/28 - 10/32	48	-20.4	-6.3	-15.1
Roosevelt F	*D*	*11/32 - 3/45*	*149*	*11.5*	*2.4*	*8.9*
Truman	*D*	*4/45 - 10/52*	*91*	*14.7*	*5.5*	*8.6*
Eisenhower	R	11/52 - 10/60	96	15.0	1.4	13.4
Kennedy	*D*	*11/60 - 10/63*	*36*	*15.1*	*1.1*	*13.9*
Johnson	*D*	*11/63 - 10/68*	*60*	*10.4*	*2.8*	*7.4*
Nixon	R	11/68 - 7/74	69	-1.3	6.0	-6.9
Ford	R	8/74 - 10/76	27	17.2	7.3	9.3
Carter	*D*	*11/76 - 10/80*	*48*	*11.0*	*10.0*	*0.9*
Reagan	R	11/80 - 10/88	96	15.2	4.5	10.3
Bush	R	11/88 - 10/92	48	14.4	4.2	9.8
Clinton	*D*	*11/92 -*				
Average from 1888 to 1992		Democrat	42.5%	9.4	4.4	4.8
		Republican	57.5%	9.3	1.5	7.7
Overall				**9.4**	**2.7**	**6.5**
Average from 1948 to 1992		Democrat	36.8%	13.4	4.1	8.9
		Republican	63.2%	11.4	4.1	7.0
Overall				**12.2**	**4.1**	**7.8**

(Stock returns taken from election date or date of taking office, whichever is earlier.)

The World Wars

The volatility of the market during World War I greatly exceeded that during World War II. The market rose nearly 100 percent during the early stages of World War I, then fell 40 percent when the United States became involved in the hostilities, and finally rallied when the Great War ended. In contrast, during the six years of World War II, the market never deviated more than 32 percent from its prewar level.

The outbreak of World War I precipitated a panic as European investors scrambled to get out of stocks and into gold and cash. After the declaration of war by Austria-Hungary on Serbia on July 28, 1914, all the major European stock exchanges closed. The European panic spread to New York and the Dow-Jones Industrials closed down nearly 7 percent on Thursday, July 30, the most since the 8.3 percent drop during the Panic of 1907. Minutes before the opening of the New York Stock Exchange on Friday, the exchange voted to close for an indefinite period.

The market did not reopen until December. Never before has the New York Stock Exchange been closed for such an extended period. Emergency trades were permitted, but only by approval of a special committee and only at prices at or above the last trade before the exchange closed. Even then, trading prohibition was observed in the breach as illegal trades were made outside the exchange (on the curb) at prices which continued to decline through October. Unofficially, by the fall prices were said to be 15 to 20 percent below the July closing.

It is ironic that the only extended period that the New York Stock Exchange was closed occurred when the United States was not at war or in any degree of financial or economic distress. In fact, when the exchange was closed, traders realized that the United States might be the beneficiary of the European conflict. Once investors realized who was going to make the munitions and provide raw materials to the belligerents, public interest in stocks soared.

By the time the exchange reopened on December 12, prices were rising rapidly. The Dow Industrials finished its historical Saturday session about 5 percent higher than the closing prices on the previous July. The rally continued, and 1915 records the best single-year increase in the history of the Dow Industrials, as stocks rose a record 82 percent.

The message of the great boom of 1915 was not lost on traders a generation later. When World War II erupted, investors took their cue from what happened at the beginning of the previous world war. When Britain declared war on Germany on September 3, 1939, the rise was so explosive that the Tokyo Exchange was forced to close early. When the market opened in New York, a buying panic erupted. The Dow Industrials gained over 7 percent and even the European stock exchanges were firm when trading reopened.

The enthusiasm which followed the onset of World War II quickly faded. The day before the Japanese attacked Pearl Harbor, the Dow was down 25 percent from its 1939 high and still less than one third its 1929 peak. Stocks fell 3.5 percent on the day following Pearl Harbor and continued to fall until they hit a low on April 28, 1942, when Germany invaded and quickly subdued France.

But when the war turned around, the market began to climb. By the time Germany signed its unconditional surrender on May 7, 1945, the Dow Industrials were 20 percent above the prewar level. The detonation of the atomic bomb over Hiroshima, a pivotal event in the history of warfare, caused stocks to surge 1.7 percent as investors recognized the end of the war was near. But World War II did not prove as profitable for investors as the First World War, as the Dow was up only 30 percent during the six years from the German invasion of Poland to V-J Day.

Post-1945 Conflicts

The Korean War took investors by surprise. When North Korea invaded its southern neighbor on June 25, 1950, the Dow fell 4.65 percent, greater than the day following Pearl Harbor. But the market reaction to the growing conflict was contained, and stocks never fell more than 12 percent below their prewar level.

The War in Vietnam was the longest and least popular of all US wars. The starting point for US involvement in the conflict can be placed on August 2, 1965, when two American destroyers were reportedly attacked in the Gulf of Tonkin.

One and one-half years after the Gulf of Tonkin incident, the Dow reached an all-time high of 995, more than 18 percent above its prewar level. But it fell nearly 30 percent in the following months after the Fed tightened credit to curb inflation. By the time American troop strength reached its peak early in 1968, the market had recovered. Two years later, the market fell again when Nixon sent troops into Cambodia, and soaring interest rates coupled with a looming recession sent the market down nearly 25 percent from its prewar point.

The Peace Pact between the North Vietnamese and the Americans was signed in Paris on January 27, 1973. But the gains made by investors over the eight years of war were quite small, as the market was held back by rising inflation, interest rates, and other problems not directly related to the Vietnamese conflict.

If the war in Vietnam was the longest American war, the war against Iraq in the Gulf was the shortest. It began on August 2, 1990, when Iraq invaded Kuwait, sending oil prices skyward and sparking a US military buildup in Saudi Arabia. The rise in oil prices combined with an already slowing US economy to drive the United States deeper into a recession. The stock market fell precipitously and by October 11, the Dow slumped over 18 percent from its prewar levels.

US offensive action began on January 17, 1991. It was the first major war fought in a world where markets for oil, gold, and US government bonds were traded around the clock in Tokyo, Singapore, and London. The markets judged the victors in a matter of hours. Bonds sold off in Tokyo for a few minutes following the news of the US bombing of Baghdad, but the stunning reports of the Allied successes sent bonds and Japanese stocks straight upward in the next few minutes. Oil prices, which were being traded in the Far East, collapsed, as Brent crude fell from $29 a barrel before hostilities to $20 on the next day.

On the following day, stock prices soared around the world. The Dow jumped 115 points, and there were large gains throughout Europe and Asia. By the time the United States deployed ground troops to invade Kuwait, the market had known for two months that victory was at hand. The war ended on February 28, and by the first week in March the Dow was more than 18 percent higher than when it started.

SUMMARY

When reviewing the causes of major market movements, it is sobering that less than one quarter can be associated with a news event of major political or economic import. Politics, war, and peace are major backdrops of market action, but few of the big moves occur for these reasons. Surprisingly, volatility during wartime has been less than during peacetime.

All this confirms the unpredictability of the market and difficulty in outguessing the major trends. Those who sold in panic at the outbreak of World War I missed out on the greatest year in the market. The victories in World War II did little to revive the market since investors were still fearful of a depression that might follow the end of the war. The postwar boom had to await the 1950s and 1960s, when investors became convinced that inflation, and not depression, was the theme of the future.

CHAPTER 13

ECONOMIC DATA AND FINANCIAL MARKETS

The thing that most affects the stock market is everything.

James Palysted Wood, 1966.

It's 8:28 Friday morning in New York, 1:28 in the afternoon in London, and 9:28 Friday evening in Tokyo—just two minutes before the most important announcement each month—the US employment statistics. Traders around the world anxiously gather around their terminals, eyes riveted on the scrolling news that displays thousands of headlines every day.

All week bond trading has been slow, but in the last hour it has dwindled to a trickle. Bond traders have already committed large positions in anticipation of the upcoming news. Foreign exchange trading has virtually dried up as traders await the announcement. Since the US stock markets will not open for one hour, many stock traders in both the equity and futures markets had closed their positions Thursday evening, knowing there would be little opportunity to unwind their trades ahead of the 8:30 announcement.

The seconds tick down. At 8:30 AM sharp, the words come across the screen:

PAYROLL DOWN 250,000, UNEMPLOYMENT AT 7.5%.

The employment news is much worse than expected.

Immediately the market moves. Bonds surge and the dollar collapses on the currency markets. Stock traders assess the information and ready their trading. There is a good bid developing in the futures market from the stock index traders as they follow bonds upwards. Despite the bad news, stocks might actually open higher. The action traders had awaited has lived up to their expectations.

The preceding description is typical of the most important day each month for bond traders: the monthly employment data released by the Bureau of Labor Statistics. It is always released on Friday (unless Friday is an exchange holiday), and almost always on the first Friday of the month. It contains the most comprehensive and timely statistics on what's happening in the economy. The numbers will also provide the best clue as to the future direction of the Federal Reserve's monetary policy.

News moves markets. Some news is unpredictable, like war, political assassinations, and the outcome of elections. But most news, especially data about the economy, comes at preannounced times that have been scheduled a year in advance. There are over 300 *scheduled* releases of economic data each year—mostly by government agencies, but increasingly by private firms. Virtually all the announcements deal with economic growth and inflation, and all have the potential to move the market significantly.

Economic data not only frame the way traders view the economy but also impact traders' expectations of how the Federal Reserve will implement its monetary policy. Stronger economic growth increases the probability the Fed will tighten monetary policy—or stop easing. Likewise, higher inflation increases the likelihood that the Fed will apply the monetary brakes. Economic releases influence the expectations of traders about the future course of interest rates, the economy, and ultimately stock prices.

PRINCIPLES OF MARKET REACTION

Markets respond to the *difference* between what the participants in the financial markets expect to be announced and what is announced. Whether the news is, by itself, good or bad, is of no importance. If the market expects that the employment release will report that 200,000 jobs were lost last month and only 100,000 jobs are lost, this will be considered "good economic news" by the financial markets. Even though this means that the economy is still contracting, it is better than expected, and will have about the same effect on financial markets as a report of a gain of 200,000 jobs when the market expected only 100,000 jobs to be created.

The reason why markets only react to data which differ from expectations is that the prices of securities in actively traded markets already include *expected* information. If a stock is expected to report bad earnings, then the stock has already been priced by the market to reflect this gloomy information. If the earnings report is not as bad as anticipated, the price will rise on the announcement. The same principle applies to the reaction of bonds, stocks, and foreign exchange to economic data.

To understand why the market moves the way is does, one must identify the *market expectation* for the data released. The market expectation, often referred to as the *consensus* estimate, is gathered by news and research organizations. They poll economists, professional forecasters, traders, and other market participants for their estimate of an upcoming government or private release. The results of their survey are sent to the financial press and widely reported in many major newspapers.[1]

INFORMATION CONTENT ON DATA RELEASES

The economic data are analyzed for their implications for future economic growth, inflation, and Federal Reserve policy. The following principle summarizes the reaction of the bond markets to the release of data relating to economic growth:

> *Stronger-than-expected economic growth increases both long- and short-term interest rates. Weaker-than-expected economic growth causes interest rates to fall.*

Faster economic growth raises interest rates for several reasons. First, a stronger economy increases private loan demands. Consumers feel more confident about borrowing and are more willing to borrow against future income. Faster economic growth also motivates firms to expand production to meet increased consumer demand. As a result, both firms and consumers in-

---

[1] Usually both the median and range of the estimates are reported. The consensus estimate does vary a bit from service to service, but usually the estimates are quite close.

crease their demand for credit. The increase in credit demand pushes interest rates higher in the money market.

A second reason why interest rates rise with a stronger-than-expected economic report is that traders believe it will be more likely that the Federal Reserve will tighten credit, or less likely that they will loosen credit, in response to the data being released. We analyzed in Chapter 9 how the Federal Reserve controls the short-term interest rate through the federal funds rate. If the economy is expanding rapidly, the Fed can use its open market operations to drain reserves from the banking system to prevent the economy from eventually overheating. Alternatively, if the economy has been weak, a strong economic report makes it less likely that the Fed will increase reserves and lower the federal funds rate. Either case—an increase in the probability of a Fed tightening or the reduction in the probability of a Fed easing—will cause traders to adjust their expectations of future interest rates upwards.

Some observers believe that faster economic growth raises interest rates because such growth increases future inflation. But this is not usually the case. Only in the latter stages of an economic expansion, when unemployment is very low and factories are working near capacity, might inflationary pressures appear. Growth associated with increases in productivity, which often occurs in the early and middle stages of a business cycle, is rarely inflationary.

If economic data show a weakening economy, interest rates will fall. In that case, both long- and short-term rates fall because of lower loan demand or the increased expectation of a Fed easing.

Let us examine how employment news affects the market. On July 2, 1992 (a Thursday, since Friday was an exchange holiday), the Bureau of Labor Statistics released the June employment report. The weakness of the report shocked the market. Wall Street had expected that payroll employment would increase at least 100,000 from the previous month and that the unemployment rate would remain stable or decrease slightly from the 7.5 percent level reached in May. Instead, the payroll dropped by 117,000 and the unemployment rate jumped to a six-year high of 7.8 percent.

Figure 13–1 depicts the impact of this announcement on the financial markets. The 30-year government bond rose from just

FIGURE 13–1
Weak Employment Report and Fed Ease (July 2, 1992)

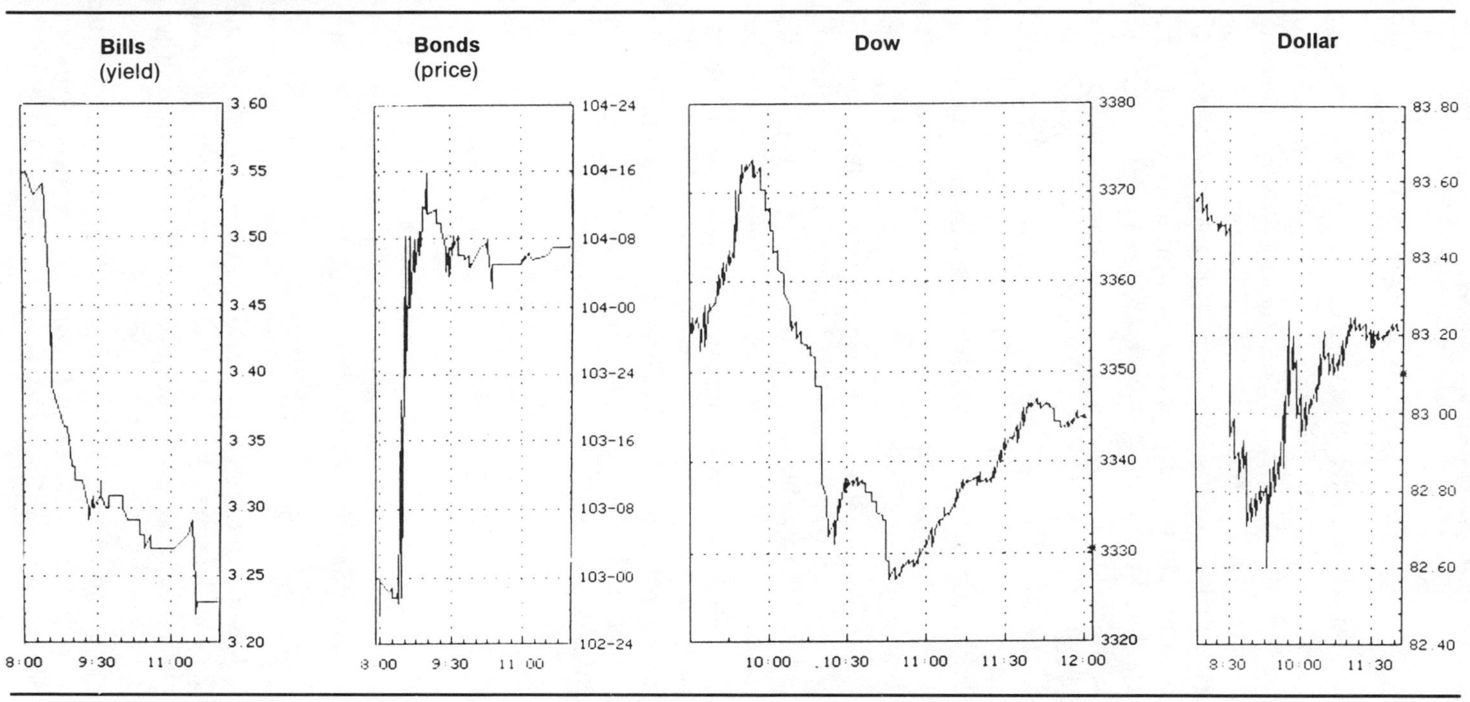

Source: Bloomberg LP.

under 103 to over 104 in a matter of seconds, and the yield fell by over 10 basis points. Yields on Treasury bills also plummeted. The 90-day bill, which had been selling at a 3.55 percent discount yield, immediately fell below 3.30 percent.

Given the surprise weakness of the employment report and the accumulation of disappointing statistics over the past week, the market had already considered a discount rate cut, and a cut in the fed funds rate, a foregone conclusion. And the traders were right. At 9:17, 47 minutes after the employment announcement, the Fed lowered the discount rate to 3 percent from 3.5 percent, the lowest level since July 1963. One can see from Figure 13–1 that the market actually moved little at the time the discount rate was cut, since such a policy action was already discounted in prices.

However, one policy question was still unresolved. The market did not know whether the Fed would cut the all-important federal funds rate by 0.25 or 0.5 percent. Traders did not get that answer until 11:30, when the Federal Reserve intervened at its usual time in the market and provided enough reserves to lower the fed funds rate by 50 basis points to 3.25 percent. You can see the reaction of the yield on the 90-day Treasury bill, which at 11:30 immediately fell further on the news of the Fed intervention.

ECONOMIC GROWTH AND STOCK PRICES

Surprisingly, the effect of a weak economic report on the stock market is not necessarily negative. There are two implications of a weak report, and each tugs the stock market in the opposite direction. Recall that the value of any stock is the present discounted value of future dividends. Certainly a weak economic report lowers the expected value of these future dividends, as earnings will probably fall short of previous expectations. But since interest rates also decline, the rate at which these lower earnings are discounted also declines.

If the interest rate effect is particularly pronounced, the stock market can rise even though the economic news is weak. This rise often confuses the general public (and the financial press) and sometimes is said to confirm the irrationality of the market. But a rising stock market in the face of a poor economic outlook is perfectly possible if interest rates drop.

Often the opposing forces of lower interest rates and lower earnings prospects will fight each other to a standstill through the day. Sometimes (but certainly not always) the impact of interest rate changes dominates stock trading right after the market opens, while the implications for corporate earnings impact the market later. This is what happened on July 2, as shown in Figure 13–1. The Dow Industrials rose nearly 20 points on lower interest rates in the early morning, only to fall later in the day, closing with a 24-point loss.

In the short run, many stock traders, especially those trading in the stock index futures market, which we shall discuss in the next chapter, look at the movements in the bond market to guide their trading. This is particularly true of investors who actively apportion their portfolio between stocks and bonds on the basis of interest rates and expected returns. When bonds rise after a weak economic report, these investors are ready to buy stocks. However, later in the day, as more stock investors recognize that the weak employment report means lower future earnings, they are apt to be more bearish about equity prospects. The stock market often gyrates wildly through such a day as investors digest the implications of the data for stock earnings and future discount rates.

But this pattern—an immediate short-run reaction to interest rates and a longer-run reaction to earnings prospects—is by no means reliable. (If it were, I would be playing it every month and be too busy to write this book!) The stock market opens in New York 60 minutes after the employment announcement (and many other important 8:30 releases), so many traders have already had some time to ponder both the earnings and interest rate implications of the news. Intra-day movements can never be predicted with certainty.

One can also see in Figure 13–1 that the dollar fell dramatically on the employment news. Lower dollar interest rates virtually guarantee a fall in the price of the dollar as investors seek higher returns elsewhere. The lower dollar enhances dollar returns on foreign markets, so Americans holding international stocks gain more on the announcement than investors holding only domestic issues.

THE EMPLOYMENT REPORT

The employment report is the key release of each month. Of the greatest importance to traders is the change in the nonfarm payroll (nonfarm because the number of farm workers is very volatile and not associated with cyclical economic trends). The payroll survey, sometimes called the "establishment survey," collects payroll data from over 300,000 business establishments, nearly one third of the total in the country. It is this survey that most forecasters use to judge the future course of the economy.

However, the unemployment rate, which is announced along with the nonfarm payroll, usually gets the top billing in the evening news and the financial press. The unemployment rate is determined from an entirely different survey than the payroll data. The unemployment rate is calculated from a "household survey," which contacts about 60,000 households and asks, among other questions, whether anyone in the household has "actively" sought work over the past four weeks. Those who answer in the affirmative are classified as unemployed. The unemployed, divided by the total labor force, yields the unemployment rate. The labor force in the United States, defined as those employed plus unemployed, comprises about two thirds of the adult population, a ratio which has risen steadily as more women successfully sought work in the 1980s.

Because the payroll and household data are based on totally different surveys, it is not unusual for payroll employment to go up at the same time that the unemployment rate rises and vice versa. This is because the payroll survey counts jobs, but the household survey counts people, so that workers with two jobs are counted once in the household survey but twice in the payroll survey.[2] Furthermore, increases in the number of workers seek-

[2] Early in 1994 the household survey was improved to include this question. Traders still pay far more attention to the payroll survey.

ing jobs—and this can arise from an increase in those seeking work and not necessarily from those who were laid off—will increase the unemployment rate. In fact, it is well known that the unemployment rate often rises in the early states of an economic recovery due to the influx of job-seekers into an improved labor market.

For these reasons, economists and forecasters have long dismissed the unemployment rate as unimportant in forecasting the business cycle. But this does not diminish the *political* importance of the unemployment rate. It is an easily understood number which represents the fraction of the workforce looking for, but not finding, work. The public looks more to this rate than to any other to judge the health of the economy. As a result, politically motivated pressures can bear on Congress, as well as the Federal Reserve, whenever the unemployment rate rises.

CYCLE OF ANNOUNCEMENTS

The employment report is just one of several dozen economic announcements that come out every month. Table 13–1 displays a typical month and the usual release dates for the data. The number of asterisks represents the importance of the report to the financial market.

The employment statistics are the culmination of important data on economic growth that come out around the turn of the month. On the first business day of each month a survey by the National Association of Purchasing Managers, or the NAPM, is released. This survey, once ignored by financial markets, has become increasingly important at providing information to help forecast the all-important employment report.

The NAPM report surveys 250 purchasing agents of manufacturing companies and inquires as to whether orders, production, employment, etc. are rising or falling. A reading of 50 means that half the firms report rising activity and half report falling activity. A reading of 53 or 54 is the sign of a normally expanding economy. Sixty would represent a strong economy where three fifths of the firms are experiencing growth. A reading below 50

TABLE 13–1
Monthly Economic Calendar (Approximate Days of Data Release)

Monday	Tuesday	Wednesday	Thursday	Friday
1 10:00 NAPM**	**2** 8:30 Leading Economic Indicator* (2 months lag) 2:45 Johnson Redbook*	**3**	**4** 8:30 Jobless Claims** 4:30 Money Supply*	**5** 8:30 Employment Report****
8	**9** 2:45 Johnson Redbook*	**10**	**11** 8:30 Jobless Claims** 4:30 Money Supply*	**12** 8:30 Retail Sales** 8:30 Producer Prices****
15	**16** 8:30 Consumer Prices**** 2:45 Johnson Redbook*	**17** 8:30 Housing Starts*** 9:15 Industrial Production*	**18** 8:30 Merchandise Trade* 8:30 Jobless Claims** 4:30 Money Supply*	**19** 10:00 Philadelphia Fed Rep* 10:00 Consumer Expect.** (Univ. of Mich., Prelim.)
22	**23** 8:30 Durable Goods Orders** 2:45 Johnson Redbook*	**24**	**25** 8:30 Jobless Claims** 4:30 Money Supply*	**26** 8:30 Gross Dom. Prod.***†
29	**30** 10:00 Consumer Expect. (Conference Board)*** 2:45 Johnson Redbook*	**31** 10:00 Chicago Purchasing Managers**		

†First report of quarter (January, April, July, and October) is of moderate importance. Other months' GDP reports of minor importance.
Stars rank importance to market (**** = most important).

represents a contracting manufacturing sector, and a reading below 40 is almost always a sign of recession.

Because of the huge importance of the monthly employment report, there is much pressure on traders to obtain earlier data that might give some hint as to the state of the economy and thereby improve the estimate of the monthly payroll change. The NAPM survey is an important indicator to the employment report. Of particular importance in the NAPM survey is the employment category, for this is the first comprehensive picture of the labor market for the previous month and provides a clue as to what might be revealed in the all-important manufacturing category of the employment report.

But traders do have access to even earlier data: the Chicago Purchasing Managers report comes out on the last business day of the previous month, the day before the NAPM report. The Chicago area is well-diversified in manufacturing so that about two thirds of the time the Chicago index will move in the same direction as the national index.

And if one wants an even earlier reading on the economy, there are the consumer sentiment indicators: one from the University of Michigan and another from the Conference Board, a business trade association. These surveys query consumers about their current financial situation and their expectations of the future. The Conference Board survey, released on the last Tuesday of the month, is considered a good early indicator of consumer spending. The University of Michigan index was for many years not released until the month following the survey. But pressure for early data has persuaded the university to release a preliminary report to compete with that of the Conference Board. And in the last few years the American Broadcasting Corporation, in conjunction with *Money* magazine, has released a *weekly* reading of consumer sentiment.

Even private firms can improve on government statistics. Traders recently discovered that the Johnson *Redbook,* which has been published for over 30 years from sales data compiled by Edward Johnson, gives a better, and more up-to-date, look at retail sales than the official data released by the Commerce Department. Every Tuesday afternoon subscribers are faxed the latest retail sales information. Increasingly this survey impacts the bond market.

One should not be surprised to find private firms entering the business of producing economic data. The way the market jumps in response to economic statistics means that anyone who can get a better handle on the numbers will have a decided advantage in the market. And with the advent of global markets, very large trades can be put on without causing undue price movement. It would not be unusual for an institutional investor who bets heavily on the outcome of the employment report to reap hundreds of millions of dollars of profits if he or she is correct.

Inflation Reports

Although the employment report forms the capstone of the news about economic growth, the market knows that the Federal Reserve is also preoccupied with inflation. The Fed does not normally ease credit unless it is assured that inflationary pressures are under control. The central bank recognizes that it must be the guardian of the currency and cannot ignore inflation. Some of the earliest signals of these pressures arrive with the midmonth inflation statistics.

The first monthly inflation release is the producer price index, or the PPI, which formerly was called the wholesale price index. The PPI measures the prices received by producers at the first commercial sale, usually to retailers. Consumer goods prices represent about three quarters of the PPI while capital goods prices comprise the rest. About 15 percent of the PPI is energy-related.

The second monthly announcement, which follows the PPI by a day or so, is the all-important consumer price index, or CPI. In contrast to the producer price index, the CPI does not include capital goods prices, but covers the prices of services as well as goods. Services, which include rent, housing costs, transportation, and medical, now comprise over half the weight of the CPI.

The consumer price index is considered the benchmark measure of inflation. When price level comparisons are made, both on a historical and an international basis, the consumer price index is almost always the chosen index. The CPI is also the price index to which so many private and public contracts, as well as Social Security, are linked.

The financial market probably gives a bit more weight to the consumer price index than to producer prices because of the CPI's widespread use and political importance. The CPI does have the advantage of including the prices of consumer services, which the PPI does not, but many economists regard the producer price index as more sensitive to early price trends. This is true because increased prices often show up at the wholesale level before they are passed on to the consumer. Furthermore, at the same time the PPI is announced, an index for the prices of intermediate and crude goods, both of which track inflation at earlier stages of production, are released.

Core Inflation

Of interest to investors are not only the month-to-month changes of the PPI and CPI but also the changes excluding the volatile food and energy sectors. Since weather has such undue influence on food prices, a rise or fall in the price of food over a month does not have much meaning for the overall inflationary trend. Similarly, oil and natural gas prices fluctuate due to weather conditions and supply disruptions which are not usually repeated in coming months. Hence the Bureau of Labor Statistics, which gathers inflation data, also releases what is called the *core* index, a price index which excludes food and energy.

Most traders regard changes in the core rate of inflation as more important than changes in the overall index, since core inflation is apt to be persistent and impact long-term inflation trends. Forecasters are usually able to predict the core rate of inflation better than the overall rate, which is influenced by the volatile food and energy sectors. A 0.3 percent error in the consensus forecast for the month-over-month rate of inflation may not be that serious. But such an error would be considered quite large for the core rate of inflation, and would have significant impact on the financial markets.

IMPACT ON FINANCIAL MARKETS

The following summarizes the impact of inflation on the financial markets:

> *A lower-than-expected inflation report lowers interest rates and boosts stock prices. Inflation worse than expected raises interest rates and depresses stock prices.*

That inflation is bad for bonds should come as no surprise. Bonds are fixed-income investments whose cash flows are never adjusted for inflation. Bondholders demand higher interest rates in response to worsening news of inflation, not only to protect their purchasing power but because of the increased concern that the Fed will tighten credit.

But worse-than-expected inflation is also bad for the stock market. As we noted in Chapter 6, stocks have proved to be poor hedges against inflation in the short run. Stock investors fear that worsening inflation increases the chance that the Federal Reserve will tighten credit, reducing corporate profits.

These observations are not at odds with our insistence that stocks are excellent long-run hedges against inflation. In the long run, inflation is primarily a monetary phenomenon, caused by an increase in the money supply at a rate in excess of the growth rate of the economy. Since stocks represent claims on real assets, they will ultimately reflect the prices of the goods produced by these assets. But in the short run, monetary factors play a subsidiary role in the inflationary process. Potential tightening by the Fed, higher effective real tax rates, and increased costs of inputs are the short-run concerns that occupy investors when inflation increases.

FED POLICY

Monetary policy is of primary importance to the financial markets. There are few fundamental or technical analyses that do not rely heavily on monetary policy indicators, such as the fed funds rate, the discount rate, and even money supplies in their forecast of future stock returns.

Martin Zweig, one of the foremost money managers, shares the opinion of others when he states:

> In the stock market, as with horse racing, money makes the mare go. Monetary conditions exert an enormous influence on stock prices. Indeed, the monetary climate—primarily the trend in interest rates and Federal Reserve policy—is the dominant factor in determining the stock market's major direction[3]

Easing monetary policy, by definition, involves lowering short-term interest rates. This is almost always extremely positive for stock prices. Stocks thrive on liquidity provided by the central bank. Not only does Fed easing lower the rate at which stocks discount future cash flows, but it also provides a monetary stimulus to future earnings. Only if Fed easing is so excessive that the market fears strong inflationary consequences might stocks react badly. But an investor should much rather be in stocks than bonds under these circumstances, as fixed-income assets are clearly hurt the most by unanticipated inflation.

SUMMARY

The reaction of financial markets to economic data is not random, but based on good economic reasoning. Strong economic growth invariably raises interest rates, but has an ambiguous effect on stock prices. Higher inflation is bad for both the stock and bond markets. And Fed easing is very positive for stocks; historically it has sparked some of the strongest rallies the market has experienced. Central bank easing associated with leaving the gold standard or a fixed exchange-rate regime are particularly powerful stimulants for the market.

Although the employment data are usually the most important monthly report for the market, the focus of traders constantly shifts. In the 1970s, the inflation announcements were center stage, but after Volcker shifted the focus to monetary

---

[3] Martin Zweig, *Martin Zweig's Winning on Wall Street* (New York: Warner Books, 1986), p. 43.

policy, the Thursday afternoon money supply announcements captured the attention of traders. Later trade statistics and the dollar were given top billing. The 1990–91 recession and subsequent slow economic recovery put the employment data back on top with traders. No single announcement always will remain most important.

This chapter focuses on the very-short-run reaction of financial markets to economic data. Many might claim that it would be best for investors to ignore such information since the data are often confusing and revised at a later date in any case. Such advice would be appropriate if you plan to stay invested for the long-run, a strategy we have advocated. But traders trying to beat the market put these bits of information together to form a picture of where the economy and market are heading. It is fascinating watching from the sidelines, but the average investor will do much better sticking to a long-run strategy for investing.

PART 4

STOCK FLUCTUATIONS IN THE SHORT RUN

CHAPTER 14

STOCK INDEX FUTURES AND OPTIONS

When I was a kid—a runner for Merrill Lynch at 25 dollars a week, I'd heard an old timer say, "The greatest thing to trade would be stock futures—but you can't do that, it's gambling."

Leo Melamed[1]

STOCK INDEX FUTURES

April 13, 1992, started as a perfectly ordinary day on the exchanges. But at about 11:45 in the morning, the two big Chicago exchanges, the Board of Trade and the Mercantile Exchange, were closed when a massive leak caused Chicago River water to course through the tunnels under the financial district, triggering extensive power outages. Figure 14–1 shows the intraday movement of the Dow Industrials and the S&P futures. As soon as Chicago futures trading was halted, the movements of stocks were markedly damped.

It almost looks like the New York Stock Exchange went "brain dead" when there was no lead from Chicago. Volume in New York dropped by more than 25 percent on the day the Chicago futures market was closed and some dealers claimed that if the futures exchanges remained inoperative, this would cause liquidity problems and difficulty in executing some trades

[1] Leo Melamed is founder of the International Money Market, the world's most successful stock index futures market. Quoted in Martin Mayer, *Markets* (New York: W. W. Norton, 1988), p. 111.

FIGURE 14–1
When the Stock Index Futures Closed Down (April 13, 1992)
(S&P 500 June Futures and Dow Jones Industrial Average)

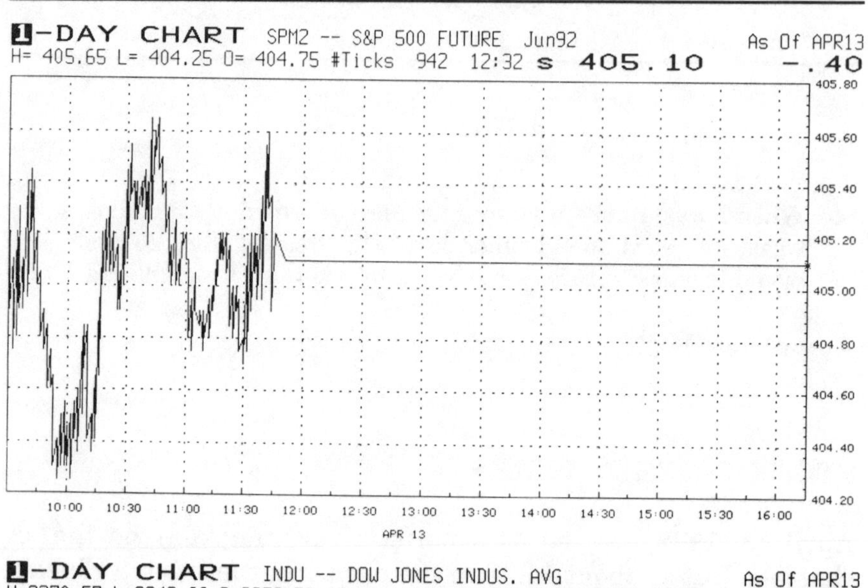

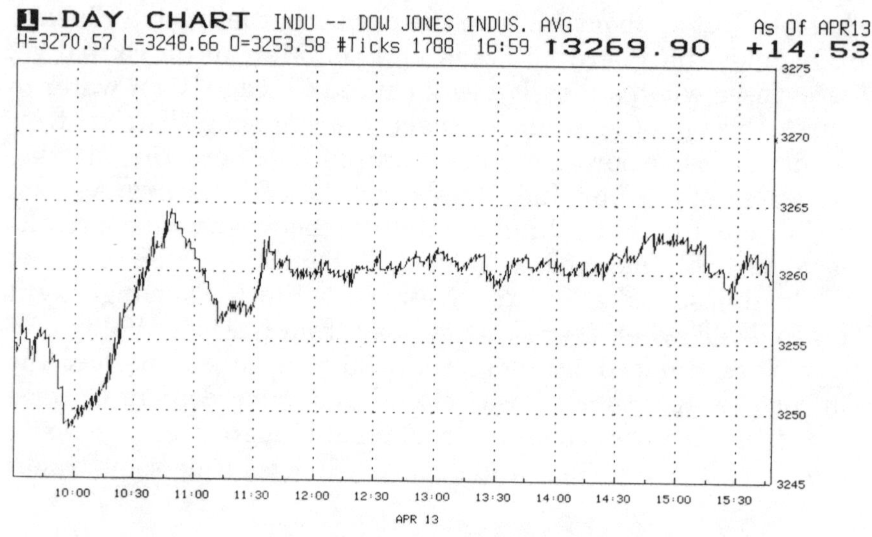

Source: Bloomberg LP.

in New York.[2] But Michael Metz, a market strategist at Oppenheimer & Co., declared of April 13, "It's been absolutely delightful; it seems so sedate. It reminds me of the halcyon days on Wall Street before the program traders took hold."[3]

But who are these program traders and what do they do? If you step onto the floor of the New York Stock Exchange, you are confronted with a constant din of people scurrying about delivering orders and making deals. But every so often the background noise is punctuated by the rat-ta-ta of dozens of automated machines printing hundreds of buy or sell tickets. These orders are almost always from stock index future arbitrageurs, a type of program trader who relies on differences between the price of stock index futures set in Chicago and the price of stocks set in New York. The tickets signal that the futures market is moving quickly in Chicago and consequently stocks are ready to move in New York. It is an eerie warning, something akin to the buzz of locusts in biblical times portending decimated crops and famine. And famine it might be, for over the past decade some of the most vicious declines in stock prices have been preceded by computers tapping out orders emanating from the futures markets.

It surprises many that, in the short run, the level of the stock market is not determined on Wall Street, but on the Chicago Mercantile Exchange located on Wacker Drive in Chicago. Specialists on the New York Stock Exchange, those dealers assigned to make and supervise markets in specific stocks, keep their eyes glued on the futures markets to find out where stocks are heading. These dealers have learned from experience: Don't stand in the way of index futures. If you do, you may get caught in an avalanche of trading such as the one that buried several specialists on October 19, 1987, that fateful day when the Dow crashed 508 points.

---

[2] "Robert Steiner, "Industrials Gain 14.53 in Trading Muted by Futures Halt in Chicago," *The Wall Street Journal,* April 14, 1992, p. C2.

[3] "Flood in Chicago Waters Down Trading on Wall Street," *The Wall Street Journal,* April 14, 1992, page C1.

IMPACT OF INDEX FUTURES

Most investors regard index futures and options as esoteric securities that have little to do with the market in which stocks are bought or sold. Many do very well trading stocks without any knowledge of these new instruments. Yet no one can comprehend the short-run market movements without an understanding of stock index futures.

Pick up a newspaper and read of the day's trading in stocks. Chances are good that you will see references to program trading, especially if the market was volatile. Program trading is the way in which large movements which originate in the Chicago futures pit are transmitted to the New York markets.

The following descriptions of volatile markets appeared in *The New York Times* on August 22, 1992:

> Stock prices plunged yesterday as a falling dollar and worries that an economic recovery would be stifled by higher interest rates set off a wave of computer-driven sell programs.
>
> The largest of seven computerized sell programs tracked yesterday by Philip H. Smyth [an analyst at Birinyi Associates, a research firm which tracks index arbitrage] began at 11:45 and lasted about 25 minutes, forcing the Dow down 30 points. It involved about 400 of the 500 stocks in the Standard & Poor's index as well as 100 smaller stocks in the Nasdaq composite index.[4]

Figure 14–2 shows the behavior of the stock and futures market on that day. Virtually all large stock movements are dominated by events which are first felt in the stock index futures markets.

BASICS OF FUTURES MARKETS

The stock index futures market is the greatest single innovation to come to stock trading since the invention of the ticker tape. Index futures now trade in virtually every major stock market

---

[4] Seth Faison, "Economic Fears Cut 50.79 from Dow," *The New York Times,* August 22, 1992, p. 36.

in the world and have become the instrument of choice for global investors who wish to change their international stock allocations.

Futures trading goes back hundreds of years. The term *futures* was derived from the promise to buy or deliver a commodity at some future date at some specified price. Futures trading first flourished in agricultural crops, where farmers wanted to have a guaranteed price for the crops they would not harvest until later. Markets developed where buyers and sellers who desired to avoid uncertainty could come to an agreement on the price for future delivery. The commitments to honor these agreements, called *futures contracts,* were freely transferable and markets developed where they were actively traded.

Stock index futures were launched in February 1982 by the Kansas City Board of Trade using the Value Line Index of about 1,700 stocks. But two months later in Chicago, at the Chicago Mercantile Exchange, the world's most successful stock index future based on the S&P 500 Index was introduced. Only 2 years after its introduction, the value of the contracts traded on this index future surpassed the dollar volume on the New York Stock exchange for all stocks. Today the S&P 500 futures trade over 70,000 contacts a day, worth over $17 billion. Although there are other stock index futures, the S&P 500 Index dominates, comprising well over 90 percent of the value of such trading.

All stock index futures are constructed similarly. The S&P index future is a promise to deliver (in the case of the seller) or receive (in the case of the buyer) a fixed multiple of the value of the S&P 500 Index at some date in the future, called a *settlement date.* The multiple for the S&P Index future is 500 (a coincidence unrelated to the number of stocks in the index), so that if the S&P 500 Index is 400, the value of one contract is $200,000.

There are four evenly spaced settlement dates each year. They fall on the third Friday of March, June, September, and December. Each settlement date corresponds to a contract. If you buy a futures contract, you are entitled to receive (if positive) or obligated to pay (if negative) 500 times the *difference* between the value of the S&P 500 Index on the settlement date and the price at which you purchased the contract.

For example, if you buy one September S&P futures contract at 400 and on that third Friday of September the S&P 500 Index is at 402, then you have made 2 points, which translates into $1,000 profit ($500 × 2 points). Of course, if the index falls to 398 on the settlement date, you would lose $1,000. For every point that the S&P 500 Index goes up or down, you make or lose $500 per contract.

On the other hand, the returns to the *seller* of an S&P 500 futures contract are the mirror image of the returns to the buyer. The seller makes money when the index falls. In our example above, the seller of the S&P 500 futures contract at 400 will lose $1,000 if the index at settlement date rises to 402, while he would make a like amount if the index fell to 398.

One source of the popularity of stock index futures is a unique settlement procedure. With standard futures contracts you are obligated at settlement to receive (if purchased) or deliver (if sold) a specified quantity of the good for which you have contracted. Many apocryphal stories abound about how traders, forgetting to close out their contract, find bushels of wheat, corn, or frozen pork bellies dumped on their lawn on settlement day.

If commodity delivery rules applied to the S&P 500 Index futures contract, delivery would require a specified number of shares for each of the 500 firms in the index. Surely this would be extraordinarily cumbersome and costly. To avoid this problem, the designers of the stock index futures contract specified that settlement be made in "cash," computed simply by taking the difference between the contract price at the time of the trade and the value of the index on the settlement date. No delivery of stock takes place. If a trader failed to close his contract before settlement, his account would just be debited or credited on settlement date.

The creation of cash-settled futures contracts was no easy matter. In most states, particularly Illinois where the large futures exchanges are located, settling a futures contract in cash was considered a wager—and wagering, except in some special circumstances, was illegal. However, in 1974, the Commodity Futures Trading Commission, a federal agency, was established by Congress to regulate all futures trading. And since there was no federal prohibition against wagering, the state laws were superseded.

INDEX ARBITRAGE

The prices of commodities (or financial assets) in the futures market do not stand apart from the prices of the underlying commodity. If the value of a futures contract rises sufficiently above the price of the commodity that can be purchased for immediate delivery in the open market (often called the *cash* or *spot* market), someone can buy the commodity, store it, and then deliver it at a profit against the higher-priced futures contract on the settlement date. If the price of a future contract falls too far below its current spot price, owners of the commodity can sell it today, buy the futures contract, and take delivery of the commodity later at a lower price—in essence, earning a return on goods that would be in storage anyway.

Such a process of buying and selling commodities against their futures contracts is one type of *arbitrage*. Arbitrage involves traders who take advantage of temporary discrepancies in the prices of identical or nearly identical goods or assets. Those who reap profits from such trades are called *arbitrageurs*.

Arbitrage is very active in the stock index futures markets. If the price of the futures contracts sufficiently exceeds that of the underlying S&P 500 Index, then it pays for arbitrageurs to buy the underlying stocks and sell the futures contract. If the futures price falls sufficiently below that of the index, arbitrageurs will sell the underlying stocks and buy the futures. Since on the settlement date, the futures price must equal the underlying index by the terms of the contract, the difference between the futures price and the index—called a *premium* if it is positive and a *discount* if it is negative—is an opportunity for profit. Investors who buy and sell futures contracts against the underlying stock index are called *index arbitrageurs*.

In recent years, index arbitrage has become a finely tuned art. The price of stock index futures usually stay within very narrow bands of the index value based on the price of the underlying shares. When the buying or selling of stock index futures drives the futures price outside this band, arbitrageurs step in and hundreds of orders to buy or sell are immediately transmitted to the exchanges which trade the underlying stocks in the index. These simultaneously placed orders to buy stock are called *buy programs* and to sell stock *sell programs*. When the market commentators refer to sell programs hitting the market, it means index arbitrageurs are selling stock in New York and buying futures which have fallen to a discount (or a small enough premium) in Chicago.

As with any arbitrage, speed is of the essence, since both ends of the transaction must be completed quickly in order to lock in a profit. Access to the stocks in the S&P 500 Index, which almost all trade on the New York Stock Exchange, is usually made through an automated order system called the DOT system, or Designated Order Turnaround. This is the system that punches out the buy and sell orders which can be heard on the Exchange floor whenever index arbitrage is occurring.

Let's take a look at the index and futures prices on August 21, 1992. As noted above, futures trading was a significant factor forcing stock prices down on that day. Figure 14–2 shows both the value of the index, the futures prices, and difference between the two from about 10:00 in the morning through 2:00 in the afternoon.

Index arbitrageurs do not engage in arbitrage whenever the index and futures price differs by small amounts. Because of transaction costs, there must be a sufficient spread between the index and the future prices before traders will undertake this arbitrage. Figure 14–2 displays the outer arbitrage limits under which index arbitrage occurs, but many engage in index arbitrage well before these limits are reached.

At around 11:45 AM the S&P futures price for September delivery began to break downward in Chicago as traders became pessimistic about the prospect for the market. As a result, the futures price fell to a significant discount to the S&P 500 Index. Index arbitrageurs found it profitable to buy the depressed index futures and sell the individual stocks comprising the index.

Look at the chart of the Dow Jones Industrial average in Figure 14–2. The character of the intraday movements in the

FIGURE 14–2
Spread between Futures and Index (August 21, 1992)
(- - - - S&P 500 Index)
(_____ September S&P 500 Futures)

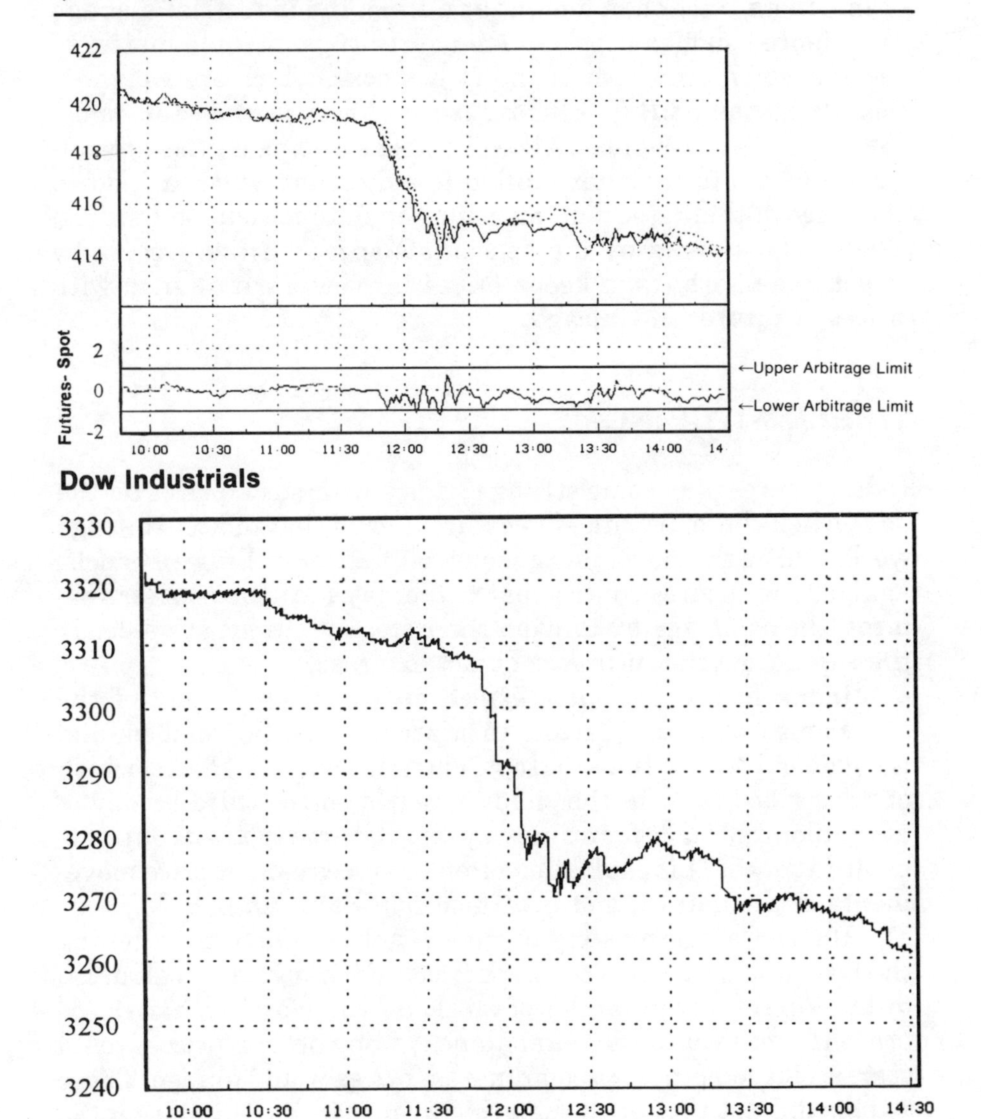

Source: Bloomberg LP.

stock average changed markedly when the sell programs kicked in. The sharp downward movements occurred when the arbitrageurs sold stock in response to the falling futures prices. Instead of moving a fraction of a point at a time, the industrial average experienced sudden drops of 5 to nearly 10 points in a matter of seconds when a number of the Dow stocks, which are weighted heavily in the S&P 500 Index, traded lower at the same time. The specialists assigned to the big stocks, seeing on their terminals that the futures have fallen to a discount, will mark down the price of their stocks in anticipation of imminent sell orders. These adjustments by the specialists speed up the process by which index arbitrage keeps prices in New York aligned with prices of futures in Chicago.

TRIPLE WITCHING

Index futures play some strange games with stock prices on the days when these instruments expire. Recall that index arbitrage works through the simultaneous buying or selling of stocks against the futures contracts. On the day that the contract expires, the arbitrageurs unwind their stock positions at precisely the same time the futures contract expires.

Index future contracts expire on the third Friday of the last month of each quarter, in March, June, September, and December. Index options and options on individuals stocks, which are described later in the chapter, settle on the third Friday of every month. Hence four times a year, all three types of contracts expire at once. This expiration often produces violent price movements in the market and is termed *triple witching*.

But there is no mystery in triple witching. On triple witching the specialists on the New York Stock Exchange are instructed to buy or sell large blocks of stock on the close, *whatever the price*. If there was a huge imbalance of buy orders, prices would soar, and if sell orders predominated, prices would plunge. These swings did not matter to the arbitrageur since the profit on the future position would offset losses on the stock position and vice versa.

In 1988, the New York Stock Exchange urged the Chicago Mercantile Exchange to change its procedures and end futures trading at the close of Thursday's trading and settle any imbalances of buy and sell orders at the Friday *open*. This change gave specialists more time to seek out balancing bids and offers and has greatly moderated the movements in stock prices at triple witching.

MARGIN AND LEVERAGE

One of the reasons for the popularity of futures contracts is that the cash needed to enter into the trade is a very small part of the value of the contract. Unlike stocks, there is no money that transfers between the buyer and seller when a futures contract is entered. A small amount of good faith collateral, or margin money, is required by the broker from both the buyer and seller to ensure that both parties will honor the contract at settlement. For the S&P 500 Index, the current margin is $12,000, or about 6 percent of the value of the contract. And this margin may be kept in Treasury bills with interest accruing to the investor. So trading a futures contract does not involve either a transfer of cash or a loss of interest income.

The *leverage*, or the amount of stock that you control relative to the amount of margin you have to put down with a futures contract, is enormous. For every dollar of cash (or Treasury bills) that you put in margin against an S&P futures contract, you command over $16 of stock. And this stock is represented by an extremely well-diversified portfolio of 500 firms. These low margins contrast with the 50 percent margin requirement for the purchase of individual stocks that has prevailed since 1974.

This ability to control $16 of stock with $1 of cash is reminiscent of the rampant speculation that existed in the 1920s before the establishment of minimum stock margin requirements. In the 1920s, individual stocks were frequently purchased with 10 percent margin. It was popular to speculate with such borrowed money, for as long as the market was rising, few lost money.

But, if the market drops precipitously, margin buyers can find that not only is their equity wiped out, but that they are indebted to the brokerage firm as well. The dangers of low margin buying are still debated in Congress and among market analysts.

ADVANTAGE TO TRADING FUTURES

Although low margins are a great advantage to those who trade in the futures markets, the greatest advantage is the substantial reduction in costs of trading stocks. Where else can you buy a diversified stock portfolio of 500 firms, such as that represented by the S&P 500 Index, for as little as a few dollars commission? Each S&P futures contract controls nearly a quarter million dollars of stock at current market averages, and the brokerage costs to an individual are as low as $25 to $30 per round-trip transaction, while professionals pay only a few dollars commission.

Of even greater importance to investors are the very low *bid-ask* spreads, or the differences between buying and selling prices of index futures. The bid-ask spread on an S&P 500 Index futures contract is often as low as .05 S&P points, which corresponds to $25 per contract, and rarely more than 0.10 points. Compared to paying the bid-ask spread on 500 stocks, the costs of trading in the futures market are minuscule.

The use of index futures greatly increases one's flexibility in managing one's portfolio. Suppose you have built up some good gains in individual stocks, but are now getting nervous about the market. You do not want to sell your individual stocks because it would involve a large tax liability. Also, you believe that these stocks will outperform the market during the decline or when stocks recover. So selling now and buying them back later would entail large transactions costs.

But with stock index futures, all this worry becomes unnecessary. You sell the number of futures contracts corresponding to the reduction in the risk that you seek, holding onto your individual stocks. If the market declines, you will profit on your futures position, offsetting the losses on your individual stocks. If the market instead goes up, contrary to your fears, you will lose on your stock index futures position, but your gains on your individual stock holdings should offset this loss. This sort of activity is called *hedging stock market risk*. Since you never sell your individual stocks, you realize no tax liability on your stock positions.[5]

Another advantage of index futures is the ability to profit from a decline in the market even if you do not own any stock. Selling index futures substitutes for *shorting* stock, or selling stock you do not own in anticipation that the price will fall and you can buy it back at a lower price. Using index futures to bet on a falling market is much more convenient than shorting a portfolio of stocks. First there are strict rules for shorting stock—specifically, stocks cannot be shorted if the price is declining. Secondly, margin requirements for shorting stock are very high. However, the margin for selling index futures is identical to that for buying a contract.

The advantages of index futures make them the ideal vehicle to increase or decrease exposure to the overall market. Suppose you are bullish on a particular stock (or a group of stocks or industry) but do not like the market. You can buy your stocks and then sell S&P 500 index futures of equal value so as to neutralize your overall exposure to the market. You will make money even if your stocks go down, as long as they outperform the market. Flexibility is what money managers value highly, and index futures market are the perfect way to respond to changing market conditions.

INDEX OPTIONS

Although index futures influence the stock market far more than options, it is the options market that has caught the fancy of many investors. And this is not surprising. The beauty of an

---

[5] Of course, your gain (or loss) on your stock index futures transactions will be taxed. In contrast to stocks, all profits and losses from futures transactions are marked to market for tax purposes as of December 31, whether realized or not.

option is embedded in its very name: you have the option, but not the obligation, to buy and sell at the terms specified.

There are two major types of options: puts and calls. *Calls* give you the right to buy a stock (or stocks) at a fixed price within a given period of time. *Puts* give you the right to sell. Puts and calls have existed on individuals stocks for decades, but organized trading did not exist until the establishment of the Chicago Board Options Exchange (CBOE) in 1974.

What attracts investors to puts and calls is that liability is strictly limited. If the market moves against the options buyer, he can forfeit the purchase price, forgoing the option to buy or sell. This contrasts sharply with a futures contract where, if the market goes against the buyer, losses can mount quickly. In a volatile market, futures can be extremely risky, and it may be impossible for an investor to exit the contract without substantial losses.

In 1978, the CBOE began trading options on the popular stock indexes, such as the S&P 500 Index.[6] Options trade in multiples of $100 per point of index value—cheaper than the $500 per point multiple on the popular S&P 500 Index futures.

An index call gives an investor the right to buy the stock index at a set price within a given period of time. Assume that the S&P 500 Index is now selling for 400. You believe that the market is going to rise. You can purchase a call option at 410 for six months for about 15 points, or $1,500. The purchase price of the option is called the *premium* and the price at which the option begins to pay off—in this case 410—is called the *strike price*. At any time within the next six months you can, if you choose, exercise your option and receive $100 for every point that the S&P 500 Index is above 410.

You need not exercise your option to make a profit. There is an extremely active market for options, and you can always sell them before expiration to other investors. In our example, the S&P 500 Index will have to rise above 425 for you to show a profit, since you paid $1500 for this option. But the beauty of

---

[6] In fact, the largest 100 stocks of the S&P 500 Index, called the S&P 100, comprise the most popularly traded index option. Options based on the S&P 500 Index became more widely used by institutional investors much later.

options is that if you guessed wrong, and the market falls, the most you can lose is the $1,500 premium you paid.

An index put works exactly the same way as a call but in this case the buyer makes money if the market goes down. Assume you buy a put on the S&P 500 Index at 390, paying a $1,500 premium. Every point the S&P 500 Index moves below 390 will recoup $100 of your initial premium. If the index falls to 375 by the expiration, you will have broken even. Every point below 375 gives you a profit on your option.

The price that you pay for an index option depends on many factors, including interest rates and dividend yields. But the most important factor is the volatility of the market itself. Clearly the more volatile the market, the more expensive it will be to buy either puts or calls. In a dull market, it is unlikely that the market will move sufficiently high (in the case of a call) or low (in the case of a put) to give the buyer of the option a profit. If this low volatility is expected to continue, the prices of options fall. In contrast, in volatile markets, the premiums on puts and calls are bid up as traders consider it more likely that the option will have value by the time of expiration.

The price of options depends on the judgments of traders as to the likelihood that the market will move sufficiently to make the rights to buy or sell stock at a fixed price valuable. But the theory of option pricing was given a big boost in the 1970s when two academic economists, Fischer Black and Myron Scholes developed the first mathematical formula to price options.

The Black-Scholes formula was an instant success. It gave traders a benchmark for valuation where previously only intuition was used. The Black-Scholes formula was programmed on traders' hand-held calculators and PCs around the world. Although there are conditions when the formula must be modified, empirical research has shown that the Black-Scholes formula closely approximates the price of traded options.

Options have opened a new market for investors. Now investors can trade the *volatility* of the market as well as the level. Those who expect that the market will be more volatile than normal will buy puts and calls while those who feel that the market will be less volatile than usual will tend to sell options. If an investor *buys volatility,* it means that he is buying either puts or calls (or both), expecting large market movements over the life of the option. If an investor *sells volatility* it means that he expects a relatively quiet market and expects the options to expire worthless or at prices far below what he paid for them. It is the fascinating truth that, even if the market is unchanged day after day, there are investors making large profits by selling options.

BUYING INDEX OPTIONS

Options are actually more basic instruments than futures. You can replicate any future with options, but the reverse is not true. Options offer the investor far more strategies than futures. Such strategies can range from the very speculative to the extremely conservative.

Suppose an investor wishes to protect himself against a decline in the market. He can buy an index put, which increases in value as the market declines. Of course you have to pay a premium for this option, very much like an insurance premium If the market does not decline, you have forfeited your premium. But if it does, the increase in the value of your put has cushioned (if not completely offset) the decline in your stock portfolio.

Another advantage of puts is that you can buy just the amount of protection that you like. If you only want to protect yourself against a total collapse in the market, then you can buy a put that is way *out of the money,* in other words a put whose strike price is far below that of the current level of the index. This option pays off only if the market declines precipitously. In addition, you can also buy puts with a strike price above the current market, so that the option retains some value even if the market does not decline. Of course these *in the money* puts are far more expensive.

There are many examples of fantastic gains in puts and calls that have been recorded. On December 20, 1991, when the Federal Reserve had just lowered the discount rate by a full point to the lowest level in 19 years, one could have purchased an S&P 500 call option with a strike price of 410 that was to expire on January 17, 1992, for 19 cents. Since the S&P 500

Index opened below 383 on that day, the market considered it highly unlikely that the S&P 500 Index could rise by 27 points (over 200 Dow points) in the next four weeks to make that option pay off.

Unlikely, maybe, but certainly not impossible. The market surged in response to the Fed easing. On the last day of the year, the S&P 500 Index rose above 418, and the 410 call traded as high as $12.50, a gain of 6,480 percent from 11 days earlier. Ignoring transactions costs, a $1,000 investment in the 410 call on December 20 would have produced nearly a $65,000 profit just 11 days later. It is profits such as these, not unlike those of lotteries or casino jackpots, that attract so many to the option markets.

But for every option that gains so spectacularly in value, there are thousands that expire worthless. Some market professionals estimate that 85 percent of those individual investors who play the options market lose. Not only does an option buyer have to be right about the direction of the market, but his timing must be nearly perfect and his selection of the strike price lucky. The option with a 420 strike price also surged after the Fed easing, but expired worthless as the S&P index closed just below 420 on the expiration date.

SELLING INDEX OPTIONS

Of course, for anyone who buys an option, someone must sell (or write) an option. The sellers, or writers, of call options, believe that the market will not rise sufficiently to make a profit for the option buyer. Sellers of call options make money most of the time they sell options, since the vast majority of options expire worthless. But should the market move sharply against the option sellers, their losses could be enormous.

For that reason, most sellers of call options are investors who already own stock. This strategy, called "buy and write," is popular with many investors since it is seen as a "win-win" proposition. If stocks go down, they collect a premium from the buyer of the call, and so are better off than if they had not written the option. If stocks do nothing, they also collect the premium on the call and are still better off.

If stocks go up, call writers still gain more on the stocks they own than they lose on the call they wrote, so they are still ahead. Of course, if stocks go up strongly, they miss a large part of the rally since they have promised to deliver stock at a fixed price. In that case call writers certainly would have been better off if they had not sold the call. But they still make more money than if they had not owned the stock at all.

LONG-TERM TRENDS AND STOCK INDEX FUTURES

The development of stock index futures and options in the 1980s was a major development for stock investors and money managers. Heavily capitalized firms, such as those represented in the Dow Industrial average, have always attracted money because of their outstanding liquidity. But with stock index futures, an investor could now buy the whole market as represented by the S&P 500 Index. The index future has higher liquidity than any highly capitalized blue chip stock. Therefore, when a money manager wants to take a position in the market, it is most easily done with stock index futures. It should not be surprising that the superior performance of the S&P 500 Index during the 1980s occurred during the period of the dramatic growth of the S&P Index futures.

International investors and those involved in global asset allocation desire index futures and options so that they can easily alter the fraction of assets they have invested in each country. For many of these money managers, the first portfolio decision is the percentage of funds invested in each country. Buying or selling stock index futures is clearly the way to alter that percentage. In fact, some money managers shun countries that do not trade index futures, since their absence deprives them of the liquidity that they so strongly desire.

Indexed instruments on the large capitalization stocks are now fully developed in the United States. The S&P 500 Index futures market increases the liquidity and hence the demand for the stocks in the S&P 500 Index. Some believe this may cause the S&P 500 stocks to become relatively overpriced relative to those not in the index, which might possibly lead to somewhat lower future returns for investors. For someone who values liquidity, the slight reduction in yield is well worth the price. But for an investor looking to the long run, liquidity is not as important. In this case, small stocks outside the S&P 500 Index may offer better long-term values in the market although they do entail greater transaction costs. Some of these issues will be discussed in Chapter 19 on investing in the market.

CHAPTER 15

MARKET VOLATILITY AND THE STOCK CRASH OF OCTOBER 1987

> The word *crisis* in Chinese is composed of two characters: the first, the symbol of danger . . . the second, of opportunity.

Compare the stock market of 1922–29 and 1980–87 shown in Figure 15–1. There is an uncanny similarity between the charts of these two periods. The editors of *The Wall Street Journal* felt the similarity so portentous that they printed a similar comparison in the edition that hit the streets on the morning of October 19, 1987. Little did they know that that day would witness the greatest drop in the history of the stock market, exceeding the great crash of October 29, 1929. In fact, the market of 1987 continued to act like that of 1929 for the remainder of the year. Many forecasters, citing the similarities between the two periods, were certain that disaster loomed and advised their clients to sell everything.

But the similarity between 1929 and 1987 ended at yearend. The stock market recovered from its October crash and by August of 1989 hit new high ground. In contrast, two years after the October 1929 crash, the Dow, in the throes of the greatest bear market in US history, had lost more than two thirds of its value and was about to lose two thirds more.

What was different? Why did the eerie similarities between these two events finally diverge so dramatically? The simple answer is that the central bank had the power to control the ultimate source of liquidity in the economy—the supply of money—and, in contrast to 1929, did not hesitate to use it. Heeding the painful lessons of the early 1930s, the Fed temporarily flooded the economy with money and pledged to stand by all bank deposits to insure that all aspects of the financial system would function properly.

FIGURE 15–1
1929 and 1987 Stock Crashes

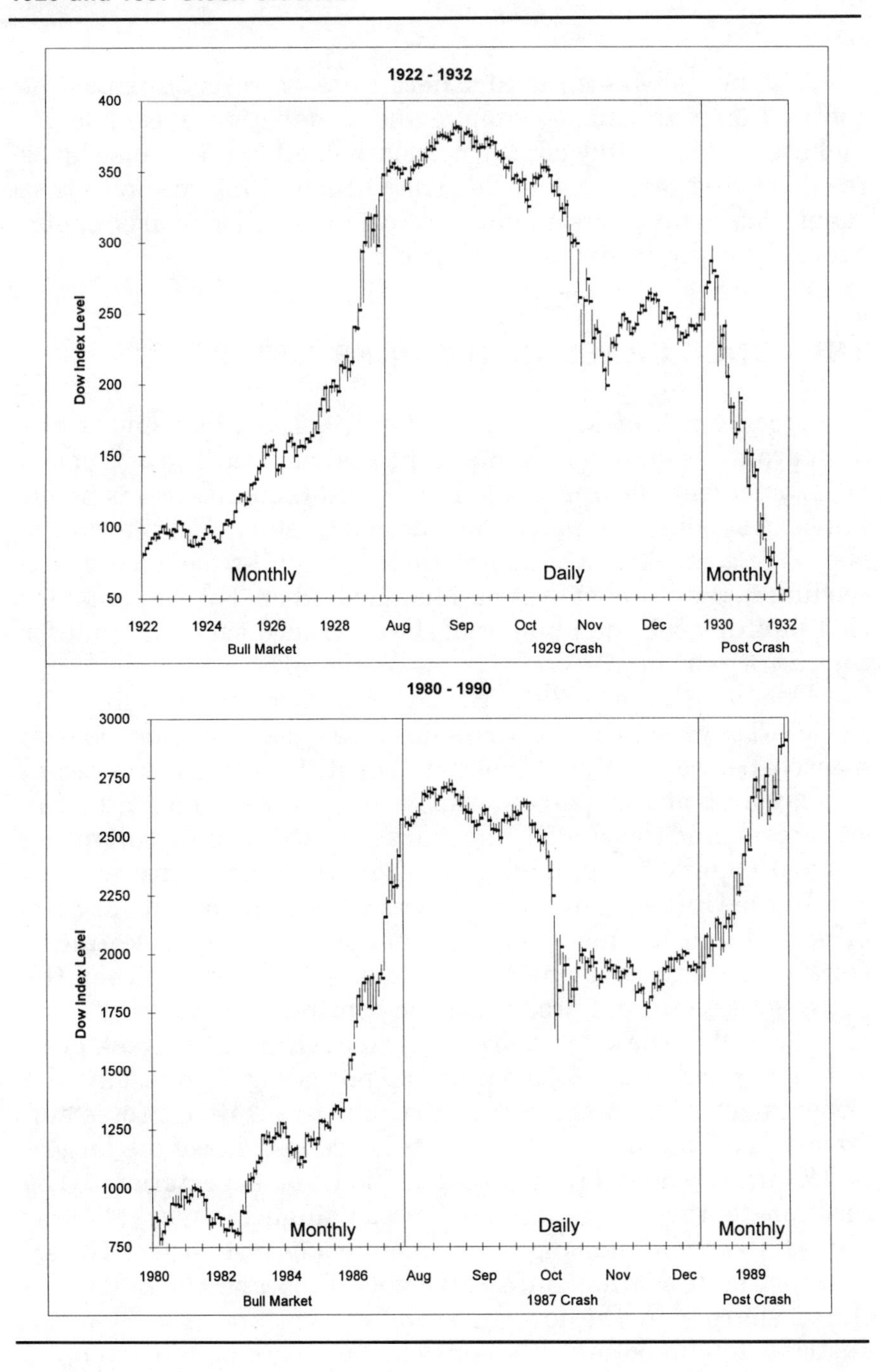

The public was assured. There were no runs on banks, no contraction of the money supply, and no deflation in commodity and asset values. Indeed, the economy itself barely paused as a result of this market debacle. The October 1987 market crash taught many investors an important lesson—crises can be opportunities for profit, not times to panic.

THE STOCK CRASH OF OCTOBER 1987

The stock crash of Monday, October 19, 1987, was one of the most dramatic financial events of the postwar era. The 508-point, or 22.6 percent, decline in the Dow Jones Industrials was by far the largest point and percentage drop in history. Volume on the New York Stock Exchange soared to an all-time record, exceeding 600 million shares on Monday and on Tuesday, and for that fateful week the number of shares traded exceeded that for the *entire* year of 1966.

The crash on Wall Street reverberated around the world—Tokyo, which two years later was going to enter its own massive bear market, fell the least, but still experienced a record one-day drop of 15.6 percent. Stocks in New Zealand fell nearly 40 percent, and the Hong Kong market closed because collapsing prices brought massive defaults in their stock index futures market. In the United States alone, stock values dropped about $500 billion on that infamous day and the total worldwide decline in stock values exceeded one *trillion* dollars. This is more than the entire gross national product of the continent of Africa.

The fall in the stock market began in earnest the week prior to Black Monday. At 8:30 AM on the preceding Wednesday, the Department of Commerce reported that the United States suffered a $15.7 billion merchandise trade deficit, one of the largest in US history and far in excess of market expectations. The reaction to the announcement in the financial markets was immediate. Yields on long government bonds rose to over 10 percent for the first time since November 1985 and the dollar declined sharply in the foreign exchange market. The Dow Industrials fell 95 points on Wednesday, a record point drop up to that time.

The situation continued to worsen on Thursday and Friday, as the Dow fell an additional 166 points. Late Friday afternoon, about 15 minutes prior to the close, heavy selling hit the stock index futures markets in Chicago. The indexes had fallen below critical support levels, which led to the barrage of selling in Chicago by those wanting to get out of stocks at almost any price.

The December S&P 500 Index future fell to an unprecedented 6 points (about 50 Dow points) below the spot index. The development of such a wide discount meant that money managers were willing to sell at a discount in order to execute large orders with speed, rather than risk sell orders that might sit, unexecuted in New York. At the close of trading on Friday, the stock market had experienced its worst week in nearly five decades.

Before the opening on Monday, ominous events hung over New York. In Tokyo overnight, the Nikkei average fell 2½ percent and there were sharp declines in stock markets in Sydney and Hong Kong. In London, prices had fallen by 10 percent and many money managers were trying to sell US stocks before the anticipated decline hit New York.

Trading on Black Monday was chaotic. No Dow Jones stock opened at the 9:30 bell. Only seven traded before 9:45 and 11 still had not opened at 10:30. Portfolio "insurers," which we describe in the next section, were selling heavily, trying to insulate their customers' exposure to the plunging market. By late afternoon, the S&P 500 Index futures were selling at a 25-point discount to the spot market, a spread that was previously considered inconceivable. By the late afternoon, huge sell orders transmitted by program sellers cascaded onto the New York Exchange through the computerized system. The Dow Industrials collapsed almost 300 points in the final hour of trading, bringing the toll to 508 points on the day.

Although October 19 is remembered in history as the day of the great stock crash, it was actually the following Tuesday—*terrible Tuesday* as it has become known—that the market almost failed. After opening up over 10 percent from Monday's low, the market began to plunge by midmorning, and shortly after noon fell below its Monday close. The S&P 500 Index futures market collapsed to 181—an incredible 40 S&P points (or 300 Dow points) under the reported index value. If index arbitrage had been working, the futures prices would have dictated a Dow at 1,450. Stock prices in the world's largest market, on the basis of this measure, were off nearly 50 percent from their high of 2,722 set just 7 weeks earlier.

It was at this point that near meltdown hit the market. The NYSE did not close, but trading was halted in almost 200 stocks. For the first and only time, trading was also halted in the S&P 500 Index futures in Chicago. The only market of any size that remained open was the Major Market Index futures, representing blue chip stocks and traded on the Chicago Board of Trade.

After the crash, an investigative report led by *The Wall Street Journal* suggested that the crash was a key to reversing the market collapse. The Major Market Index, a stock index future patterned after the Dow Industrials, was selling at such deep discounts to the prices in New York that the values seemed irresistible. And it was the only market that was open. Buyers stepped in and the futures market shot up an equivalent of 120 Dow points in a matter of minutes. When traders and the exchange specialists saw the buying come back into the blue chips, prices rallied in New York, and the worst of the market panic passed.

CAUSES OF THE STOCK CRASH

There was no single precipitating event—such as a declaration of war, terrorists acts, assassination, or bankruptcy—that caused Black Monday. However, ominous trends had threatened the buoyant stock market for some time: sharply higher interest rates, caused by a falling dollar on international currency markets, program trading, and portfolio insurance. The latter was born from the explosive growth of stock index futures markets, markets that did not even exist six years earlier.

Exchange Rate Policies

The roots of the surge in interest rates that preceded the October 1987 stock market crash are found in the futile attempts by the United States and other G7 countries (Japan, United Kingdom,

Germany, France, Italy, and Canada) to prevent the dollar from falling in the international exchange markets.

The dollar had bounded to unprecedented levels in the middle of the 1980s on the heels of huge Japanese and European investment in the United States. Foreign investment was rooted in the optimism about the US economic recovery and the high real dollar interest rates, in part driven by record US budget deficits. By February 1985, the dollar became massively overvalued and United States exports became very uncompetitive in world markets, causing a severe trade deficit.

The initial fall of the dollar was cheered by central bankers, but they grew concerned when the dollar continued to decline and the US trade deficit worsened. Finance ministers met in February 1987 at the Louvre in Paris, with a goal to support the price of the dollar. Foreign central bankers were worried that if the dollar became too cheap, their own exports to the United States, which had grown substantially when the dollar was high, would suffer.

The Federal Reserve reluctantly participated in the dollar stabilization program, which was dependent either on an improvement in the deteriorating US trade position or, absent such an improvement, a commitment by the Federal Reserve that interest rates would be raised to support the dollar. But the trade deficit did not improve, and in fact worsened after the initiation of the exchange stabilization policies. Traders, nervous about the deteriorating US trade balance sending billions of dollars abroad, demanded higher and higher interest rates to hold US assets. Leo Melamed, chairman of the Chicago Mercantile Exchange, was blunt when asked about the origins of Black Monday: "What caused the crash was all that f------ around with the currencies of the world."[1]

The stock market initially ignored the rising interest rates. The US market, like most equity markets around the world, was booming. The Dow Jones Industrials, which started 1987 at 1,933, reached an all-time high of 2,725 on August 22, 250 percent above the August 1982 low reached five years earlier. Over

---

[1] Martin Mayer, *Markets* (New York: W. W. Norton, 1988), p. 62.

the same five-year period the British stock market was up 164 percent, the Swiss 209 percent, German 217 percent, Japanese 288 percent, and Italian 421 percent.

But rising bond rates and falling dividend yields spell trouble for the equity markets. The long-term government bond rate, which began the year at 7 percent, topped 9 percent in September and continued to rise. As the Dow rose, the dividend yield fell, and in August it reached a postwar low of 2.69 percent. The gap between the real yield on bonds and the earning yield on stocks reached a postwar high. On the morning of October 19, the long-term bond yield reached 10.47 percent. The record gap between earnings and dividend yields on stocks and real returns on bonds set the stage for the stock market crash of October 19, 1987.

The Stock Crash and the Futures Market

One cannot overemphasize the importance of the S&P 500 futures market in contributing to the market crash.

But to say that heavy futures selling was one reason why stocks crashed begs the question of what caused the heavy influx of sales in the futures market. Since the introduction of the stock index futures market, a new trading technique, called *portfolio insurance,* had been introduced into portfolio management.

Portfolio insurance was, in concept, not much different than an oft-used technique called a *stop-loss order*. If an investor buys a stock and wants to protect herself from a large loss (or if it has gone up and she wants to protect her profit), it is possible to place a sell order, below the current market, which is triggered when the price of the stock falls to, or below, this limit.

But stop-loss orders are not guarantees that you can get out of the market. If the stock falls below your specified price, your stop-loss order becomes a market order to be executed at the *next best price*. If the stock "gaps" downward, your order could be executed far below your specified price. One can see how a panic might develop if many investors place stop-loss orders around the same price. A price decline could trigger a flood of sell orders which could overwhelm the market.

Portfolio insurers, who used the stock index futures market, felt they were immune to such problems. It seemed inconceivable that the S&P 500 Index futures could ever gap in price. Although individual stocks might gap, it seemed impossible that the whole US capital market, the world's largest, could fail to find buyers.

But the entire market did gap on October 19, 1987. During the week of October 12, the market declined by 10 percent and a large number of sell orders flooded the markets. Portfolio insurers began to sell index futures to protect their clients' profits. The stock index futures market collapsed. There was no liquidity.

What was once inconceivable, that many of the stocks of the world's largest corporations would have no market, happened. Portfolio insurers were shell-shocked, and since the prices of index futures were so far below the prices of the stocks selling in New York, investors halted their buying of shares in New York altogether.

Portfolio insurance, withered rapidly after the crash. It was shown not to be an insurance scheme at all, since the continuity and liquidity of the market could not be assured. There was an alternative form of portfolio protection—index options. With the introduction of these options markets in the 1980s, insurance against market declines could be purchased explicitly by buying puts on a market index. With puts, you never needed to worry about price gaps or being able to get out of your position.

Certainly there were factors other than portfolio insurance contributing to the stock debacle. But portfolio insurance, and its ancestor, the stop-loss order, abetted the fall. All of these schemes are rooted in the basic trading philosophy of letting profits ride and cutting losses short. Whether implemented with stop-loss orders, index futures, or just a mental note to get out of a stock once it declines by a certain amount, this philosophy can set the stage for market gaps.

THE NATURE OF MARKET VOLATILITY

Although most investors express a strong distaste for market fluctuations, volatility must be accepted to reap the superior returns offered by stocks. For risk and volatility are the essence of above-average returns: You cannot make any more than the safe rate of return unless there is some possibility that you can make less.

While the volatility of the stock market deters many investors, it fascinates others. The ability to monitor a position on a minute-by-minute basis fulfills the need of many to know quickly whether their judgment, upon which not only money but also ego lies, has been validated. For many the stock market is truly the world's largest gambling casino.

Yet this ability to know exactly how much you are worth at any given moment can also provoke anxiety. Many investors do not like the instantaneous verdict of the financial market. Some retreat into investments such as real estate, for which daily quotations are not available. They believe that not knowing the current price makes an investment somehow less risky. As Keynes stated over 50 years ago about the investing attitudes of the endowment committee at Cambridge University:

> Some Bursars will buy without a tremor unquoted and unmarketable investment in real estate which, if they had a selling quotation for immediate cash available at each Audit, would turn their hair grey. The fact that you do not know how much its ready money quotation fluctuates does not, as is commonly supposed, make an investment a safe one.[2]

HISTORICAL TRENDS OF STOCK VOLATILITY

Is the stock market becoming more volatile over time? Until recently, many investors would respond to this question in the affirmative, as the record one-day drop in 1987 and the sharp intra-day movements caused by program selling and index arbitrage gave the impression that the market has been more volatile. There is evidence that the market has become more volatile *within the trading day,* undoubtedly the result of instantaneous communications and arbitrage from the index futures markets. But there is little evidence that the market has be-

---

[2] "Memo for the Estates Committee, King's College, Cambridge, May 8, 1938," in *Classics,* ed. Charles D. Ellis (Homewood, Ill.: Dow Jones-Irwin, 1989), p. 79.

come more volatile measured by monthly or even daily fluctuations.

Figure 15–2 plots the annual variability (measured by the standard deviation) of the monthly returns on stocks, calculated yearly from 1834 to the present. One can see that the period of greatest volatility was during the Great Depression, and the year of highest volatility was 1932. The annualized volatility of 1932 was over 65 percent, 17 times higher than 1964, which is the least volatile year on record. The volatility of 1987 was the highest since the Great Depression. But on the whole, volatility shows no overall trend and, excluding 1987, has not been higher since the introduction of stock index futures in 1982.

Most of the periods of high volatility occur when the market has declined. In recessions, the average volatility is about 23 percent while it is less than 16 percent in expansions. There are two reasons why volatility increases in a recession. First, as we noted in Chapter 6, a decline in the market frequently portends an economic slowdown and therefore generates uncertainty for investors. Secondly, if the market declines because of lower earnings forecasts, then investors become much more concerned about the debt and other fixed-income obligations of the firm. Since the bondholders have first claim on the assets of the firm, the probability of severe financial stress and bankruptcy increases when earnings decline. This leads to increased volatility in the equity value of the firm.

If the market believes that the value of the firm is at or below that of the indebtedness to bondholders or banks, the stock market often becomes extremely volatile. Since stockholders only lay claim to value of the firm above debt obligations, the valuation of the stock of a firm which is in trouble becomes much like that of an "out-of-the-money" option which pays off only if the firm does well, and otherwise is worthless. Such options are notoriously volatile.

DISTRIBUTION OF LARGE DAILY CHANGES

We noted in Chapter 12 that there were 120 days from 1885 through the present when the Dow Jones Industrials changed by 5 percent or more—exactly one-half up and one-half down.

FIGURE 15–2

Annual Volatility of Stock Returns (Annualized Standard Deviation of Monthly Returns 1834–1992)

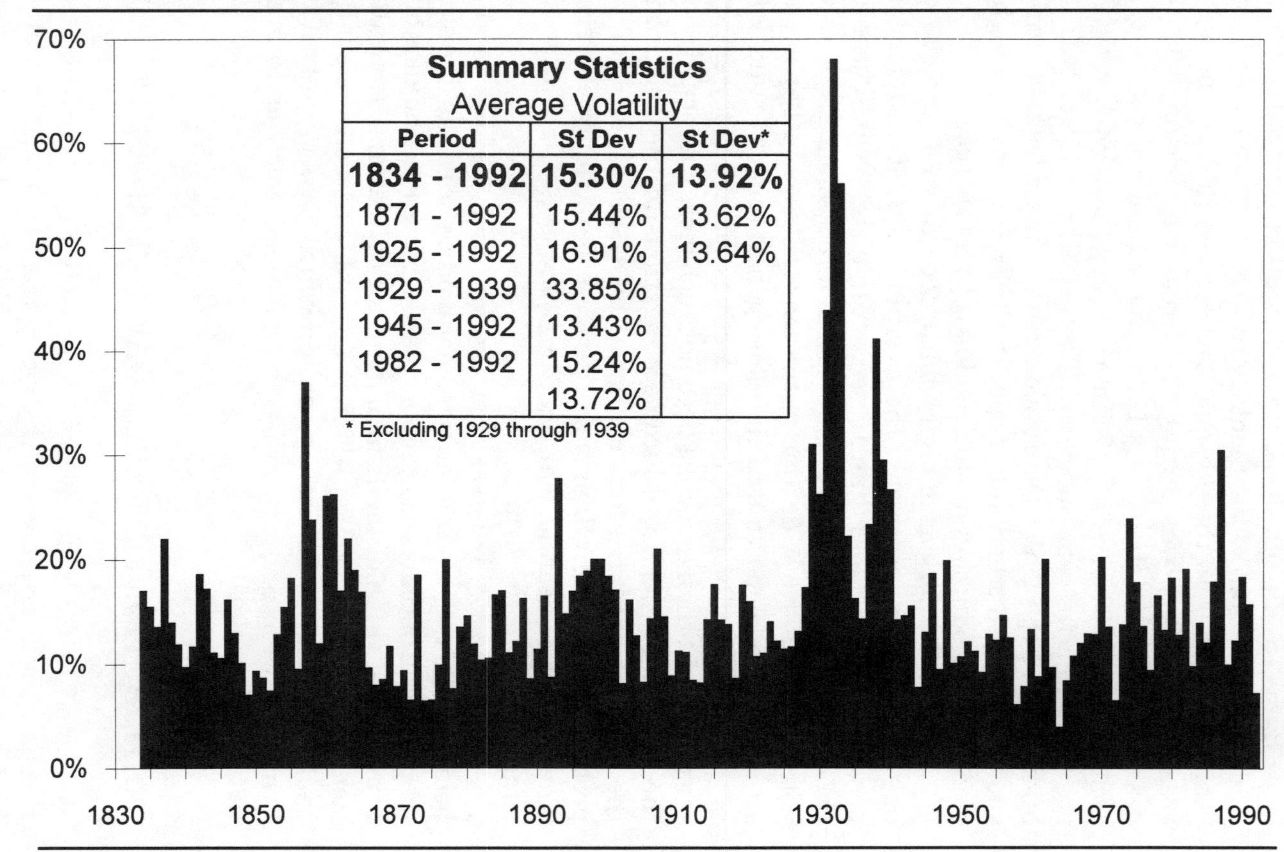

Period	St Dev	St Dev*
1834 - 1992	**15.30%**	**13.92%**
1871 - 1992	15.44%	13.62%
1925 - 1992	16.91%	13.64%
1929 - 1939	33.85%	
1945 - 1992	13.43%	
1982 - 1992	15.24%	
	13.72%	

* Excluding 1929 through 1939

Seventy-six of these days, or nearly two-thirds of the total, were in the period from 1929 through 1933. The most volatile year by far in terms of daily changes is 1932, which contained 32 days when the Dow moved by at least 5 percent. The longest period of time between two successive changes of at least 5 percent was the 17-year period that preceded the October 19, 1987 stock crash.

Figure 15–3 records some of the distributional properties of large daily changes. Monday has seen only slightly more large changes than the rest of the week, and Tuesday has seen significantly fewer. Monday has the largest number of down days, but Wednesday has by far the highest number of up days.

Twenty-eight of the large changes occurred in October, which has notoriously been a month of great volatility in the stock market. This reputation is fully justified. Not only has October witnessed 28 out of the 120 largest changes, but it has also seen the two greatest stock crashes in history. It is interesting to note that over 60 percent of the days with large declines have occurred in the last four months of the year. We shall study the seasonal aspects of stock price changes in Chapter 17.

One of the most surprising bits of information about large market moves relates to the period of the greatest stock market collapse. From September 3, 1929, through July 8, 1932, the Dow Jones Industrials collapsed nearly 89 percent. During that period, there were 37 episodes when the Dow changed by 5 percent or more. Surprisingly, 21 of those episodes were *increases!*

Many of these sharp rallies were the result of short-covering, as those speculators who thought the market was on a one-way street downward rushed to sell stock they did not own. They were forced to buy back, or cover their positions once the market rallied. It is not uncommon for markets which appear to be trending in one direction to experience occasional sharp moves in the other direction. This often happens in the market for small stocks, where the expression "Up the staircase, Down the elevator," is an apt description of their price performance. Traders who play the trend are quick to bail out when they see a correction coming, making it hazardous to ordinary investors who believe it simple to spot major trends in financial markets.

FIGURE 15–3
Distribution of Dow Industrial Changes Over 5 Percent (1885–1992)

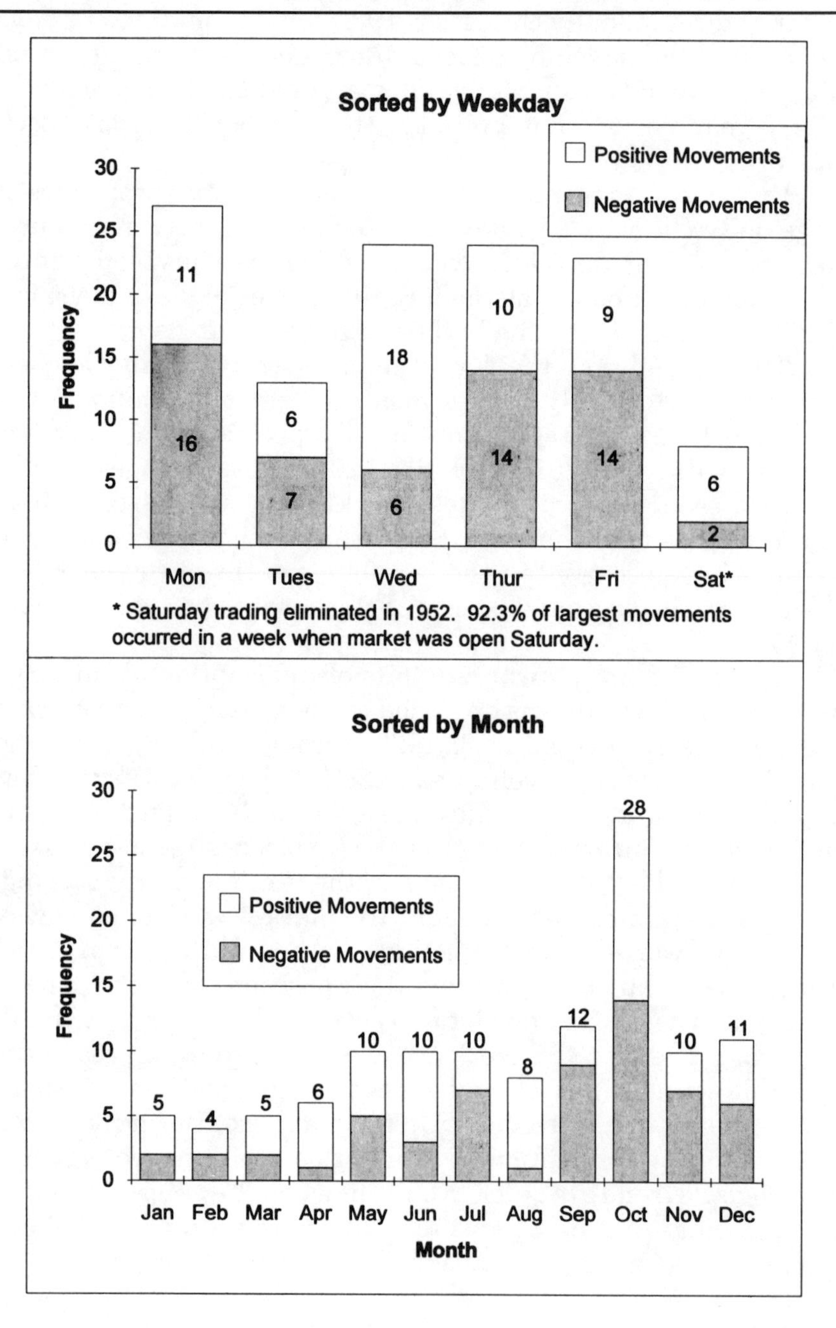

FIGURE 15–3 (*concluded*)

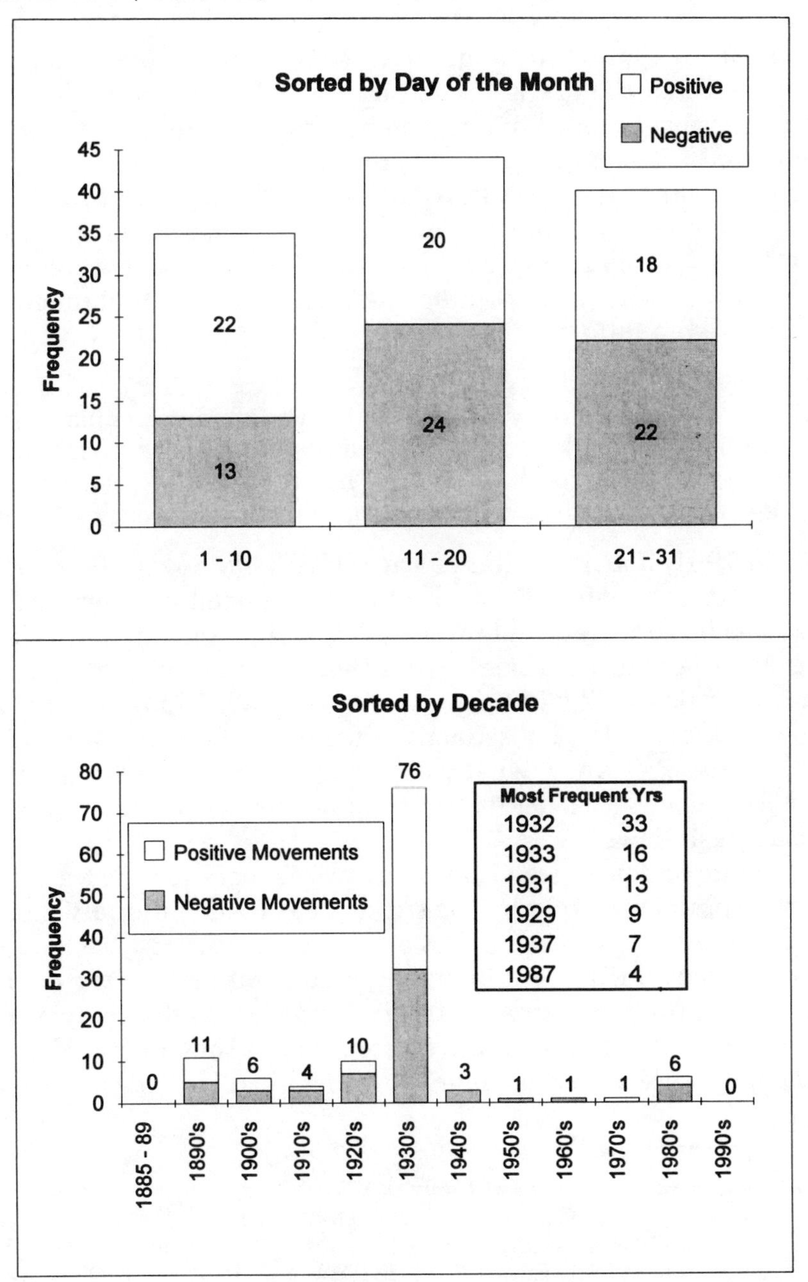

THE ECONOMICS OF MARKET VOLATILITY

Many of the complaints about market volatility are grounded in the belief that the market reacts excessively to changes in news. But how news *should* impact the market is so difficult to determine that few can quantify the proper impact of an event on the price of a stock. As a result, traders often "follow the crowd" and try to predict how *other* traders will react when news strikes.

Over half a century ago, Keynes illustrated the problem of the investor who tries to value stock by economic fundamentals as opposed to following the crowd:

> Investment based on genuine long-term expectation is so difficult today as to be scarcely practicable. He who attempts it must surely lead much more laborious days and run greater risk than he who tries to guess better than the crowd how the crowd will behave; and, given equal intelligence, he may make more disastrous mistakes.[3]

In 1981, Robert Shiller of Yale University devised a method of determining whether stock investors tended to overreact to changes in dividends and interest rates, the fundamental building blocks of stock values.[4] From the examination of historical data, he calculated what the value of the S&P 500 Index *should have been* given the subsequent realization of dividends and interest rates. We know what this value is because, as we learned in Chapter 4, stock prices are the present discounted value of future cash flows.

What he found was that stock prices were far too variable to be explained merely by the subsequent behavior of dividends and interest rates. Stock prices appeared to *overreact* to changes in dividends, failing to take into account that most of the deviations from the trend growth in dividends were only temporary. In other words, investors priced stocks as if they expected dividends in a recession to go much lower while dividends in a boom

---

[3] John Maynard Keynes, *General Theory*, p. 157.

[4] Robert Shiller, *Market Volatility* (Cambridge, Mass.: M.I.T. Press, 1989). The seminal article which spawned the excess volatility literature was "Do Stock Prices Move Too Much to Be Justified by Subsequent Changes in Dividends?" *American Economic Report*, 71 (1981), pp. 421–435.

would keep increasing, completely contrary to historical experience.

The word *cycle* in *business cycle* implies that ups in economic activity will be followed by downs, and vice versa. Since earnings and profits tend to follow the business cycle, they too should behave in a cyclical manner, returning to some average value over time. Under these circumstances, a temporary drop in dividends (or earnings) during a recession should have a very minor effect on the price of a stock, which discounts dividends into the infinite future.

Yet we have seen in Chapter 6 that stock prices fall precipitously before and during the early stages of most economic recessions. This would be true if investors do not really believe that bad times will necessarily be followed by good times, and that the economy could instead slide into an ever-worsening depression.

When stocks are collapsing, such worst-case scenarios loom larger in investors' minds. On May 6, 1932, with stocks having plummeted 85 percent from their 1929 high, Dean Witter issued the following memo to its clients:

> There are only two premises which are tenable as to the future. Either we are going to have chaos or else recovery. The former theory is foolish. If chaos ensues nothing will maintain value; neither bonds nor stocks nor bank deposits nor gold will remain valuable. Real estate will be a worthless asset because titles will be insecure. No policy can be based upon this impossible contingency. Policy must therefore be predicated upon the theory of recovery. The present is not the first depression; it may be the worst, but just as surely as conditions have righted themselves in the past and have gradually readjusted to normal, so this will again occur. The only uncertainty is when it will occur. . . . I wish to say emphatically that in a few years present prices will appear as ridiculously low as 1929 values appear fantastically high.[5]

Two months later the stock market hit its all-time low and rallied strongly. In retrospect, these words reflected great wisdom and sound judgment about the temporary dislocations of stock prices. Yet at the time they were uttered, investors were so

---

[5] Memorandum from Dean Witter, May 6, 1932.

disenchanted with stocks and so filled with doom and gloom, that these words fell on deaf ears.

EPILOGUE TO THE CRASH

Despite the drama of the October 1987 market collapse, which was often compared with 1929, there was amazingly little lasting effect on the world economy or even the financial markets from the 1987 stock crash. Because this stock crash did not augur either a further collapse in stock prices or a decline in economic activity, it will probably never attain the notoriety of the crash of 1929. Yet its lesson is perhaps more important. Economic safeguards, such as prompt Federal Reserve action to provide liquidity to the economy and assure the financial markets *can* prevent an economic debacle of the nature that beset our economy during the Great Depression.

This does not mean that the markets are exempt from violent fluctuations. Since the future will always be uncertain, psychology and sentiment often dominate economic fundamentals. As Keynes perceptively stated 60 years ago in *The General Theory,* "The outstanding fact is the extreme precariousness of the basis of knowledge on which our estimates of prospective yield have to be made."[6] Precarious estimates are subject to sudden change and prices in free markets are often volatile.

---

[6] Keynes, *The General Theory,* p. 149.

CHAPTER 16

TECHNICAL ANALYSIS AND INVESTING WITH THE TREND

The stock market has no memory.
The central proposition of charting is absolutely false.

Burton Malkiel[1]

I can't overemphasize the importance of staying with the trend of the market, being in gear with the tape, and not fighting the major movements. Fighting the tape is an open invitation to disaster.

Martin Zweig[2]

THE NATURE OF TECHNICAL ANALYSIS

Flags, pennants, saucers, and head-and-shoulders formations. Stochastics, moving average convergence divergence indicators, and candlesticks. Such is the arcane language of the technical analyst, an investor who forecasts future returns by the use of past price trends. Few areas of investment analysis have attracted more critics, yet no other area has a core of such dedicated, ardent supporters. Technical analysis, often dismissed by academic economists as being no more useful than astrology, is being given a new look, and some of the recent evidence is surprisingly positive.

---

[1] Burton Malkiel, *A Random Walk Down Wall Street* (New York: W. W. Norton, 1990), p. 133.

[2] Martin Zweig, *Winning on Wall Street* (New York: Warner Books, 1990), p. 121.

Technical analysts, or *chartists* as they are sometimes called, stand in sharp contrast to fundamental analysts, who use such variables as dividends, earnings, and book values to forecast stock returns. Chartists ignore these fundamental variables, maintaining that virtually all useful information is summarized by past price patterns. These patterns may be the result of market psychology or of informed traders who are accumulating or distributing stock. If these patterns are read properly, chartists maintain, they can be used by other investors to share in the gains of those more knowledgeable about a stock's prospects.

CHARLES DOW—TECHNICAL ANALYST

The first well-publicized technical analyst was Charles Dow, the creator of the Dow Jones averages. But Charles Dow did not only analyze charts. In conjunction with his interest in market movements, Dow founded *The Wall Street Journal* and published his strategy in editorials in the early part of this century. Dow's successor, William Hamilton, extended Dow's technical approach and published *The Stock Market Barometer* in 1922. Ten years later, Charles Rhea formalized Dow's concepts in a book entitled *Dow Theory*.

Charles Dow likened the ebb and flow of stock prices to the movement of water in an ocean. He claimed that there was a primary wave which, like the tide, determined the overall trend. Upon this trend were superimposed secondary waves and minor ripples. One can identify which trend the market is in by analyzing a chart of the Dow Industrial average, the volume in the market, and the Dow Jones Rail average (now called the Transportation average).

It is widely acknowledged that the use of Dow Theory would have gotten an investor out of the stock market before the October 1929 stock crash, but not before the crash of October 1987. Martin J. Pring, a noted technical analyst, argues that, starting in 1897, an investor who purchased stock in the Dow Jones Industrial average and followed each Dow theory buy and sell signal, would have seen an original investment of $100 reach $116,508 by January 1990, as opposed to $5,682 with a buy-and-hold strategy (these calculations exclude reinvested dividends).[3] But confirmation of profits by using Dow Theory is difficult because the buy and sell signals are subjective and not given to precise numerical rules.

RANDOMNESS OF STOCK PRICES

Although Dow Theory may not be as popular as it once was, the idea that one can identify the major trends in the market, riding bull markets while avoiding bear markets, is still the fundamental thrust of technical analysis. Yet most economists still attack the fundamental tenet of the chartists—that stock prices follow predictable patterns. To these academic researchers, the movements of prices in the market more closely conform to a pattern called a *random walk* than to trends and designs which forecast returns.

In 1959, Harry Roberts, a professor at the University of Chicago, simulated movements in the market by plotting price changes which resulted from completely random events, such as flips of a fair coin. These simulations looked like the charts of actual stock prices, forming shapes and following trends which are considered by chartists as significant predictors of future returns. But since next period's price change was produced by a completely random event, such patterns could not logically have any predictive content. This early research supported the belief that the apparent patterns in past stock prices were the result of completely random movements.

But did the randomness of stock prices make economic sense? Factors influencing supply and demand do not occur randomly and are often quite predictable from one period to the next. Should not these predictable factors make stock prices move in nonrandom patterns?

---

[3] Martin Pring, *Technical Analysis Explained,* 3rd ed. (New York: McGraw-Hill, 1991), p. 31. Also see David Glickstein and Rolf Wubbels, "Dow Theory Is Alive and Well!" *Journal of Portfolio Management,* April 1983, pp. 28–32.

In 1965, Professor Paul Samuelson of MIT showed that the randomness in security prices did not contradict the laws of supply and demand.[4] In fact, such randomness was a result of a free and efficient market in which investors have already incorporated all the *known* factors influencing the price of the stock. If this is true, prices will change only when new, *un*anticipated information is released to the market. Since unanticipated information is as likely to be good or bad, the resulting movement in stock prices is random. Price charts will look like a random walk since the probability that stocks go up or down is completely random and cannot be predicted.[5]

If stock prices are indeed random, then their movements should not be distinguishable from counterfeits generated randomly by a computer. Figure 16–1 extends the experiment conceived by Prof. Roberts over 30 years ago. Instead of generating only closing prices, we programmed the computer to generate intraday prices, creating the popular high/low/close bar graphs that are found in most newspapers and chart publications.

Figure 16–1 contains eight charts. Four of these charts have been simulated by a computer, using a random-number generator. In these graphs, there is absolutely no way to predict the future from the past, since future movements are designed to be totally independent from the past. The other four charts were chosen from actual data of the Dow Jones Industrial average over recent years. Before reading further, try to determine which are real historical prices and which have been created by a computer.

Such a task is quite difficult. In fact, most of the top brokers at a leading Wall Street firm found it impossible to tell the difference between real and counterfeit data. Only Figure 16–1D, which depicts the period around the October 19, 1987, stock crash, was correctly identified by two thirds of the brokers. Of the

---

[4] Paul Samuelson, "Proof that Properly Anticipated Prices Fluctuate Randomly," 1965, *Industrial Management Review*, 6, (1965), p. 49.

[5] More generally, the sum of the product of each possible price change times the probability of its occurrence is zero. This is called a *martingale*, of which a random walk (50 percent probability up, 50 percent probability down) is a special case.

FIGURE 16–1
Real and Simulated Stock Indexes

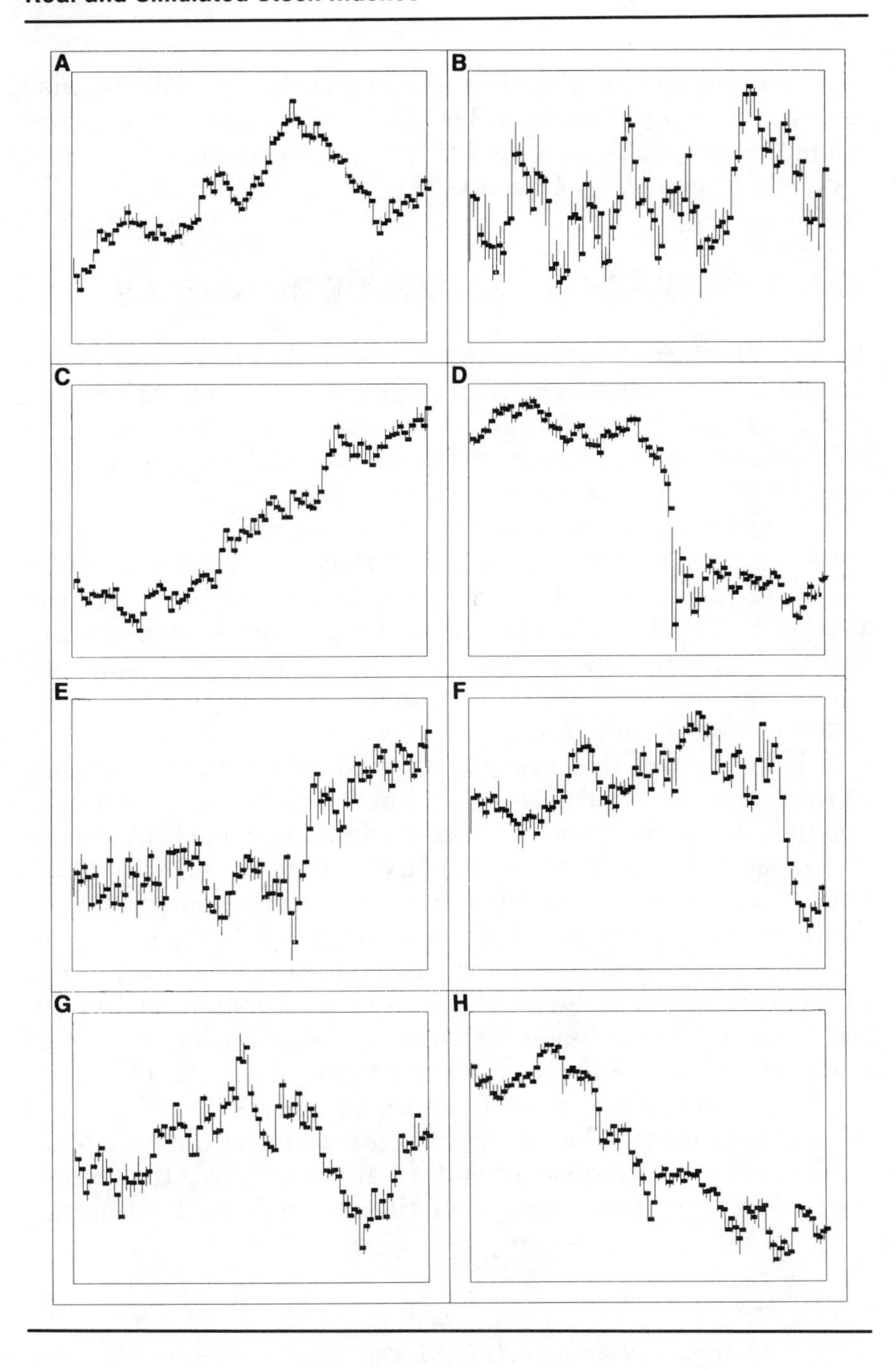

remaining seven graphs, they showed no ability to distinguish actual from counterfeit data. The true historical prices are represented by graphs B, D, E, and H, while the computer-generated data are graphs A, C, F, and G.[6]

TRENDING MARKETS AND PRICE REVERSALS

Despite the fact that many trends are in fact the result of the totally random movement of stock prices, many traders will not invest against a trend they have identified. Two of the most well-known sayings of market timers are "Make the trend your friend," or "Trust the thrust."

When a trend appears established, technical analysts draw *channels* which enclose the path of stock prices. A channel is drawn to enclose the upper and lower bounds within which the market has traded. The lower bound of a channel is frequently called a *support level* while the upper bound a *resistance level.* When the market breaks the bounds of the channel, a large market move often follows.

The very fact that many traders believe in the importance of the trend can induce behavior that makes trend-following so popular. While the trend is intact, traders sell when prices reach the upper end of the channel and buy when they reach the lower end, attempting to take advantage of the apparent back-and-forth motion of stock prices. If the trend line is broken, many of these traders will reverse their positions: buying, if the market penetrates the top of the trend line, and selling if it falls through the bottom. This behavior often accelerates the movement of stock prices and reinforces the importance of the trend.

Option trading by trend followers reinforces the behavior of the market timers. When the market is trading within a channel, traders will sell put and call options at strike prices that represent lower and upper bounds of the channel. As long as the

---

[6] Graph 16–1B covers February 15 to July 1, 1991, graph 16–1E covers January 15 to June 1, 1992, and graph 16–1H from June 15 to November 1, 1990.

market remains within the channel, these speculators collect premiums as the options expire worthless.

If the market penetrates the trading range, option sellers are exposed to great risks. Recall that sellers of options (as long as they do not own the underlying stock) face a huge potential liability, a liability that can be many times the premium that they collected upon sale of the option. When such unlimited losses loom, these option writers run to cover, accelerating the movement of prices.

MOVING AVERAGES

Successful technical trading requires not only identifying the trend but, more importantly, identifying when the trend is about to reverse. A popular tool used to determine when the trend may change examines the relation between the current price and a *moving average* of past price movements, a technique that goes back to at least the 1930s.[7]

A moving average is simply the arithmetic average of a given number of past closing prices of a stock or index over a fixed interval of time. For example, a 200-day moving average is the average of the past 200 days of closing prices. For each new trading day, the oldest price is dropped and the most recent price is added to compute the average.

Moving averages fluctuate far less than daily prices. When prices are rising, the moving average trails the market and, technical analysts claim, forms a support level for stock prices. When prices are falling, the moving average is above current prices and forms a resistance level. Analysts claim that a moving average allows investors to identify the basic market trend without being distracted by the day-to-day volatility of the market. When prices penetrate the moving average, this indicates that

---

[7] See William Brock, Josef Lakonishok, and Blake LeBaron, "Simple Technical Trading Rules and the Stochastic Properties of Stock Returns," *Journal of Finance* 47, no. 5 (December 1992), pp. 1731–64. The first definitive analysis of moving averages comes from a book by H. M. Gartley, *Profits in the Stock Market* (New York: H. M. Gartley, 1930).

powerful underlying forces are signaling a reversal of the basic trend.

The most popular moving average uses prices for the past 200 trading days, and is therefore called the *200-day moving average.* The 200-day moving average is frequently plotted in newspapers and investment letters as a key determinant of investment trends. One of the early supporters of this strategy was William Gordon, who indicated that over the period 1897 through 1967, buying stocks when the Dow broke above the moving average produced nearly seven times the return as buying when the Dow broke below the average.[8] Colby and Meyers claim that for the United States the best moving average for weekly data is 45 weeks, just slightly longer than the 200-day moving average.[9]

Testing the Moving Average Strategy

In order to test the 200-day moving average strategy, I examined the daily record of the Dow Jones Industrial average from 1885. In contrast to the previous studies of this strategy, the holding period returns include the reinvestment of dividends when in the market and interest when out of the stock market. Annualized returns are examined over the entire period as well as the subperiods.

The following criteria were adopted to determine the buy-sell strategy: Whenever the Dow Jones Industrial average *closed* at least 1 percent above its 200-day moving average, stocks were purchased at these closing prices. Whenever the Dow Industrials closed by at least 1 percent below its 200-day moving average, stocks were sold. When you are out of the market, it is assumed you are invested in Treasury bills.

There are two noteworthy aspects of this strategy. The 1 percent band around the 200-day moving average is used in order to reduce the number of times an investor would have to move in and out of the market. Without this band, investors using the

---

[8] William Gordon, *The Stock Market Indicators* (Palisades, NJ: Investors Press, 1968).

[9] Robert W. Colby and Thomas A. Meyers, *The Encyclopedia of Technical Market Indicators* (Homewood, IL: Dow Jones-Irwin, 1988).

200-day moving average strategy are often *whipsawed,* a term used to describe the frequent buying and then selling and then buying again of stocks in an attempt to beat the market. Such trades dramatically lower investor returns because of the large transaction costs which are incurred.

The second aspect of this strategy assumes an investor buys or sells stock at the closing price rather than at any time reached during the day. Only in recent years has the exact intraday level of the averages been computed. Using historical data, it is impossible to determine times when the market average penetrated the 200-day moving average during the day, but closed at levels that did not trigger a signal. By specifying that the average must close above or below the signal, we present a theory which could have been implemented in practice.[10]

Results

Figure 16–2 shows the daily and the 200-day moving average of the Dow Jones Industrial average during two select periods: from 1924–36 and 1980–93. The time periods when the investor is out of the stock market are shaded, while during the unshaded periods the investor is fully in stocks.

To the eye, it looks like the strategy works extremely well. An investor is in stocks during all the important bull markets, and out of stocks during all the major bear markets.

The strategy worked extremely well during the bull and bear market of the 1920s. Using the criteria outlined above, an investor would have bought stocks on June 27, 1924 when the Dow was 95.33 and, with only two minor interruptions, ridden the bull market to the top at 381.17 on September 3, 1929. An investor would have exited the market on October 19, 1927 at 323.87, 10 days before the Great Crash. Except for a brief period in 1930, the strategy kept one out of the market through the

---

[10] Historically, the daily high and low levels of stock averages were calculated on the basis of the highest or lowest price of each stock reached *at any time* during the day. This is called the *theoretical* high or low. The *actual* high is the highest level reached *at any given time* by the stocks in the average.

FIGURE 16–2

Dow Industrials and 200-Day Moving Average

Shaded areas = out of market

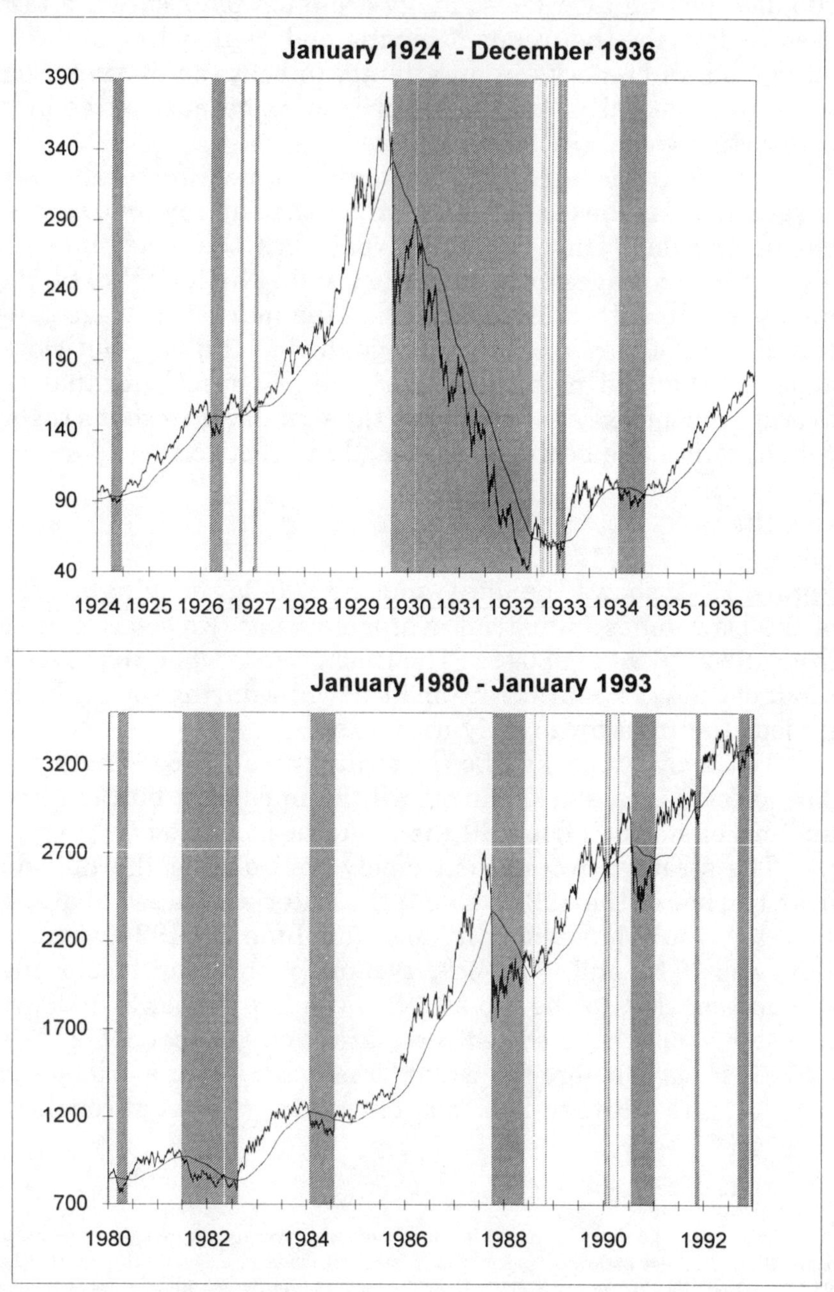

Shaded areas = out of market

entire decline before reentering the market on Aug. 6, 1932, at 66.56, just 25 points higher than its postcrash low. Over the entire 107-year history of the Dow Jones average, the 200-day moving average strategy had its greatest triumph during the boom and crash of the 1920s and early 1930s.

An investor following the 200-day moving average strategy would also have avoided the October 19, 1987, crash and have sold out on the previous Friday, October 16. However, in contrast to the 1929 crash, the market did not continue downward. Although the market fell 23 percent on October 19, an investor would not have reentered the market until the following June when the Dow was only about 5 percent below the exit level of October 16. Nonetheless, following the 200-day moving average strategy would have avoided October 19 and 20, traumatic days for many investors who were long in the market.

Table 16–1 analyzes the entire period from 1885 through 1992, including three subperiods. The first subperiod covers the period Oct. 13, 1885, when the Dow Industrial average was begun, through 1925. The second, covering 1926 through 1945, covers the 1920s boom, the Great Depression, and World War II. The final subperiod covers the postwar experience.

In each of the subperiods, the timing strategy did outperform the buy-and-hold strategy. But, except for the second subperiod, the differences were very small. The excess annual compound return of the timing strategy over the buy-and-hold strategy was about 0.7 percent in the first subperiod, 0.4 percent in the third subperiod, but a whopping 5.74 percent in the second subperiod. Over the whole period there is a 1.52 percent annual excess return from following the 200-day moving average strategy over the buy-and-hold strategy.

All the excess return in the second period resulted from getting out of the market before the Great Crash and staying out until the market bottomed. If the 1929 peak to the 1932 trough is excluded, the return to the buy-and-hold strategy actually exceeds the timing strategy in the second period and by a tiny margin over the entire 107 years of the study.

Of course, it is no small feat to avoid the Great Crash of 1929. Yet, if one believes that another episode when the Dow drops by nearly 90 percent in less than three years is unlikely

TABLE 16–1
Timing and Holding Strategy Annualized Returns

	Holding Strategy		Timing Strategy				Percent	Number
	Annualized		Annualized Return		Net Trans Costs		in	of
Period	Return	Risk	Return	Risk	Return	Risk	Market	Switches
Overall	**9.46%**	23.09%	**10.98%**	17.06%	**9.51%**	17.60%	**61.78%**	**284**
Subperiods								
1885 - 1925	**9.22**	23.74	**9.91**	17.31	**8.25**	17.58	**57.08**	**122**
1926 - 1945	**6.34**	33.11	**12.08**	23.15	**10.52**	23.96	**62.69**	**56**
1946 - 1992	**11.03**	17.35	**11.43**	13.87	**10.17**	14.50	**65.41**	**106**
Excl. 1929-1932 Crash								
1926 - 1945	**17.46**	27.41	**14.04**	22.77	**12.30**	23.70	**72.73**	**53**
Overall	**11.36**	21.53	**11.27**	16.68	**9.77**	17.23	**63.41**	**281**

(and no other episode before or since has come close), it is important to consider how successful the strategy would be excluding those unique years.

The above results are calculated assuming that there are no transaction costs to buying or selling. If the transaction costs of implementing the timing strategy are included in the calculations, the excess returns vanish over all but the second subperiod, even when all the data around the Great Crash are included. Transaction costs include brokerage costs and bid-ask spreads, as well as the capital gains tax incurred when stocks are sold. All of these costs are far higher under the 200-day moving average strategy, which requires frequent buying and selling, than under the buy-and-hold strategy.

Each 0.1 percent of transaction costs lowers the compound annual returns by 29 basis points. Table 16–1 shows the annual distribution of returns if the investor incurs a 0.5 percent transaction cost on the buy and on the sell. During much of the period, a 0.5 percent transaction cost probably underestimates the true costs of getting into and out of stocks.

In the postwar period, transaction costs cause the timing strategy to underperform the buy-and-hold strategy by an average of 86 basis points a year. Accumulated over the postwar period, this means that $1 invested and reinvested from January 1, 1946 turns into $9,400 by the end of 1992 using the timing strategy, but accumulates to $13,600 using a buy-and-hold strategy.

Despite the fact that the timing strategy does not raise overall returns, it does lower risk substantially. Over the whole period, risk (measured by the standard deviation of annual returns) is reduced from 23 percent to under 18 percent, while returns (after transactions costs) are about the same. Even in the postwar period, after transaction costs, risk are reduced by almost three percentage points while returns are reduced by less than one percentage point.

There is no question that the 200-day moving average strategy avoids large losses while reducing overall gains only slightly. But this timing strategy also reduces some of the big gains since it does not get you into the market until it has already risen, so some of the spectacular gains realized when the market bounces off its lows are lost.

The real difference between the timing and buy-and-hold strategy comes in the large number of small losses that the timing strategy entails. These occur when the stock market does not take on a definite trend and, despite the use of the 1 percent band to reduce whipsawing, an investor finds himself moving in and out of the market frequently, incurring transactions costs and trading losses.

CONCLUSION

Technical analysis, its proponents claim, helps the investor identify the major trends of the market and when these trends might reverse. Yet there is considerable debate about whether such trends exist, or whether they are just runs of good and bad returns that are really the result of random price movements.

Burton Malkiel has been quite clear in his denunciation of technical analysis. In his best-selling work, *A Random Walk Down Wall Street,* he proclaims:

> Technical rules have been tested exhaustively by using stock price data on both major exchanges going back as far as the beginning of the 20th century. The results reveal conclusively that past movements in stock prices cannot be used to foretell future movements.[11]

Yet this contention, once supported nearly unanimously by academic economists, is cracking. A recent paper by academic economists has shown that such simple trading rules as 200-day moving averages can be used to improve returns.[12]

Despite the ongoing academic debate, technical analysis and trend following draw huge followings on Wall Street and from many savvy investors. Our analysis gives a cautious nod to the strategy based on moving averages, as long as transactions costs

---

[11] Malkiel, *A Random Walk Down Wall Street,* p. 133.

[12] William Brock, Josef Lakonishok, and Blake LeBaron "Simple Technical Trading Rules and the Stochastic Properties of Stock Returns," *Journal of Finance* 47, no. 5 (December 1992), pp. 1731–64

are not high. But this strategy must be monitored closely. In October 1987, the Dow fell below its 200-day moving average on the Friday before the crash. If you failed to get through to your broker that Friday afternoon in order to sell all your stock, it would have spelled disaster.

CHAPTER 17

CALENDAR ANOMALIES

> October. This is one of the peculiarly dangerous months to speculate in stocks. The others are July, January, September, April, November, May, March, June, December, August, and February.
>
> *Mark Twain*

The dictionary defines an *anomaly* as something inconsistent with what naturally is expected. And, what is more *un*natural than to expect to beat the market by predicting stock prices based solely on the day or week or month of the year? Yet, it appears that one can. Recent research has revealed that there are predictable times during which stocks as a whole, and certain classes of stocks in particular, excel in the market.

The most important calendar anomaly is that small stocks far outperform larger stocks in one specific month of the year—January. In fact, January is the only reason that small stocks have greater total returns than large stocks over the past 67 years! This phenomenon has been dubbed *the January effect.* Its discovery in the early 1980s by Don Keim, at that time a graduate student at the University of Chicago, was the first, and in some ways the most significant, finding in a market where researchers had previously failed to detect any predictable pattern to stock prices.

The January effect may be the granddaddy of all calendar anomalies, but it is not the only one. For inexplicable reasons, stocks generally do much better in the first half of the month than the second. They also fare much better on Fridays than on Mondays. Furthermore, they do exceptionally well on any day before a big holiday, particularly December 31 which is actually the day that launches the January effect.

Why these anomalies occur is not well understood, and whether they will continue to be significant in the future is an open question. But their discovery has put economists on the spot. No longer can researchers be so certain that the stock market is thoroughly unpredictable and impossible to beat.

THE JANUARY EFFECT

Of all of these calendar-related anomalies, the January effect is the most important. From 1925 through 1992, the value-weighted S&P 500 Index experienced an average annual arithmetic return of 12.4 percent, while the small stock index, which is comprised of the bottom 20 percent of all stocks ranked by size, produced an average return of 17.6 percent. For the 68 Januaries during this period, the average return on the S&P 500 Index was 1.6 percent, while the average returns on the small stocks came to 6.9 percent. The 5.3 percent average excess returns to small stocks in January *exceeds* the entire yearly difference in returns between large and small stocks. In other words, from February through December the arithmetic returns on small stocks—which as a group are significantly riskier than large stocks—have a lower return than large stocks. The only time to hold small stocks as a group is the month of January!

To see how important the January effect is, look at Figure 17–1. It shows the total return index on large and small stocks, and what the total return index on small stocks would be if the January return on small stocks was identical to the stocks in the S&P 500 Index. A single dollar invested in small stocks in 1926 grows to $2,279 by the end of 1992, while the same dollar grows to only $727 in large stocks. Yet if the January effect is eliminated, the total return to small stocks accumulated to only $88, merely 12 percent of that in large stocks!

Figure 17–2 shows the January effect from another angle. It displays the difference in the return from investing in smaller stocks (ranked by decile) over the return of the largest decile stocks. The results are similarly startling. From 1926 through 1992, the average rate of return on the smallest 10 percent of stocks in January is 11.47 percent. If this January bonanza would continue all year, an investor would more than triple his money in small stocks in 12 months. But these spectacular returns stop

FIGURE 17–1
Small-Stock Index without January Effect (1926–92)

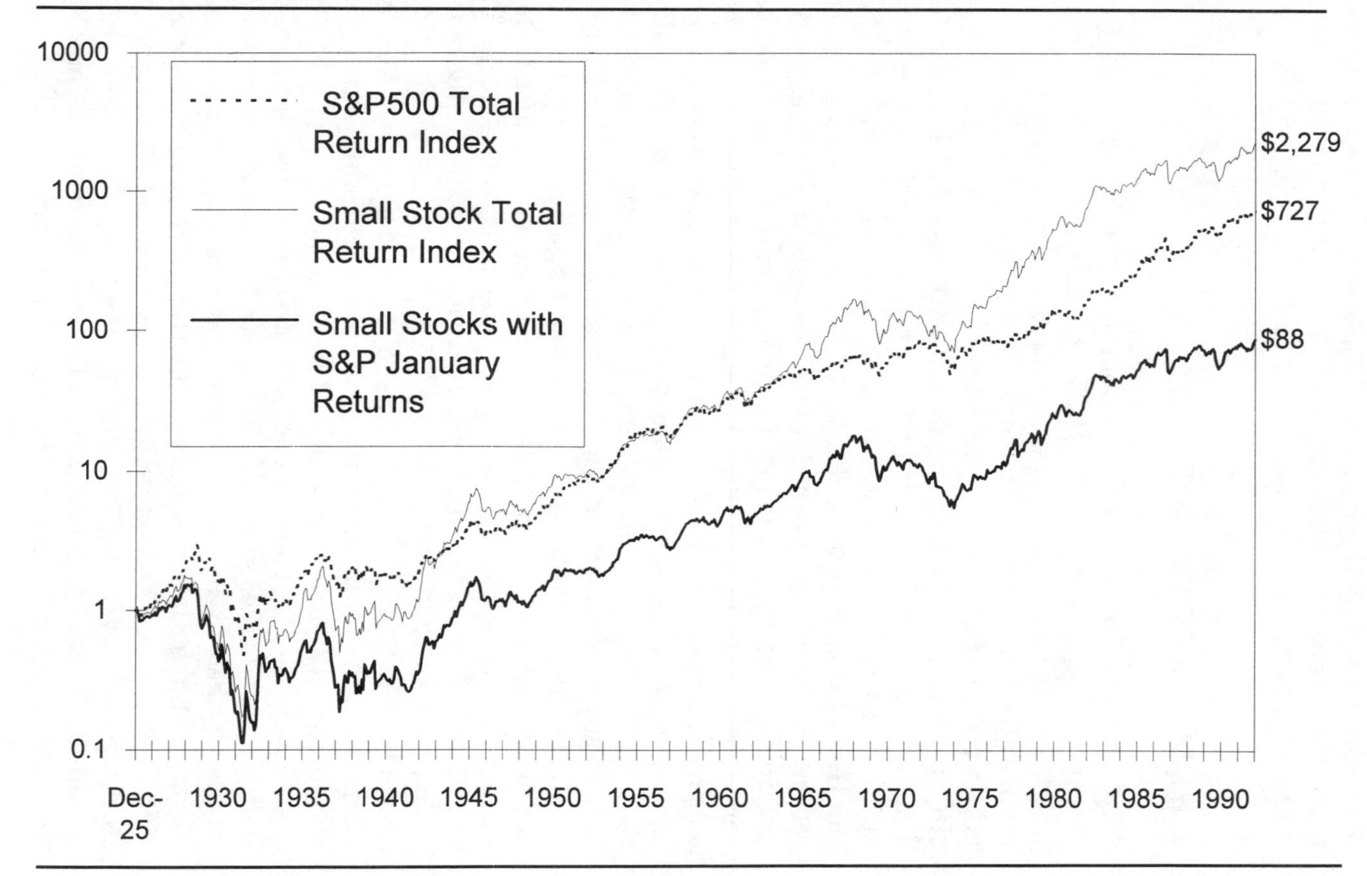

FIGURE 17–2
The January Effect (Average Monthly Return Ranked by Market Capitalization 1926–92)

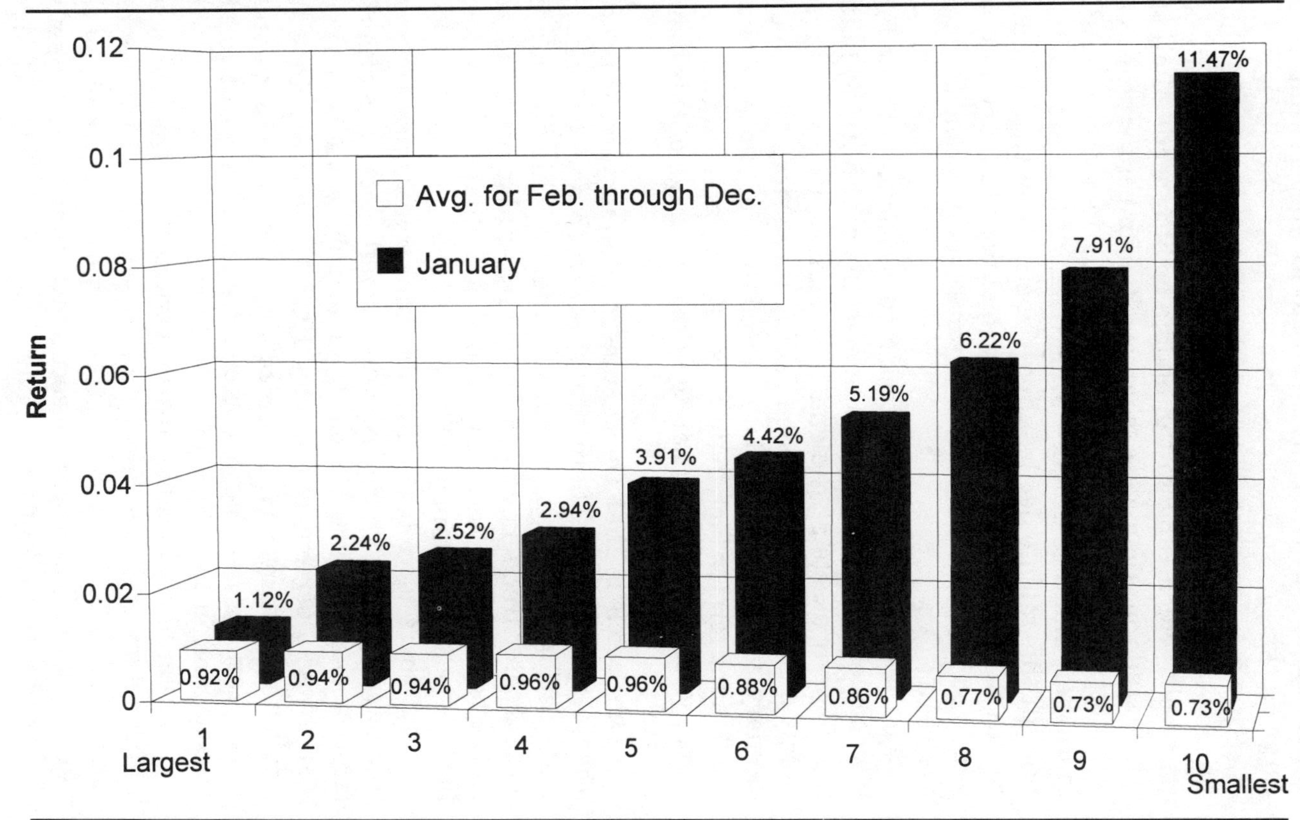

dead at the end of January. In seven of the remaining 11 months, the average returns for the small stocks are less than those for large stocks.

One can see from Figure 17–2 that as the size of the firm increases, the January effect diminishes. But it is still strong for stocks which rank in the middle or fifth decile of all stocks which trade on organized exchanges. Remember that the average size stock traded on either the New York, American, or NASDAQ is still very small, averaging far less than $100 million capitalization. In this middle decile, almost one third of the total annual return on these stocks comes in the month of January, four times what you would expect if returns were evenly spread throughout the year.

If these January small-stock returns continue in the future, it would lead to some astounding investment results. By liquidating all your assets at the end of December, using the proceeds to buy small stocks, and then selling these stocks at the end of January, your returns will far exceed those of almost all investment managers! In fact, logic dictates that you should borrow and leverage as much as you can to take advantage of this January anomaly.

One catch is that these superior January returns do not *always* materialize. There are years when small stocks have underperformed larger stocks in January. This has happened with greater frequency in recent years: small stocks (measured as the bottom quintile of capitalization value) underperformed larger stocks in January 1982, 1987, 1989, and 1990.

But there have been only six other years since 1925 when this happened. Furthermore, when small stocks underperform large stocks, it is usually not by much: the worst underperformance was 5 percent in January 1929. In contrast, since 1925, small-stock returns have exceeded large stock returns in January in 26 years by at least 5 percent, in 13 years by at least 10 percent, and in two years by over 20 percent.

The January effect has also prevailed during the most powerful bear market in our history. From August 1929 through the summer of 1932, when small stocks lost over 90 percent of their value, small stocks posted consecutive January *monthly* returns of plus 13 percent, 21 percent, and 10 percent in 1930, 1931, and

1932. It is testimony to the power of the January effect that investors could increase their wealth by 50 percent during the greatest stock crash in history by buying small stocks at the beginning of January of those three years and selling them at the end of the month, putting their money in cash for the rest of the year!

A fascinating feature of the January effect is that you do not have to wait the entire month to see the big returns from small stocks roll in. Most of the buying in small stocks begins on the last trading day of December (often in the late afternoon), as some investors pick up the bargains that are dumped by others on New Year's eve. Strong gains in small stocks continue on the first trading day of January and continue with declining force through the first week of trading. On the first trading day of January alone, small stocks earn nearly four percentage points more than large stocks.[1] By the middle of the month, in fact, the January effect is largely exhausted.

When any anomaly such as the January effect is found, it is important to examine its international reach. When researchers turned to foreign markets, they found that the January effect was not just a US phenomenon. In Japan, the world's second-largest capital market, the excess returns on small stocks in January come to 7.2 percent per year, more than in the United States. As we shall see below, in many other countries of the world, January is the best month for both large *and* small stocks. [2]

How could such a phenomenon go unnoticed for so long by investors, portfolio managers, and financial economists? Because in the United States, January is nothing special for large stocks, and these stocks form the base of the popular indexes, such as the Dow Industrials or the S&P 500. That's not to say that January is not a good month for those stocks too. As we shall see below,

---

[1] Robert Haugen and Josef Lakonishok, *The Incredible January Effect* (Homewood, IL: Dow Jones-Irwin, 1989), p. 47.

[2] For an excellent summary of all this evidence see "On the Predictability of Common Stock Returns: World Wide Evidence," by G. Hawawini and Don Keim, in R. A. Jarrow, W. T. Ziemba, and V. Moksimovich, Eds., *Finance* (North Holland, 1993).

large stocks do quite well in January, particularly in foreign markets. But in the United States, January is by no means the best month for stocks of large firms.

Causes of the January Effect

Why do investors tend to favor small stocks in January? No one knows for sure, but there are several hypotheses. Small stocks are disproportionately held by individual investors, rather than institutions. Individual investors are more sensitive to the tax consequences of their trading. Small stocks, especially those which have declined in the preceding 11 months, are subject to tax selling in December. This selling depresses the price of individual issues.

There is some evidence in support of this explanation. Stocks which have fallen throughout the year fall even more in December, and then often rise dramatically in January. Furthermore, there is some evidence that before the introduction of the US income tax in 1913, there was no January effect. And in Australia, where the tax year runs from July 1 through June 30, there are abnormally large returns in July.

If this is a factor, however, it cannot be the only one, for the January effect holds in countries which do not have a capital gains tax. Japan did not tax capital gains for individual investors until 1989, but the January effect was still present. Furthermore, before 1972, capital gains were not taxed in Canada, and yet in that country, too, there was a January effect. Finally, stocks which have risen throughout the previous year still rise in January, although not as much as stocks which have fallen the previous year.

There are other potential explanations for the January effect. Individuals often receive an influx of funds, such as bonuses and monies that become available from tax loss selling, at year-end. These individuals often wait several days to invest their cash and then buy in the first week of January. Data show that there is a sharp increase in the ratio of public buy orders to public sell orders around the turn of the year. Since the public holds a large fraction of small stocks, this could be an important clue to understanding the January effect.[3]

Another possible explanation is that portfolio managers will often load up with risky stocks, which are often small stocks, at the beginning of the year, but sell them by the time their balance sheets are inspected at year-end. They do this because if their risky stocks have done well, the managers can lock in their superior performance, in other words, "beat the S&P", by indexing on the S&P 500 stocks for the rest of the year. And if they have not done well, they will also sell them because they do not want their clients to see them on their year-end balance sheet!

Yet another factor contributing to the January effect is the fact that returns are calculated on the basis of the last price recorded on the day. If the last sale, no matter how small, is motivated by a buyer, the final price will be registered at the asked or offer price. For small stocks, this could be 5 percent or more above the "bid" price at which the last sale was made. A buying flurry at the end of the day, especially centered in small stocks, could cause a substantial rise in small stock indexes. This appears to be important at the end of calendar quarters and especially on December 31. But researchers have concluded that it can explain just a small part of the January effect.[4]

Although all these explanations appear quite reasonable, none jibes with what is called an *efficient capital market*. If money managers know that stocks (especially small ones) will surge in January, they should be bought well before New Year's Day to capture these spectacular returns. That would cause a boom in small stocks in December, which would prompt other managers to buy them in November, and so on. In the process of acting on the January effect, the price of stocks would be smoothed out over the year and the phenomenon would disappear.

---

[3] Jay Ritter, "The Buying and Selling Behavior of Individual Investors at the End of the Year," *Journal of Finance* 43, (1988), pp. 701–17

[4] Marshall E. Blume, and R. F. Stambaugh, "Biases in Computed Returns: An Application to the Size Effect, *Journal of Financial Economics,* 12, (1983), pp. 387–404.

Of course, to eliminate the January effect, money managers and investors with significant capital must know of the effect and feel comfortable about acting on it. Those in a fiduciary position may feel uneasy justifying what appears to be a very unusual investment strategy to their clients, especially if it does not work out. And others are reluctant to take advantage of a phenomenon which seems to have no economic rationale. In the back of many investors' minds is a lingering suspicion that the January effect won't last when more investors catch on by reading this and other books that have been written about it.

MONTHLY RETURNS

There are other seasonal patterns to stock returns besides the January effect. Table 17–1 displays the monthly returns on the Dow Industrials and S&P 500 Index.[5] Since 1885, December has been the second-best month of the year as measured by the Dow Jones Industrial average, and first-best since World War II. Over the entire period, August has been the best month and July has been third, although most of these great summer returns were registered before the war.

But after the summer holidays, watch out! September is by far the worst month of the year, and the only one to have a negative return. September is followed closely by October, which,

---

[5] The estimates of the monthly dividends returns are taken from Josef Lakonishok and Seymour Smidt, "Are Seasonal Anomalies Real? A Ninety-Year Perspective," *The Review of Economic Studies* 1, no. 4 (1988), pp. 403–25. It should be remembered that the Dow Industrials, like virtually all price indexes, exclude dividends. Since the total returns include dividends as well as price changes, they must be added to the changes in any price index series.

Most large corporations, such as those in the Dow Industrials, pay dividends in the middle month of each quarter (February, May, August, and November), with a nearly even distribution the other eight months. (Currently 17 of the 30 Dow Industrial stocks pay dividends in the middle month of the quarter, eight pay in the last month, and five pay in the first month.) In past years, many corporations paid special dividends in December, but this practice has been largely discontinued. The effect of including dividends is to boost the yield of the months in the middle of the quarter by about 0.5 percent, but the overall pattern of monthly returns remains largely unchanged.

TABLE 17–1

Monthly Returns on the Dow Jones Industrials and S&P 500 (Monthly rank below in italics)

	Average	Jan	Feb	Mar	Apr	May	June	July	Aug	Sept	Oct	Nov	Dec
Cap Appreciation													
1885 - 1992	**0.49%**	1.08%	-0.17%	0.42%	0.96%	-0.29%	0.29%	1.15%	1.61%	-1.04%	0.04%	0.60%	1.20%
		4	*10*	*7*	*5*	*11*	*8*	*3*	*1*	*12*	*9*	*6*	*2*
1885 - 1925	**0.47**	0.77	-0.69	1.31	0.81	0.01	-0.64	0.22	2.22	-0.42	0.79	0.47	0.75
		5	*12*	*2*	*3*	*9*	*11*	*8*	*1*	*10*	*4*	*7*	*6*
1926 - 1945	**0.30**	0.86	0.96	-3.17	0.02	-1.27	2.99	3.12	4.11	-2.53	-1.85	0.01	0.34
		5	*4*	*12*	*7*	*9*	*3*	*2*	*1*	*11*	*10*	*8*	*6*
1946 - 1992	**0.58**	1.44	-0.20	1.18	1.48	-0.14	-0.06	1.11	0.02	-0.95	0.18	0.95	1.95
		3	*11*	*4*	*2*	*10*	*9*	*5*	*8*	*12*	*7*	*6*	*1*
Cap Appr + Est Div													
1885 - 1992	**1.01**	1.25	0.47	0.92	1.20	0.43	0.83	1.32	2.26	-0.57	0.22	1.55	2.20
		5	*9*	*7*	*6*	*10*	*8*	*4*	*1*	*12*	*11*	*3*	*2*
1885 - 1925	**0.99**	0.94	-0.05	1.81	1.05	0.73	-0.10	0.39	2.87	0.05	0.97	1.42	1.75
		7	*11*	*2*	*5*	*8*	*12*	*9*	*1*	*10*	*6*	*4*	*3*
1926 - 1945	**0.82**	1.03	1.60	-2.67	0.26	-0.55	3.53	3.29	4.76	-2.06	-1.67	0.96	1.34
		6	*4*	*12*	*8*	*9*	*2*	*3*	*1*	*11*	*10*	*7*	*5*
1946 - 1992	**0.99**	1.62	0.51	1.42	1.64	0.64	0.16	1.27	0.81	-0.76	0.46	1.81	2.28
		4	*9*	*5*	*3*	*8*	*11*	*6*	*7*	*12*	*10*	*2*	*1*
S&P500 (incl. div)													
1926 - 1992	**0.99**	1.59	0.58	0.41	1.35	0.45	1.33	2.15	1.84	-0.97	0.10	1.32	1.72
		4	*8*	*10*	*5*	*9*	*6*	*1*	*2*	*12*	*11*	*7*	*3*
1946 - 1992	**1.01**	1.65	0.34	1.47	1.38	0.79	0.34	1.35	0.67	-0.64	0.81	1.84	2.17
		3	*11*	*4*	*5*	*8*	*10*	*6*	*9*	*12*	*7*	*2*	*1*

we learned in Chapter 15, already has a disproportionate percentage of crashes.

Some of the monthly patterns of stock returns seem to have changed since World War II. The big returns generated in July and August, which make these months number one and two in the returns on the S&P 500 Index since 1926, are primarily generated before World War II. In the postwar period, July and August offer investors quite mediocre returns. There is really no evidence of the "summer rally" which is much trumpeted by brokers and investment advisers. On the other hand, September and October have remained the worst months throughout the century.

These monthly patterns have a worldwide reach. Although January is a good, but not great, month in the United States, it is a far better month for most countries abroad. Figure 17–3 shows the January return for the 20 countries covered by the Morgan Stanley Capital Market Index. In every country but Austria, January returns are greater than average. Outside the United States, January returns constitute 30 percent of total stock returns on a value-weighted basis. If the United States is included, January returns amount to about one quarter of the total returns experienced during the year, three times what would be expected.

The data presented in Figure 17–3 are from a value-weighted stock index calculated on large stocks. As we noted above, there is evidence that smaller stocks experience even higher January returns. So the January returns shown in Figure 17–3 are probably much lower than those that can be gained in the average stock. January also seems to infect its neighboring months of December and February. Nearly *two thirds* of all returns outside the United States occur in the three months of December through February.

Another anomaly is the prevalence of poor returns in September. It is amazing that September is the only month of the year which has negative returns in the value-weighted (or equal-weighted) world index and in *each of the 20* countries examined! We have shown that September exhibited negative returns in the United States throughout the century. In fact, the underperformance of stocks worldwide in September is of equal magnitude

FIGURE 17–3

International January and September Effects (Average Monthly Returns in local currencies 1970–92)

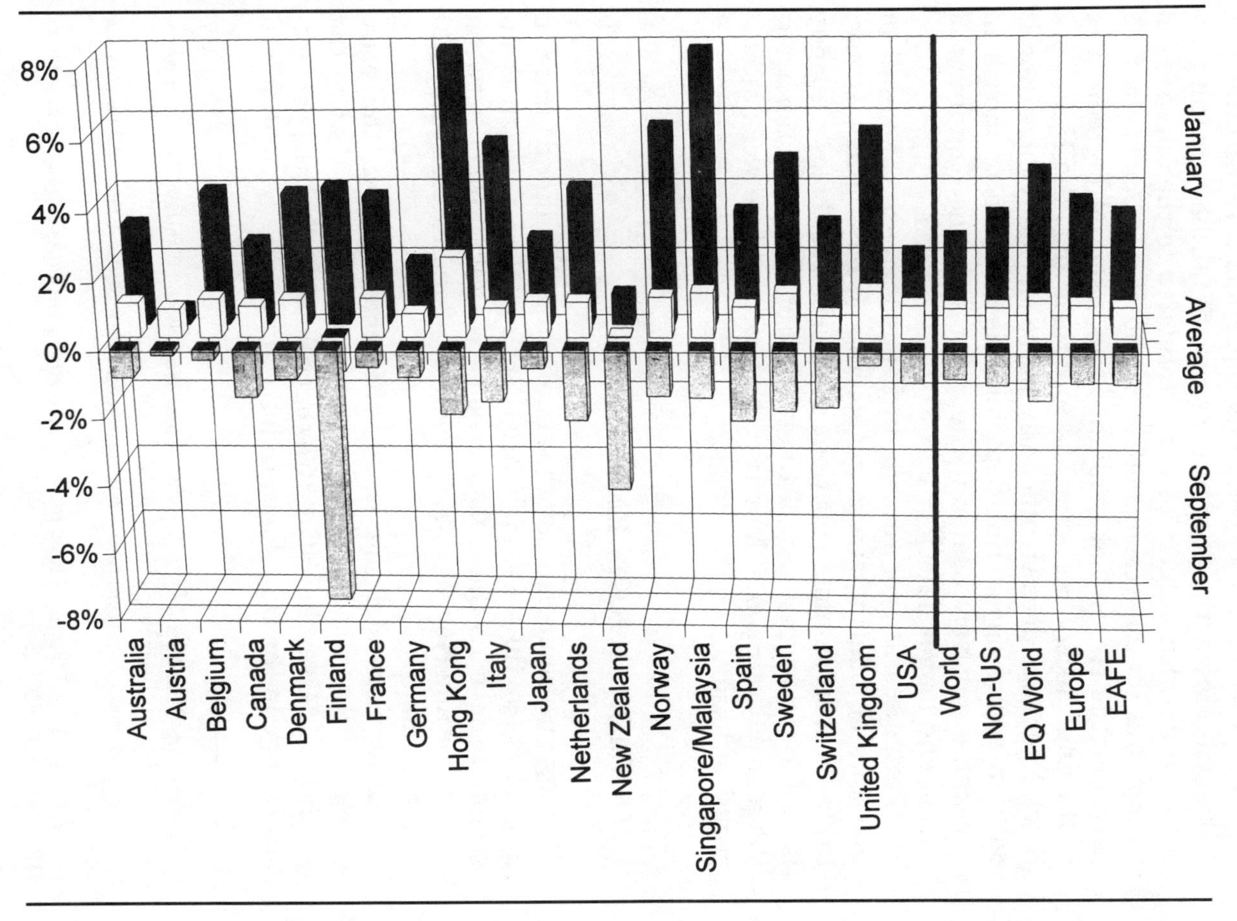

to the overperformance in January. Yet this phenomenon has gone largely unnoticed, and there has been no research to date on this "September effect."

Why the market experiences these monthly variations is unknown. Maybe the poor returns in late fall have nothing directly to do with economics but are related to the approach of winter and the depressing effect of the shorter days. In fact, psychologists stress that sunlight is an essential ingredient to well-being. Recent research has confirmed that the New York Stock Exchange does significantly worse on cloudy days than it does on sunny days.[6] But September is also a poor month in Australia and New Zealand where it marks the beginning of spring and longer days.[7]

Perhaps, the poor returns in September are the result of investors liquidating stocks (or holding off buying new stocks) to pay for their summer vacations. As we shall see below, Monday is by far the poorest day of the week. For many, September is the monthly version of Monday: the time you face work after a period of leisure.

INTRAMONTH RETURNS

Although psychologists say that many silently suffer depression around the joyful season of Christmas and New Year, stock investors believe 'tis the season to be jolly. Daily returns between Christmas and New Year's, as Table 17–2 indicates, average *13* times normal.

Even more striking is the difference between the price change in the first half of the month compared to that in the second half.[8] Over the entire 107-year period studied, the percentage change in the Dow Jones Industrial average in the first half

---

[6] Edward M. Saunders, Jr., "Stock Prices and Wall Street Weather," *American Economic Review* 83 (December 1993), pp. 1337–45.

[7] Of course, many investors in the Australian and New Zealand market live north of the equator.

[8] R. A. Ariel, "A Monthly Effect in Stock Returns," *Journal of Financial Economics* 18, (1987), pp. 161–74.

TABLE 17–2
Average Daily Returns

	1885 - 1992	1885 - 1925	1926 - 1945	1946 - 1992
Overall Averages				
Whole month	**.021%**	.019%	.012%	.027%
First half of month	**.038**	.019	.062	.046
Second half of month	**.004**	.019	-.035	.009
Last day of month	**.089**	.108	.063	.083
Days of the Week				
Monday	**-.121**	-.087	-.211	-.113
Tuesday	**.035**	.038	.047	.028
Wednesday	**.061**	.028	.066	.088
Thursday	**.028**	.001	.063	.037
Friday	**.076**			
With Sat	**.070**	.099	.006	.091
Without Sat	**.084**			.084
Saturday	**.056**	.033	.096	.096
Holiday Returns				
Day before holiday				
July 4th	**.329**	.212	.817	.224
Christmas	**.374**	.452	.363	.309
New Year's	**.396**	.596	.393	.223
Holiday average	**.366**	.420	.524	.252
Christmas week	**.278**	.346	.300	.200

of the month—which includes the last trading day of the previous month up to and including the 14th day of the current month—is more than *seven* times the gain which occurs the second half. Since 1925, *more than* the entire 3,300 point gain in the Dow Jones Industrial average has come in the first half of the month!

The gain in the Dow Industrials is particularly powerful on the last trading day of the month, averaging some six times greater than the average daily gain. But even if the last trading day is removed from the first half of the month and put in the second half, the gain in the Dow Industrials is still strikingly stronger in the first half of the month.[9]

DAY-OF-THE-WEEK EFFECT

Most people hate Mondays. After two days of relaxing and doing pretty much what one likes, having to face work on Monday is not fun. And stock investors apparently feel the same way. Monday is by far the worst day of the week for the market, and has been throughout all the time periods examined. Over the past 107 years, the return on Monday has been decisively negative—seven times less than average.

Although investors hate Monday, they relish Friday. Friday is the best day of the week, giving returns about four times the average. Even when markets were open Saturday (every month before 1946 and nonsummer months before 1953), Friday returns were the best.

Once again, we find that the Monday effect is not confined to US equity markets. Throughout most of the world, Monday is a poor day, garnering negative returns not only in the United States but also in Canada, the United Kingdom, Germany, France, Japan, Korea, and Singapore. On the other hand, none of the major countries have negative returns on Wednesday, Thursday, or Friday. Tuesday is also a poor day for the market, especially in Asia and Australia. This may be due to the poor Monday just experienced in Western countries, since daily returns in the United States have been found to influence Asian markets the next day.

---

[9] The difference in the returns to the Dow stocks between the first and second halves of the month is accentuated by the inclusions of dividends. Currently, about two thirds of the Dow Industrial stocks pay dividends in the first half of the month, which means that the difference between the first and second half returns are accentuated even more.

The daily patterns in returns, although conforming to the conventional popularity of the workweek, do not correspond with economic rationale. Since the return on Monday covers the three-day period from Friday's close, one might think the return should be three times larger than that for other days, given that capital is committed for three times the length of time (and with more risk). But this is not the case.[10]

Fridays are not the only good days in the market. As mentioned earlier, the market does well before virtually any holiday. Returns before three big holidays, July 4, Christmas, and New Year's Day are shown in Table 17–2. They are, on average, *18* times the average daily return. Research on behavior before other exchange holidays shows the same pattern. And the last day of the month is a winner, too.

Finally, there appears to be a diurnal pattern of stock returns. Evidence has shown that there is usually a sinking spell in the morning, especially on Monday, a rising trend after lunch, a pause and then a spurt in the last half hour of trading. This often leads the market to close at the highest levels of the day.

WHAT'S AN INVESTOR TO DO?

These anomalies are an extremely tempting guide to formulating an investing strategy. But those who choose to play by them should be aware of two additional issues: risks and transactions costs. As noted earlier, these calendar-related returns do not always occur, and, as investors become more aware of them, they may not occur as frequently, or at all in the future. Secondly, investing in these anomalies requires the buying and selling of stock, which incurs transaction costs.

It is true that the advent of no-load mutual funds and futures markets has made the cost of trading extremely low. However, unless one is investing with tax-sheltered funds, realizing the gains from playing these anomalies can incur significant taxes.

---

[10] Dividends are fairly evenly spread during the week. They were slightly higher on Monday during the early period, but higher on Friday more recently.

Chapter 6 demonstrated that realizing capital gains each year, rather than deferring them to the future, substantially lowers one's total returns. Nevertheless, investors who have already decided to buy or sell but have some latitude in choosing the exact time of their transaction, would be well advised to take these calendar anomalies into account.

PART 5

BUILDING WEALTH THROUGH STOCKS

CHAPTER 18

FUNDS, MANAGERS, AND LONG-TERM INVESTING

How can institutional investors hope to outperform the market . . . when, in effect, they *are* the market?

Charles D. Ellis[1]

Throughout this book we have spoken of the superior long-run performance of stocks. But how does one actually go about achieving these returns? Despite the recent cover story entitled "Just Do It!" in a popular business weekly featuring successful investors who shun mutual funds and money managers, most people prefer to have someone else handle their money. The spectacular 16-fold increase in the value of mutual fund holdings over the past six years, from $100 billion in 1986 to $2 trillion at the end of 1993, is testimony to the desires of investors to let someone else manage their money.

PERFORMANCE OF EQUITY MUTUAL FUNDS

Unfortunately, the record of such managed funds is not very good. From 1970 through 1992, the average equity mutual fund returned 10.8 percent annually while the return on the stock market was 12.0 percent.[2] During this 20-year period, there were only seven years when more mutual funds beat the market than fell short. Five of those years occurred from 1977 through 1982, when, as we saw in Chapter 5, small stocks spectacularly

---

[1] Charles D. Ellis, "The Loser's Game," *Financial Analysis Journal,* July/August 1975.

[2] See John C. Bogle, *Bogle on Mutual Funds* (Burr Ridge, IL: Irwin Professional Publishing, 1994), p. 171. The market here is defined as the Wilshire 5000, a value-weighted index of virtually all stocks traded on all US exchanges.

outperformed large stocks. Equity funds generally do better when small stocks do well, as many mutual funds seek to outperform the averages by overweighing smaller issues. During the last 10 years, only in 1990 did the average equity mutual fund outperform the market as measured by the Wilshire 5000 Index.

As poor as the above data make mutual funds look, they actually overstate the performance of the average equity fund. First, mutual fund returns ignore the sales and redemption fees that most of the funds impose. Secondly, these surveys suffer from what is called a *survivorship bias:* Mutual funds that did poorly were terminated and were not included in the survey. The strongest funds survived, making the overall record look even better than it was. It has been estimated that this bias adds nearly one percentage point to the returns on all equity funds.[3]

The underperformance of mutual funds did not begin in the 1970s. In 1970, Becker Securities Corporation startled Wall Street by compiling the track record of managers of corporate pension funds. Becker showed that the median performance of these managers lagged behind the S&P 500 by one percentage point, and that only one quarter of them were able to outperform the market.[4] This study followed on the heels of academic articles, particularly by William Sharpe and Michael Jensen, which also confirmed the underperformance of equity mutual funds.[5]

Figure 18–1 displays the distribution of the difference between the returns of 242 mutual funds and the S&P 500 Index over the 14-year period 1978 through 1992. Also displayed is what the theoretical distribution of these 242 mutual funds would be if they invested in a fairly diversified group of stocks chosen at random.[6]

---

[3] *Bogle on Mutual Funds,* p. 161.

[4] Malkiel, *A Random Walk Down Wall Street, p. 362.*

[5] For an excellent review of the studies on mutual funds, see Richard A. Ippolito, "On Studies of Mutual Fund Performance, 1962–1991," *Financial Analysts Journal,* January–February 1993, pp. 42–50

[6] The expected returns will be identical to that of the S&P 500 Index. The average annual standard deviation of the S&P 500 Index during this period (measured with annual data) is 13.08 percent. The standard deviation of the average mutual fund is slightly higher, assumed to be 15 percent, with a correlation coefficient of .85.

FIGURE 18–1

Performance of 242 Mutual Funds Relative to the S&P500 1978–92

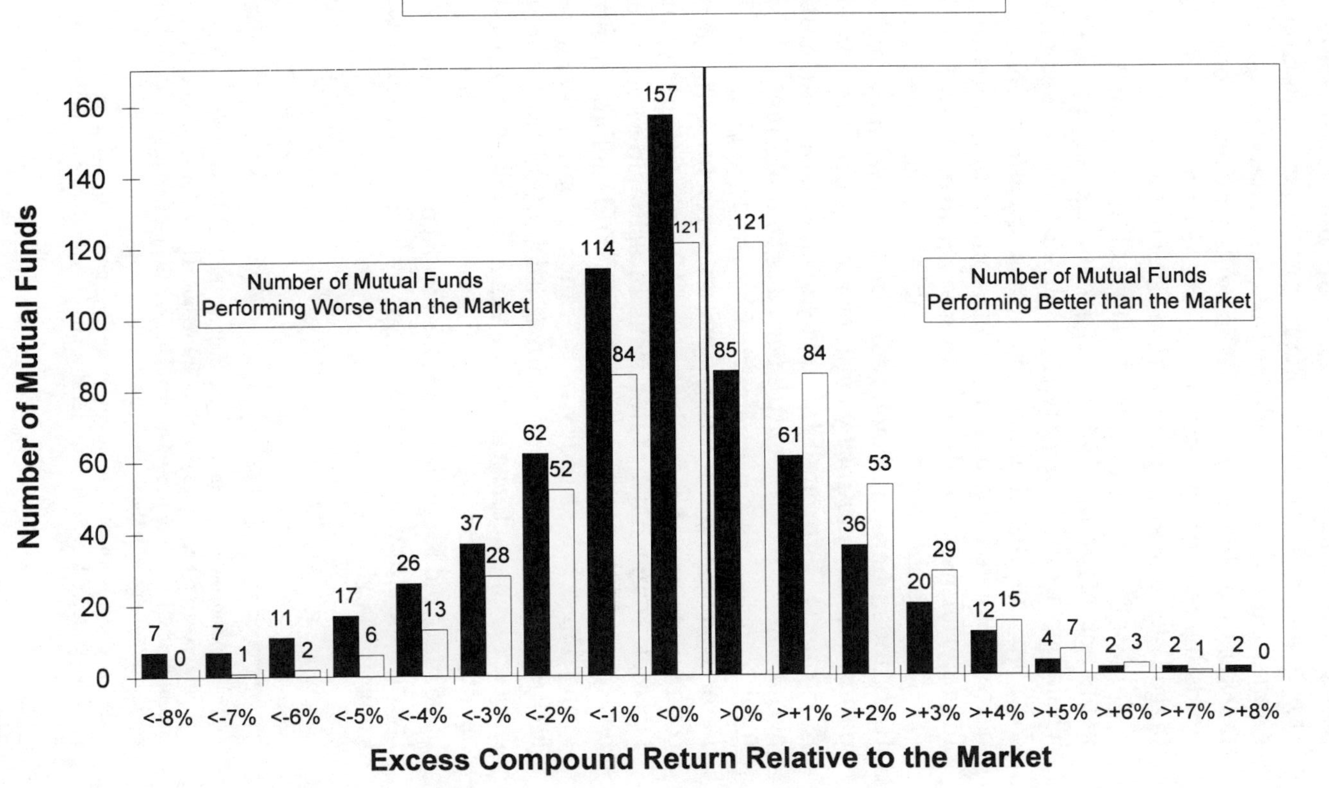

From 1978 through 1992, only one in three funds has been able to outperform the market at all, one in four funds has been able to outperform the market by more than a 1 percent average annual rate of return, while only one in seven has bettered the market by at least 2 percent.[7] In contrast, nearly one half of the funds lagged the market by 1 percent or more, and one in four lagged the market by more than 2 percent.

The generally poor performance of funds relative to the market is not due to the fact that these managers pick losing stocks. Their performance lags because funds impose fees and trading costs on the shareholder. These costs, which average about 2 percent per year on assets, are the most important reason why fund performance falls behind market averages.

Despite the generally miserable performance of equity mutual funds, there are some real winners. Two mutual funds outperformed the market by eight or more percentage points annually from 1978 through 1992. The most outstanding mutual fund performance over the entire period is that of Fidelity's Magellan fund, run for most of the period by the legendary stock picker, Peter Lynch. The Magellan fund outperformed the market by a compound annual rate of return of 10.3 percent per year. Magellan took somewhat greater risks in achieving this return,[8] but notwithstanding, the probability that Magellan would outperform the S&P 500 Index by so much over a 14-year period by luck alone is only 1.8 percent. If all mutual funds adopted the same risk characteristics of the Magellan fund over that period, about four of the 242 equity funds that have survived would have matched Magellan's stellar record by luck alone. Was Peter Lynch's outstanding record gained by luck or skill? We will never know for sure.

---

[7] These performance ratings do not include the "load," or front-end (and sometimes back-end) fees and commissions that are frequently charged when buying and selling mutual funds. Including these fees would lower the performance of these funds relative to the market even further.

[8] Its average standard deviation over the period is 22.11 percent compared to 12.84 percent for the S&P 500 Index, while its correlation coefficient with S&P was only .82.

DETECTING SKILLED MONEY MANAGERS

To show how difficult it is to detect whether superior returns of money managers are due to skill or luck, Table 18–1 computes the *probability* that a manager will outperform the market given that he picks stocks of average risk, but above-average expected returns.[9] The results are surprising. Even if the money manager chooses stocks that have an *expected* return of 1 percent better than the market, after 10 years there is only a 60 percent probability he will exceed the average market return, and after 30 years the probability rises to only two thirds.

On the other hand, detecting a bad manager is equally difficult. In fact, your money manager would have to underperform the market on average by 4 percent a year for 30 years before

TABLE 18–1
Probability of Outperforming the Market

Expected Excess Return	Holding Period						
	1	2	3	5	10	20	30
1%	53.2%	54.5%	55.6%	57.2%	60.1%	64.1%	67.1%
2	56.4	59.0	61.0	64.0	69.4	76.4	81.1
3	59.5	63.3	66.1	70.4	77.6	85.9	90.6
4	62.5	67.4	71.0	76.2	84.3	92.3	96.0
5	65.4	71.2	75.4	81.2	89.5	96.2	98.5

[9] The money manager is assumed to expose his clients to the same risk as the market and has a correlation coefficient of .85 with market returns, which is typical of equity mutual funds.

you can be *statistically certain* (defined to mean being less than one chance in 20 of being wrong) that he is actually a poor manager and not just having bad luck. By that time, your assets will have accumulated to only one third the total cumulative return attained in the market.

Even extreme cases are hard to identify. Take the Wall Street guru Peter Lynch, manager of the Magellan Fund, the outstanding mutual fund on Wall Street from 1987 through 1992. Surely you would think that a Peter Lynch would easily and quickly stand out among money managers.

But not necessarily. Even if the Magellan Fund could continue its outstanding stock-picking ability, beating the market *on average* by 10.3 percent per year, after one year there is only a 71 percent probability that Magellan would outperform the market. And the probability rises to only 79 percent that the Magellan Fund would still be outperforming the market after two years. (It did in fact underperform the market in four of the last 14 years.)

Assume you gave the young Peter Lynch an ultimatum: that he would be fired if he did not at least match the market after two years. There is a one in five chance that you would have fired him, judging him incapable of picking winning stocks!

REASONS FOR UNDERPERFORMANCE OF MANAGED MONEY

There are several reasons why money managers fall short of the market. First, in seeking superior returns, a manager generally must actively buy and sell stocks. This involves brokerage commissions and paying the bid-ask spread, or the difference between the buying and the selling price of shares. And secondly, investors pay management fees (and possibly load fees) to those who are trying to beat the averages. Finally, managers are often competing with other managers with equal or superior skills at choosing stocks. It is a mathematical impossibility for everyone to do better than the market—for every dollar which outperforms the average, there must be some other investor's dollar which is underperforming the average.

Figure 18–2 depicts the influence of trading activity and investor information on stock returns. Left to right indicates the amount of trading activity ranging from zero, when a fixed portfolio is held with no trading, to continual trading. Since stocks have to be bought, absolutely zero trading costs are impossible. A simple indexed portfolio, where stocks are held in proportion to their market value, involves almost no trading.[10] The returns on an index fund will fall slightly below the market, as illustrated in Figure 18–2. Increased trading, holding information content, reduces an investor's return.

The depth in Figure 18–2 indicates the amount of information possessed by the investor. As noted above, to achieve excess returns, one must know more than the average informed investor. The average informed investor who influences market prices is usually a money manager or large investor who has researched the stock and has an informed opinion of its value.

Figure 18–2 illustrates the excess returns of an average money manager, who lags the market, a successful manager, who beats the market, and an average investor, who falls far short of achieving the average market return. It is possible to beat the market, but it requires a very large amount of information. Stock investors are always fighting uphill against transaction costs and the knowledge of other investors. The average investor, as well as the average money manager, will lag the market.

A LITTLE LEARNING IS A DANGEROUS THING

Although stocks may appear to be incorrectly priced to an investor who is just beginning to understand market valuation, this is often not the case. For example, let us take the novice—an investor who is just learning about stock valuation. This is the investor to whom most of the books titled *How to Beat the Market* are sold. Our novice may note that the stock has just reported

---

[10] Even in this case there may be minimal trading costs associated with maintaining proper proportions due to changes in the index, mergers, etc.

FIGURE 18–2
Excess Return Due to Trading and Information

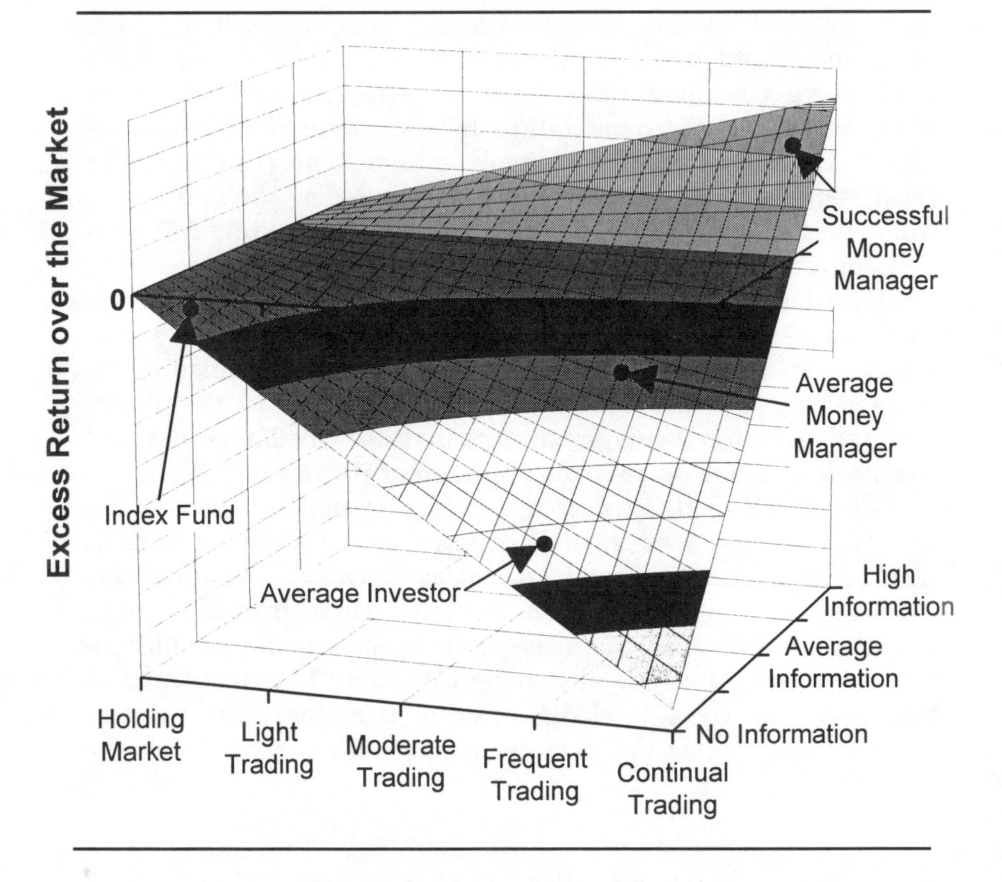

very good earnings, but its price does not rise as much as he believes is justified by this good news. He might think the price should have gone up much more, and so buys the stock.

Yet informed investors know that special circumstances caused the earnings to increase and that these circumstances will not likely be repeated in the future. Informed investors are therefore more than happy to sell the stock to our novice, realizing that even the small rise in the price of the stock is not justified. The informed investors make a return on their special knowledge. They make their return from our novice who believes he has found a bargain. The uninformed investor, who does not even know what the earnings of the company are, does better than one who is just beginning to learn what equities are worth.

The saying, "A little learning is a dangerous thing," proves itself to be quite apt in financial markets. Many seeming anomalies or discrepancies in the price of stocks (or most other financial assets for that matter) are due to the trading of informed investors with special information. Although this is not always the case, when a stock looks too cheap or too dear, the easy explanations—that the stock is irrationally priced by emotional or stupid traders—are often wrong. This is why novices who try to analyze individual stocks often do quite badly.

PROFITING FROM INFORMED TRADING

As a novice becomes more informed, he will no doubt find some stocks that are genuinely under- or overvalued. Trading these stocks will begin to offset his transaction costs and poorly informed trades. At one point, the novice may become well enough informed to overcome the transaction costs and match, and perhaps exceed, the market return. The key word here is *may,* since the number of investors who have consistently been able to outperform the market is small indeed. And for individuals who do not devote much time to analyzing stocks, the possibility of outperforming the averages *consistently* is remote.

Yet the apparent simplicity of picking winners and avoiding losers lures many investors into active trading. Many are convinced that they are at least as smart as the next guy who is playing the same investing game. Yet being just as smart as the next guy is not good enough. For being average at the game of finding market winners will result in underperforming the market, since transactions costs will diminish returns. The money management industry would like you to believe that there are enough ill-informed traders for most professionally managed portfolios to beat the average. But the facts belie such claims.

In 1975 Charles D. Ellis, a managing partner at Greenwood Associates, wrote an influential article called "The Loser's Game." In it he showed that, with transactions costs taken into account, the average money managers must outperform the market by margins which are not possible given that they themselves are the major market players. Ellis concludes that "Contrary to their oft articulated goal of outperforming the market averages, investment managers are not beating the market: The market is beating them."[11]

POWER OF COMPOUND RETURNS

Fees of 2 or 3 percent a year might seem small for investors who are gunning for 20 or 30 percent annual market returns. Furthermore, such fees appear insignificant compared to the year-to-year volatility of the market. But annual fees are extremely detrimental to long-term wealth accumulation. One thousand dollars invested at a compound return of 11 percent per year, the average nominal return on stocks since World War II, will accumulate over 30 years to $23,000. A 1 percent annual fee will reduce the final accumulation by almost one third. With a 3 percent annual fee, the accumulation amounts to just over $10,000, less than one half the market return. For a young investor aged 25, *one* extra percentage point return on one's investment will enable her to retire *two* years earlier, without sacrificing her standard of living either while working or during retirement.

WHAT'S AN INVESTOR TO DO?

The performance of managed funds reported in this chapter may sound discouraging. The fees that most money managers charge do not provide the investor with superior returns and can be a significant drag on wealth accumulation. Furthermore, a good money manager is extremely difficult to identify, for luck plays some role in all successful investment outcomes.

---

[11] Charles D. Ellis, "The Loser's Game," *Financial Analysts Journal,* July/August 1975, p. 19.

But there is a solution to this problem. In the next chapter we shall discuss ways in which the typical investor can keep costs down and still enjoy the benefits of the superior returns on equity. One will not be able to avoid all fees, for no investment can be made costlessly. But it is not difficult to match the market return and perhaps even beat it by following some simple rules. Performing as well as the top third of equity money managers is a goal well within the reach of all investors.

CHAPTER 19

INVESTING FOR THE LONG RUN

> [The] *long run* is a misleading guide to current affairs. *In the long run* we are all dead. Economists set themselves too easy, too useless a task if in tempestuous seasons they can only tell us when the storm is long past, the ocean will be flat.
>
> *John Maynard Keynes*[1]

No one can argue with Keynes' statement that in the long run we are all dead. But vision for the long run must be used as a guide to current action. Those who keep their focus and perspective during trying times are far more likely to emerge successful. The knowledge that the sea will be flat after the storm is not useless, but of enormous comfort.

It is particularly important that the principles of investment strategy be guided by long-run expectations. Keynes is right when he wrote that "our knowledge of the factors which will govern the yield of an investment some years hence is usually very slight and often negligible."[2] But the fact that such expectations are subject to such radical revision does not justify their abandonment. The well-known statement—that the most successful are those who keep their heads about them when everyone else is losing theirs—is particularly applicable for investment decisions.

---

[1] *A Tract on Monetary Reform,* 1924, p. 80.

[2] John M. Keynes, *The General Theory,* (New York: MacMillan, 1936), p. 149.

RISK AND RETURN

The conventional wisdom is that long-run investments in stocks are risky, the lucky get rich quickly, but many lose everything. But the conventional wisdom is not true. In the long run, not only do stocks have higher returns than bonds, but also lower risk. This is because bondholders can never be compensated for unexpected inflation, a factor that cannot be ignored in our current world of paper money.

Since, over time, the risk of stocks shrinks faster than bonds, the best portfolio for investors will depend on their planning horizon. Figure 19–1 displays the after-inflation risks and returns for various combinations of stocks and bonds over different holding periods. These risk-return trade-offs are based on the entire 190-year history of US data. The bottom of each curve represents a portfolio which is 100 percent in bonds, while the top represents 100 percent in stocks. Movement along the curve measures the risk and return for shifts in the allocation between bonds and stocks in a portfolio.

For all holding periods, stocks have higher average real returns than bonds and, for holding periods up to 10 years, stocks also have higher risk. But once the holding period exceeds a decade, stocks have lower risk than bonds. The inflation hedging quality of stocks makes equity a safer asset for the long-term investor.

It should be noted that the risk-return trade-offs are bowed to the left. This is because stock and bond returns are imperfectly correlated. Chapter 3 showed the benefits of diversification: combining risky assets enables an investor to lower risk. Similarly, adding stocks to an all-bond portfolio enables an investor to lower total risk, even though stocks by themselves may be riskier than bonds. Of course, as stocks become a large fraction of the portfolio, total risk rises as the diversification benefit disappears.

BEST PORTFOLIO ALLOCATIONS

Risk-return analysis indicates an investor should always include enough stocks to *at least* achieve a portfolio which minimizes

FIGURE 19–1
Risk/Return-Trade-offs for Various Holding Periods 1802–1992

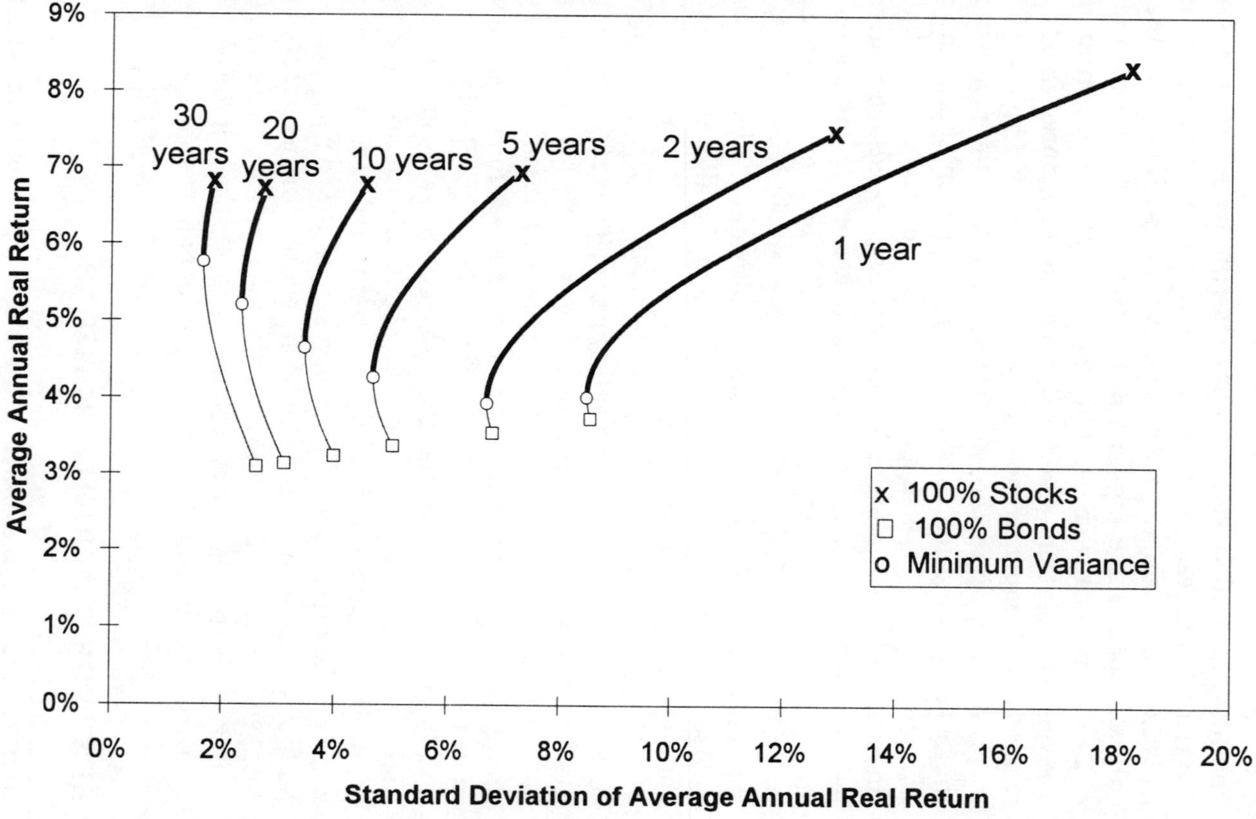

risk. Owning any less stock than this will *lower* your return and *increase* your risk, clearly an inferior strategy for any investor. But the minimum risk portfolio should only be entertained by the ultraconservative investors. Increasing the percentage of stocks allows the investor to trade off between risk and return.

The percentage of your portfolio that you put in stocks is dependent on both the horizon over which you plan to hold your investments and your willingness to trade off risk and return. Because the risks of holding stocks decrease over time, the percentage of your portfolio committed to stock rises substantially as your horizon increases.

Table 19–1 displays the best portfolios of investors with different risk-return trade-offs. We shall assume that the investor's risk-return trade-offs for a one-year horizon are used to determine the best stock-bond allocation over longer holding periods. An ultraconservative investor will accept only a minimum risk portfolio and will not be willing to accept any additional risk, no matter how large the additional return. A conservative investor will accept small risks for extra returns, inducing him to

TABLE 19–1
Percentage of Portfolio in Stocks for Various Holding Periods

Risk Tolerance	Holding Period		
	1 year	10 years	30 years
Minimum Risk	6.2%	40.0%	72.1%
Conservative	25.0	62.3	91.8
Moderate	50.0	87.9	115.5
Risk-taking	75.0	106.9	134.6

maintain, for example, 25 percent in a stock portfolio geared for a one-year horizon. An investor of average risk tolerance may keep 50 percent of his one-year portfolio in stocks, while a high-risk investor might hold 75 percent in equity.

As the investment horizon increases, investors dramatically increase the proportion invested in equity, especially for conservative investors. Even the ultraconservative investor, who would hold less than 10 percent stock if planning over a one-year horizon, should put nearly three quarters of his financial assets in stocks for 30-year horizons. Those with average risk tolerance should hold more than 100 percent of their financial assets in stocks, in effect borrowing against other assets to increase their equity holdings.

It is apparent that investing for the long run is quite different from investing for the short run. There is no such thing as a safe, or inflation-protected and risk-free long-term asset. Money markets, which are a good haven for short-term assets, become risky in the long run when inflation is factored in. But those who roll over these short-term assets in a long-horizon portfolio, assuming it is good to have some cash handy as a hedge against stock market risk, will often find themselves far worse off in the long run. The risks in the long run are borne by the bondholder, not the stockholder.

The difference between stock holdings in a long- and short-run portfolio occurs because stock market risk decreases more quickly than would be predicted by market models that assume the independence of returns over time. If next period's returns are independent of this period's returns, an investor would not alter her portfolio over time, holding as much in equity when she is young as when she is old. But our data show that the young *should* hold a higher proportion of their portfolio in stocks.

HISTORICAL RETURNS AND ASSET ALLOCATION

The portfolio allocations recommended above are based on long-term historical data. Yet we have maintained that during the last 50 years, real bond returns appeared abnormally low, due primarily to the emergence of persistent and unexpected inflation. If investors finally understand the inflationary consequences of paper money standards and build these expectations into future interest rates, then the past might not be an accurate portrayal of the future. Portfolio allocations based on historical data would bias one against holding bonds.

But this is not necessarily so. Although real bond returns are likely to be higher in the future than they were in the past half century, the risks to bonds have also increased. When the gold standard reigned, as they did over most of the historical period examined, bonds served as the most desirable asset to hedge against depressions and deflation. Bad economic times were associated with falling prices, a condition when bonds thrived.

Today, bad economic times are often associated with inflation, as governments print money to attempt to buy themselves and the economy out of recession. Inflation strips bonds of their ability to hedge against many economic risks, meaning that bond returns will in the future be more correlated with those of equity.

If bond returns become more correlated with equity returns, the diversification properties of bonds will be reduced. In terms of Figure 19–1, the risk-return trade-off will be less bowed out. Bonds under these conditions lose their attractiveness to stocks. Although future bond returns may be higher, their hedging ability will probably be reduced, and it is uncertain whether bonds in the future will be any more attractive than they have been in the past for the long-term investor.

EQUITIES—DOMESTIC AND GLOBAL

International equities must be part of any long-term portfolio of common stocks. This is not because foreign stock returns are likely to be greater than returns in the United States, although they may, but because foreign equities enable stockholders to diversify their risks far more effectively than portfolios containing only domestic securities.

Figure 19–2 displays risk and return trade-offs for foreign and US equities based on return data from 1970. Comprehensive

FIGURE 19–2
International Risk/Return Trade-off (Historical Risk and Return)

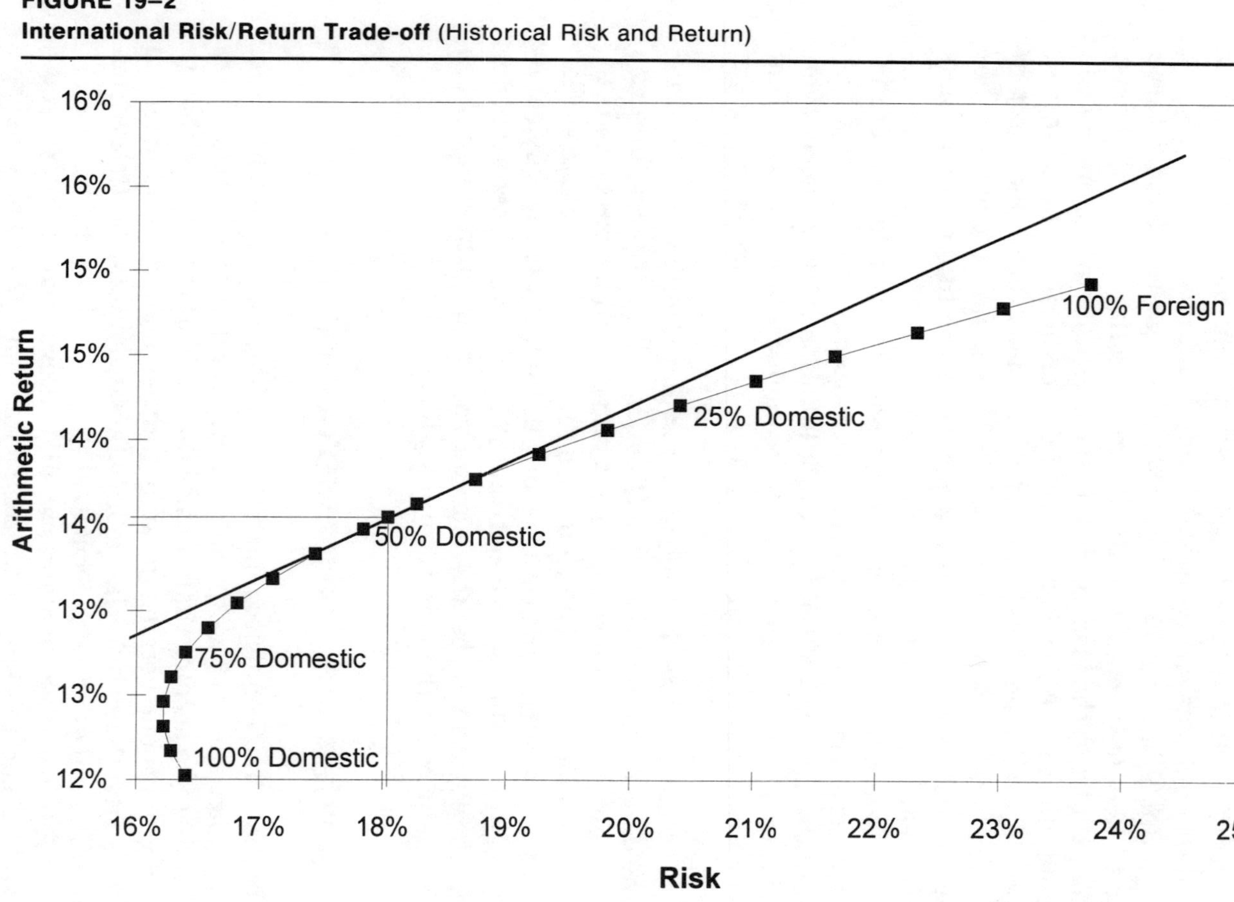

(US risk = 16.4%, US return = 12.0%, foreign risk = 23.7%, foreign return = 14.9%)

returns on international equities, save for the countries discussed in Chapter 1, have come mostly from the postwar period. Chapter 8 analyzed foreign returns and made the case for investing in international equities.

Figure 19–2 reports the percentage of one's stock portfolio that should be in foreign securities at various risk-return tradeoffs. The minimum risk portfolio is weighted 12.5 percent in foreign equities. During the historical period under consideration, the average short-term rate was 7.5 percent, indicating that slightly over one half of a dollar investor's portfolio should be in foreign equities. At the lower interest rates that exist today one might argue that a lower percentage should be foreign, but even at 3 percent dollar interest rates, one third of one's portfolio should be devoted to foreign stocks. Even if foreign stock returns do not exceed US returns in the future, the diversification properties of foreign equities indicate that to maximize returns, between one quarter and one half of one's stock portfolio should be in foreign stocks.

It is very difficult to motivate most investors to put this high a percentage of their stock portfolio into foreign stocks. Americans feel comfortable with US stocks—they are familiar with the firms whose stock they are buying and realize that their fortunes are dictated by events occurring in an economy that they understand far better than any abroad. Nationalism may also play a role in the bias against foreign equities. But the fortunes of American corporations are increasingly intertwined with the world economy. The greatest growth in demand for many American products will occur in the world's emerging nations.

PRACTICAL ASPECTS OF STOCK INVESTING

1. *Invest in a highly diversified mutual fund with very low expense ratios.*

To replicate the returns described in the book, it is necessary to hold a highly diversified portfolio of stocks. Unless one is successful in choosing individual stocks, it can be shown that maximum diversification is achieved by holding each stock in proportion to its value to the entire market. Since there are over 6,000 stocks traded on US markets, this is a virtually impossible task.

However, the mutual fund industry offers investments, called *index funds,* which yield returns extremely close to those of the major market indexes, such as the S&P 500 Index. An index fund does not attempt to beat the market, but by holding a large number of stocks in the proper proportion, such a fund is able to match the market with extremely low costs. The oldest and largest of these mutual funds is Vanguard Group Mutual Fund's 500 Portfolio, a fund indexed to the S&P 500 Index. Begun in 1976, the fund has more than 8 billion in assets and has a total expense ratio that is less than 0.3 percent per year.

Chapter 18 showed that the market has outperformed at least two out of three mutual funds since 1978. By matching the market year after year, as you can with index funds, you can guarantee you will be near the top of the pack when the final returns are tallied. And matching the market is sufficient to achieve the superior returns that have been achieved through stocks over time.

Although the value of the S&P 500 Index comprises a good part of the market, thousands of smaller stocks still sum to over one quarter of the total value. To match the total market requires an investment in over 6,000 stocks, a strategy that would be prohibitively expensive.

To approximate total market returns, small-stock index funds choose a representative subset of small stocks to approximate the returns of those stocks not in the S&P 500 Index. The small-stock funds, which have somewhat higher expenses than the large-stock index funds, replicate such indexes as the Wilshire 4500 (the smallest 4,500 stocks of the top 5,000) or the Russell 2000 (the smallest 2,000 stocks of the top 3,000). For those investors who do not want to put together large and small index funds, there are mutual funds, such as Vanguard's Total Stock Market Fund, which put them together for you.

2. *Use the same principles as above to pick international stocks.* Do not buy closed-end country funds unless they sell at a discount, especially when regular, open-ended funds are available. Do not substantially overweigh "emerging nations."

It is not unreasonable to invest one third or more of your portfolio in international stocks. Choose international mutual funds that have low expenses and are as broadly diversified as possible. However, because costs are higher in international markets, you cannot achieve expense ratios that are as low as those you can achieve with domestic indexed funds. This is particularly true of foreign small-stock funds.

Closed-end country funds, which represent fixed pools of money which are invested in foreign countries, trade like stocks. They may be good buys if they are selling below the value of their underlying shares, which frequently happens. But when foreign investing is in vogue, these funds sell at a premium and the investor is often better off investing in an open-end mutual fund.

There is a tendency for investors to jump to the emerging markets where promises of growth and capital appreciation are high. But these are extremely risky. The market capitalization of many small countries is less than many individual stocks of developed countries, and often far more risky. Small country stocks should make up no more than 20 percent of the foreign sector of your portfolio.

3. *Do not overweigh small stocks in your portfolio.*

Small stocks have outperformed large stocks since 1926. But we have seen that they have done so primarily because of the nine good years from 1975 through 1983. Excluding that period leaves small stocks with inferior total performance and higher risk.

The over- or underperformance of small stocks has come and gone in streaks that last several years. For the intermediate-term investor, these streaks appear to increase the probability that small stocks will underperform the market averages.

This does not mean that you should avoid small stocks. Since almost 30 percent of the domestic market resides outside the S&P 500 Index, you should hold nearly one third of your portfolio in small stocks. Even if S&P 500 stocks may be slightly overpriced due to the development of the stock index futures markets, holding much more than one third of your portfolio in small stocks exposes the investor to too much risk.

4. *Hold value stocks in your pension fund, growth stocks in your personal portfolio.*

Value stocks are stocks with high earnings, book values, and dividends, relative to their price while growth stocks have the opposite characteristics. Over time, value stocks, like small stocks, have tended to outperform growth stocks, but it is uncertain whether this will characterize the future.

We have seen in Chapter 7 how taxes can devastate the returns on your portfolio. You can minimize the tax bite by separating out high- and low-dividend-paying stocks. By placing *value* stocks in tax-exempt accounts, such as IRA, Keogh, or 401(k) plans, their total returns will accumulate untaxed. *Growth* stocks, which have achieved a much greater part of their return through capital gains, can be kept outside of tax-exempt accounts.

In 1992, Vanguard divided the S&P 500 Index into growth and value stocks. By combining equal values of each of these funds, the total S&P 500 Index is recreated. By holding the value fund in a tax-exempt account and an equal proportion of the growth fund on personal account, you have replicated the S&P 500 Index while lowering taxes. For tax savings, small-stock funds can be held in personal accounts because their returns have also come primarily through capital gains and not dividends.

5. *Take advantage of calendar anomalies and technical trading from your tax-exempt, not personal, trading account.*

For investors who closely follow the market, evidence presented in Chapters 16 and 17 suggests that there have been regular calendar patterns in stock returns and that stock risks might be reduced by pursuing trend-following strategies. The biggest anomaly is the January effect which documents the superb returns that accrue to small stocks in that month.

The January effect makes it very tempting to buy a small stock fund late in December and dispose of it toward the end of January. Even after transaction costs, this strategy has been a superior investment. But remember that selling your large stocks to buy small stocks incurs capital gains taxes, and these taxes can greatly reduce the total return on your long-term portfolio.

To avoid these taxes, play the January effect from funds in your tax-exempt account. Any capital gains are not taxed, so that your only costs are the fees imposed by the small-stock fund. Choose a fund with very low fees to minimize your transactions costs.[3]

Because of tax reasons, technical trading should also be done from your tax-exempt account. Transaction costs can easily eat up the gains otherwise. If you choose to follow the 200-day moving average strategy as outlined in this book, keep careful records and follow the market closely. Remember how important it was to sell on Friday, October 16, 1987, the day before the great crash.

These yield-enhancing strategies are not necessary to achieve extremely good long-run returns on the market. If following these strategies involves high transactions costs or subjects you to anxiety, forget them. You will do quite well with a buy-and-hold strategy pegged to an index or other well-diversified, low-cost fund. But if you like the hunt, and get a thrill out of beating the market, this is the way to do it.

6. *If you are short on cash but want to invest in the stock market, use stock index futures.* These futures are also an ideal way to adjust your portfolio or play calendar anomalies with a minimum tax effect.

Chapter 14 describes how stock index futures enable you to buy diversified portfolios of stocks with less than 10 percent cash margin. If your funds are tied up in other investments, or if you want to have ready cash on hand for contingencies, buying and selling these futures are an ideal way to get into the market.

Remember, if the market goes down, you must come up with more cash against your futures contract. If you cannot, you will be sold out at a loss. Yet buying one S&P 500 Index futures contract, representing about a quarter million dollars of stocks, is absolutely no more risky than putting a like amount of money

---

[3] In recent years, there have been funds designed to take advantage of these calendar anomalies. Check their fee structure and make sure they, at minimum, play the January effect.

in an S&P 500 Index fund. Stock index futures representing smaller sums are also available.

Futures are also an ideal way to adjust your portfolio if you are pursuing technical analysis or playing calendar anomalies. There are small-stock futures (such as the Russell 2000, and to some extent, the Kansas City Value Line) which can be bought late in December and sold in January.

The advantage of dealing with futures for technical or calendar trading is that you do not have to disturb your original portfolio, with possibly adverse tax consequences and transaction costs. If technical or calendar trading is done in the futures market, taxes are only paid on the profits from futures trading, not on the accumulated capital gains on the stocks you own.

CONCLUSION

To be a successful long-term investor is easy in principle, but difficult in practice. Easy in principle since to buy and hold a diversified portfolio of stocks, foregoing any forecasting ability, is available to all investors, no matter what their intelligence, judgment, or financial status. Yet it is difficult in practice since tales of those who have achieved great wealth quickly tempt one to play a very different game than the long-term investor.

How many times have those of us who follow the market closely exclaim: "I *knew* that stock (or the market) was going up! If I had only relied on my judgment, I would have made a lot of money." But hindsight plays tricks on our minds. We forget the doubts we had when we made the decision not to buy. Hindsight often distorts the past and encourages us to play hunches and outguess other investors, who in turn are playing the same game.

For most of us, trying to beat the market leads to disastrous results. We take far too many risks, our transaction costs are high, and we often find ourselves giving in to the emotions of the time: pessimism when the market is down and optimism when the market is high. Our actions lead to much lower returns than can be achieved by just staying in the market.

Keynes lamented the lack of long-term players in the market, and the predominance of short-term traders whose major preoccupation was outguessing other players: He wrote:

> Life is not long enough;—human nature desires quick results, there is a peculiar zest in making money quickly, and remoter gains are discounted by the average man at a very high rate.[4]

Keynes goes on to say that those who try to beat the market must "pay the appropriate toll"—higher transaction costs, greater risks, and often lower returns.

But one can build wealth and still enjoy the drama of the market. I have reassured the long-term investor that superior gains are possible in stocks with far less risk than one is led to believe by watching the daily ups and downs of the averages. But I have also tried to enrich your understanding of this most complex but fascinating subject. The stock market stands not only as the quintessential symbol of capitalism but, as the proliferation of stock exchanges all around the world attests, represents a driving force behind the enrichment of all peoples everywhere.

---

[4] Keynes, *The General Theory,* p. 157.

INDEX

OPTIONS

Essential Concepts and Trading Strategies

The Options Institute, The Educational Division of the Chicago Board Options Exchange

Describes the different trading strategies you can use to predict the winners and avoid the losers. The world's leading options trading educators give you proven options pricing and forecasting theories so you can work better. (400 pages)

ISBN: 1-55623-102-4

LEAPS (LONG-TERM EQUITY ANTICIPATION SECURITIES)

What They Are and How to Use Them for Profit and Protection

Harrison Roth

Discover why thousands of individual and institutional investors are using LEAPS to implement investment strategies ranging from bullish to bearish and everything in between! Harrison Roth shows readers how they can use LEAPS with fewer risks than more common options. Detailing conservative, moderate, and aggressive strategies, Roth's comprehensive guide includes: thorough, historical perspective of LEAPS emphasizing why they are different from conventional examples readers can use to better understand how to implement basic LEAPS strategies; experience-based warnings so investors know what to watch out for and how to protect their position over time. (360 pages)

ISBN: 1-55623-819-3

THE ENCYCLOPEDIA OF TECHNICAL MARKET INDICATORS

Robert W. Colby and Thomas A. Meyers

The most complete and comprehensive description of technical stock market indicators ever published! Separates Wall Street myth from reality and shows you the true forecasting value of over 110 indicators. (581 pages)

ISBN: 1-55623-049-4

Available at fine bookstores and libraries everywhere.